Maturin Murray Ballou

Under the Southern Cross

Or, Travels in Australia, Tasmania, New Zealand, Samoa, and other Pacific islands

Maturin Murray Ballou

Under the Southern Cross
Or, Travels in Australia, Tasmania, New Zealand, Samoa, and other Pacific islands

ISBN/EAN: 9783337209742

Printed in Europe, USA, Canada, Australia, Japan

Cover: Foto ©Andreas Hilbeck / pixelio.de

More available books at **www.hansebooks.com**

UNDER THE SOUTHERN CROSS

UNDER

THE SOUTHERN CROSS

OR TRAVELS IN

AUSTRALIA, TASMANIA, NEW ZEALAND, SAMOA, AND OTHER PACIFIC ISLANDS

BY

MATURIN M. BALLOU

AUTHOR OF "DUE WEST; OR, ROUND THE WORLD IN TEN MONTHS," "DUE NORTH;
OR, GLIMPSES OF SCANDINAVIA, RUSSIA, AND RUSSIAN POLAND,"
"DUE SOUTH; OR, CUBA PAST AND PRESENT," ETC.

> . . . Of antres vast and deserts idle,
> Rough quarries, rocks, and hills whose heads touch heaven,
> It was my hint to speak, — such was the process;
> And of the cannibals that each other eat,
> The Anthropophagi. — SHAKSPEARE.

BOSTON
TICKNOR AND COMPANY
211 Tremont Street
1888

Copyright, 1887,
BY MATURIN M. BALLOU.

All rights reserved.

𝔘𝔫𝔦𝔳𝔢𝔯𝔰𝔦𝔱𝔶 𝔓𝔯𝔢𝔰𝔰:
JOHN WILSON AND SON, CAMBRIDGE.

PREFACE.

Dr. Johnson is reported to have said that the best way to travel is to sit by one's own fireside and read how others have done it; but though this may be the safest mode it certainly is not the pleasantest. This any travelled writer knows; and he also knows that could he succeed in adequately inspiring the reader with his accounts of the delights of foreign experiences, especially those of the grand, beautiful, and marvellous exhibitions of Nature, he would surely induce him to add to his own enjoyment by similar personal experiences. That there is a degree of pleasure in recording these observations we freely confess; but that one constantly feels how inadequate is language to convey a realizing sense of what is actually enjoyed in travel we must as freely admit. Madame Swetchine was more sarcastic than truthful when she pronounced travel to be the frivolous part of serious lives, and the serious part of frivolous ones. To an observant person nothing can be more instructive than travel; in fact it may be said to be the only royal road to learning. Travel is a magician, — it both enchants and disenchants; since while it delights the eye, it often proves the winding-sheet of many cherished illusions. There is always some bitter to be tasted with every sweet; but even the bee which finds a thorn on every rose comes home laden with honey.

M. M. B.

Boston, January, 1888.

CONTENTS.

CHAPTER I.

Journey across the American Continent. — The Giant City of the West. — A Chinese Community. — Embarking for a Long Sea-voyage. — About Ocean Birds. — Navigating the Pacific. — Peculiarities of Life at Sea. — Curiosities of the Deep. — Ambergris. — City of Honolulu. — An Island Paradise. — Early Paganism at Hawaii. — Wholesale Human Sacrifices. — Royalty at the Race-course. — Not a Kingly Monarch 1–25

CHAPTER II.

Ladies Riding Astride. — Passion for Flower Decorations. — A Sailor on a Bucking Horse. — A Weekly Gala-day. — Hawaiian Ladies' Costume. — A Famous Battle-ground. — The Native's Staff of Life. — Ubiquitous John Chinaman. — Largest Apple-orchard in the World. — Hawaiians as Cannibals. — An Active Volcano. — Colony of Lepers. — Unwelcome Visitors. — Our Political Relations with the Sandwich Islands 26–49

CHAPTER III.

The Samoan Islands. — A Unique Race of Savages. — Diving for Money. — A Genuine Samoan Mermaid. — German Aggressiveness. — A South-Sea Nunnery. — A Terrible Disease. — Christianity *vs.* Paganism. — Under the Southern Cross. — Grandeur of the Heavens at Sea. — Landing at Auckland. — A Stormy Ocean. — The Famous Harbor of Sydney. — England and her Australian Colony. — The Modern Eldorado. — Early Settlers 50–75

viii   *CONTENTS.*

CHAPTER IV.

PAGE

Interesting Statistical Facts. — Emigration. — Heavy Indebtedness. — Curious Contrasts. — New South Wales. — A Populous City. — A Splendid Harbor. — The Yacht "Sunbeam." — Street Scenes. — Gin Palaces. — Public Gardens of Sydney. — A Noble Institution of Learning. — Art Gallery. — Public Libraries. — Pleasure Trip to Parametta. — Attractive Drives. — A Sad Catastrophe in Sydney Harbor 76–98

CHAPTER V.

A Zigzag Railway. — Wonderful Series of Caves. — Immense Sheep-Runs. — Sheep-Shearing. — Central Australia. — City Characteristics. — Fine Architectural Development. — Steam Tramways. — Labor Unions. — Colonial Federation. — The Tariff. — Loyalty to England. — Spirit of Local Rivalry. — The St. Giles of Sydney. — City Clubs. — The Laughing Jackass. — Public Parks. — Gold Mines 99–125

CHAPTER VI.

The Capital of Queensland. — Public Gardens. — Gold Mines and Gold Mining. — Pleasant Excursion. — Inducements to Emigrants. — Coolie Principle of Labor. — Agricultural Products. — Sugar Plantations. — Australian Aborigines. — Cannibalism. — Civil Wars. — Indian Legends. — Fire-arms and Firewater. — Missionary Efforts. — A Brief Romance. — The Boomerang. — The Various Tribes. — Antiquity of these Lands   126–151

CHAPTER VII.

Morning in the Forest. — Flying Foxes. — A Startling Snake-story. — Geographical. — Want of Irrigation. — Droughts. — Immense Sheep-Runs. — Seeking a Shepherd Life. — Wonderful Gold Nuggets — A "Welcome" Discovery. — Wool is King in Queensland. — The Chinese Population. — Education in Australia. — Peculiar Banking Business. — Waging War upon Kangaroos. — Journalism in Australia. — Proposed New Colony 152–176

CHAPTER VIII.

An Inland Journey. — The Capital of Victoria. — Grand Public Buildings. — Water-Supply of the City. — Public Parks and Gardens. — Street Scenes. — Dashing Liveries. — Tramways. — Extremes. — Melbourne Ladies. — Street Beggars. — Saturday Half-Holiday. — Public Arcades. — The City Free Library. — The Public Markets. — China-Town, Melbourne. — Victims of the Opium Habit 177-201

CHAPTER IX.

A Melbourne Half-Holiday. — Inconsistency of Laborers. — Vice-Royal Residence. — Special Gold-Fields of Victoria. — Ballarat. — Great Depths in Mines. — Agricultural Interests. — Sandhurst. — The Giant Trees of Australia. — The Kangaroo. — In Victorian Forests. — Peculiar Salt Lakes. — The Bower-bird's Retreat. — The Wild Dog. — Desirable and Undesirable Emigrants. — No Place for the Intemperate 202-222

CHAPTER X.

From Melbourne to Adelaide. — Capital of South Australia. — New Gold-Fields. — Agricultural Interests. — City Institutions. — Inducements to Immigrants. — Public Buildings. — A City of Churches. — Australian Ladies. — Interior of the Country. — Irrigation. — German Settlers. — The Botanical Gardens. — West Australia. — Perth the Capital. — The Pearl Fisheries. — Commercial Advantages Considered 223-245

CHAPTER XI.

From Australia to Tasmania. — The River Tamar. — Bird Life. — City of Launceston. — Aborigines of the Island. — Tattooing. — Van Diemen's Land. — A Beautiful Country. — Rich Mines. — Mount Bischoff. — Down in a Gold Mine. — From Launceston to Hobart. — Rural Aspects. — Capital of Tasmania. — Street Scenes. — A Former Penal Depot. — Mount Wellington. — Personal Beauty. — An Unbecoming Fashion . . . 246-268

CHAPTER XII.

Lake District of Tasmania. — Mount Wellington. — Kangaroos. — The Big Trees. — A Serenade. — The Albatross. — Marksmanship at Sea. — Dust of the Ocean. — A Storm. — Franklin's Proposition. — A Feathered Captive. — Bluff Oysters. — Most Southerly Hotel in the World. — Invercargill. — Historical Matters. — Geographical. — The Climate of New Zealand. — Colonial Hospitality 269–298

CHAPTER XIII.

The City of Dunedin. — Scotch Residents. — The Enchanter's Wand. — Chain-Cable Tramways. — Volcanic Effects. — The Salvation Army. — Local Gold-Fields. — Enormous Aggregate Product. — Trees and Flowers. — The Rabbit Pest. — Port Littleton. — Market Day in Christchurch. — An Interesting City. — Wonderful Extinct Bird. — Strange Record of an Unknown Race. — The New Zealand Forests 299–321

CHAPTER XIV.

Capital of New Zealand. — About the Native Race. — A City of Shops. — Local Earthquakes. — Large Glaciers. — McNab's Gardens. — A Public Nuisance. — Napier. — Maori Peculiarities. — Native Language. — Mythology. — Christianizing Savages. — Gisborne. — Cruelty to Dumb Animals. — Shag Island. — Sir George Gray's Pleasant Home. — Oysters Growing on New Zealand Trees ! 322–343

CHAPTER XV.

Historical Glance at Auckland. — A Remarkable Volcanic Region. — City Institutions. — Queen Street and Its Belongings. — Mount Eden. — Comprehensive View. — Labor Unions. — The Public Debt. — Kauri Forests. — Production of Kauri Gum. — Environs of Auckland. — The Native Flora. — An Admirable Climate. — A Rich Mineral District. — Agricultural Development 344–364

CHAPTER XVI.

A Journey to the King's Country. — An Experienced "Whip." — Volcanic Hills. — A New Zealand Forest. — A Strangely Afflicted Boy. — Lake Rotorua. — Ohinemutu. — Funeral of a Maori Chief. — Wailing and Weeping. — Moonlight on the Lake. — Wonderland. — Spouting Geysers and Boiling Pools. — Savage Mode of Slaughter. — Maori Houses. — Chivalry and Cannibalism. — Savage and Civilized Life 365–385

CHAPTER XVII.

The Maori Dog. — A Romantic Island. — Sinking of a Maori Fort. — Volcanic Destruction. — A Country of Boiling Springs. — Idleness. — A Lazy Race of Savages. — Native Religion. — A Fitful Geyser. — Sophia, the Famous Guide. — A Funeral Dance. — The "Haka" Performance. — Maori Improvidence. — Rubbing Noses. — Native Babies. — Church-Going and Card-Playing. — The King's Country. — Eloquent Aborigines. — A Sanitarium. — Sulphur Point. — Future of New Zealand 386–405

UNDER THE SOUTHERN CROSS.

CHAPTER I.

Journey across the American Continent. — The Giant City of the West. — A Chinese Community. — Embarking for a Long Sea-voyage. — About Ocean Birds. — Navigating the Pacific. — Peculiarities of Life at Sea. — Curiosities of the Deep. — Ambergris. — City of Honolulu. — An Island Paradise. — Early Paganism at Hawaii. Wholesale Human Sacrifices. — Royalty at the Race-course. — Not a Kingly Monarch.

WHEN the author resolved upon a journey to the Antipodes he was in London, just returned from Norway, Sweden, and Russia, and contemplated reaching the far-away countries of Australia and New Zealand by going due east through the Mediterranean, the Suez Canal, the Red Sea, and then crossing the Indian Ocean. But this is not the nearest route to Oceania. The English monthly mail for that part of the world is regularly forwarded from Liverpool to Boston or New York, thence across the continent of America, and by steamboat from San Francisco. These mail steamers touch at the Sandwich Islands, after which the course lies southwest into the island-dotted latitudes of the widespread South Pacific. Auckland, in New Zealand, is reached by this route in thirty-seven days from London; and Sydney, in Australia, five days later, — the two great English colonies being separated by over a thousand miles of unbroken ocean. The latter route was adopted by the writer of these pages as being both more comfortable and more expeditious. Having already experienced the sirocco-like heat of the Red Sea throughout its whole length, from Adin to Suez, the prospect of a second journey in that exhausting region was anything but attractive. The Atlantic Ocean was therefore crossed to the westward, and a fair start made from much nearer home; namely, by the American Central Pacific route.

The journey by rail across our own continent was easily accomplished in one week of day-and-night travel, covering a distance of thirty-four hundred miles from Boston to San Francisco. Comfortable sleeping-cars obviate the necessity of stopping by the way for bodily rest, provided the traveller be physically strong and in good health. On a portion of the road one not only retires at his usual hour, but he also breakfasts, dines, and enjoys nearly all the domestic conveniences in the train, while it is moving at a rate varying from thirty-five to forty-five miles per hour, in such well-adjusted cars as hardly to realize that he is all the time being rapidly and surely forwarded to his destination.

The pleasing variety of scenery presented to the eyes of the watchful traveller from the car windows is extremely interesting and peculiarly American, embracing peaceful, widespread, fertile fields, valleys of exquisite verdure, foaming torrents and mountain gorges, together with Alpine ranges worthy of Switzerland. Now the route skirts the largest lakes on the face of the globe, navigated by mammoth steam ships; now follows the silvery course of some broad river, or crosses a great commercial water-way, hundreds of feet above its surface, by iron bridges skilfully hung in air. For scores of miles the road may run parallel with some busy canal crowded with heavily-laden barges, slowly making their way to market. Besides winding through mountain gorges, plains, parks, and primeval forests, one passes *en route* through grand and populous cities numbering half a million and more of people each, as well as through pleasant towns, thrifty villages, pioneer hamlets, and Indian reservations, where the plains are as far-reaching as the open sea, the blue of the sky overhead and the yellow buffalo-grass which carpets the earth forming the only blending colors, — until by and by a distant glimpse of the waters of the Pacific signifies that the land-journey draws near its close, and soon after the young but wonderful giant city of the West, San Francisco, is reached.

Five years had elapsed since we last visited this thriving metropolis, during which brief period whole streets of substantial houses have been erected in what was formerly a suburb of the town, and many noble architectural structures have been reared upon the long avenues previously established. In population forty thousand inhabitants have in that space of time been added to its aggregate numbers, while it is to-day growing in wealth, numbers, and political importance faster than ever before. What a panorama of living interest was afforded by its streets, alleys, and broad boulevards! How impressive to watch its cosmopolitan life, to note the exaggerated love of pleasure exhibited on all hands, the devotion of each active member of the community to money-making, the artificial manners and customs so widely prevailing, the iniquitous pursuits of the desperate and dangerous classes, and the ripe aptitude of their too willing victims! It is the solitary looker-on who sees more than the actors in the great drama of every-day life. It is "the hearing ear and the seeing eye" that enrich the memory and ripen the judgment. Is it not curious to observe how the lines of barbarism and civilization intersect along these teeming avenues?

Of our own country we do not propose to treat at length in these pages; but probably not many of our readers have visited the hidden corners of Chinatown in the metropolis of California, — a section of the city contiguous to its very centre, and yet at total variance with its every aspect. It required but a slight stretch of the imagination after passing its borders to believe oneself in Canton, Pekin, or Hong-Kong, except that the thoroughfares in the Asiatic capitals are mere alleys in width, shut in overhead and darkened by mats, while here we have broad streets after the American and European fashion, open to the sky. They are, however, lined with Chinese shops decked in all their national peculiarities exhibiting the most grotesque signs, while the windows are crowded with outlandish trash, and the whole is surrounded by an Oriental atmosphere. This section is entirely peopled by the Mongolians, and by such poor, fallen, abandoned men and women of other nationalities as seek among these surroundings to hide themselves from the shame and penalty of their crimes. There are but few native Chinese women here, and those that are seen have been smuggled in, it being the rule that none of them shall be landed in this country.

The Chinaman appears thoroughly at home here, and revels in his native dress,—pigtail, odd shoes, and silk attire,—even though he may adopt the American style while working as a stevedore on the wharves, or while engaged in various avocations about the other parts of the city. Here without the least attempt at disguise all the many vices of the race are freely indulged in, especially as regards sensuality, opium-smoking, and gambling. A Chinaman rarely touches spirituous liquors, so that there is no drunkenness to be seen in the district, but only that insensibility which is the effect of indulgence in opium. The thirty thousand Asiatics who live in Chinatown are packed together at night like dried herring in a box. Twenty of them often sleep in the same small room, lying upon the floor, without even an apology for a bed. Here they cook and eat mysterious dishes after the custom of their race, amid smells and filth which no American or European stomach could endure.

A couple of hours sufficed to give us all the personal experience of this locality we had the least wish to acquire, though our official guide of the police force proposed to introduce us to other peculiar sights and into deeper cellars, — places usually hidden from the curious eyes of the general public. The vile practices, indecent and gross exhibitions, which are indulged in by these Mongolians, no respectable paper would publish in detail. In short, Chinatown is the repository of vice of the most brutal and disgusting character, affording the fullest entertainment for the low tastes of the most depraved. Finding that this pandering to the curiosity of a certain class of whites brings them in money, the Chinamen give them all the grossness they are willing to pay for.

The reader, however, must not entertain a wrong idea with regard to Chinatown, since in the midst of all this squalor, dirt, immorality, and wickedness, there are some of this race living here who keep themselves untainted by the objectionable associations that surround them. They are the exceptions, to be sure. We were told of several Chinese gentlemen, for instance, who have amassed large fortunes by legitimate trade, within the last ten or fifteen years, — men who, as reliable and honorable merchants, stand high among the commercial people of San Francisco. Three names were given us by a gentleman who was well informed in the matter, of Asiatics who were each worth over a million dollars. To these were added the names of two who are worth over two millions. These men will not return to China, because the property tax is so high there. Like many of our own citizens, these Chinese find their great satisfaction in accumulating wealth, and so go on adding daily to their possessions. We have said that there are thirty thousand Chinese in this district, but we were officially informed that forty thousand would be much nearer the true aggregate.

The impression prevails that the open immigration of this race has ceased at San Franciso, but the arrival of several hundreds by steamer the day before we visited their miserable quarter of the town, was duly announced in the papers. These came by the way of Japan. A sickening odor adheres to one's clothing for hours after returning from the Asiatic section of San Francisco,—a flavor of musk, opium, stale tobacco, and sandal-wood, the latter being freely burned as an incense before the Chinese gods; for amid all his filth and vileness, John does not forget scrupulously to fulfil the conventional requirements of his idolatrous faith.

After a few days devoted to renewing acquaintance with the familiar localities of the city, passage was taken on board the Union Steamship Company's mail-packet "Zealandia" bound for Australia. Once before the Golden Gate, as the entrance into the harbor of San Francisco is called, had been passed by the author when bound upon a twenty days' sea-voyage. Japan then formed the objective point, the route being a northerly one; but the "Zealandia" was bound for the tropics and the far southern sea, — that vast region forming the largest expanse of ocean in the world and containing fully one half of its water surface. The Pacific measures nine thousand miles from north to south, and is ten thousand miles broad between Quinto, South America, and the Moluccas, or Spice Islands; while at the extreme north, where Behring Strait divides the continents of Asia and America, it is but about forty miles in width, and in clear weather one can distinctly see the shore of Asia from that of our own continent.

The harbor of San Francisco presented much the same busy scene which so impressed us five years before; it was full of commercial activity and the occupations incident to various forms of maritime life. The noise of steam-whistles from the ferry-boats, the hoarse signals from ocean-going vessels starting on long voyages, and the boatswain's shrill whistle were half deafening as they mingled in direst discord. Big white sea-gulls in myriads flew fearlessly in and out among the shipping, uttering defiant screams, or floated like corks upon the water alongside of the ship. In no other part of the world are there so many snow-white sea-gulls to be seen as frequent this spacious and charming bay. They are large, graceful, dignified birds, and are never molested, being looked upon as picturesque ornaments to the harbor; besides which they are the most active sort of scavengers in removing the floating carrion and the débris thrown from the wharves and the cook's galley. The gulls one sees off the coast of Norway and among the Loffoden Islands are thousands in number, but they are not nearly so large as are these bird-monarchs of the Pacific. Their rank, fishy flavor renders them unfit for the table, though the Chinamen about the wharves secretly snare and eat them. Their breeding-places are not known, but they must be hundreds of miles away on unfrequented rocks and reefs. Distance, however, is of little account to these buoyant navigators of the atmosphere.

One of the ship's officers told us of a sea-gull which was caught within the last year just off the Golden Gate, and detained for a brief period on board a steamship bound for Japan. A short piece of red tape was securely tied to one of its legs, after which the bird was released. This identical gull followed the ship across the Pacific into the harbor of Yokohama,—a distance of over four thousand miles. Until this experiment was tried, it had been doubted whether the same individual birds continue with a ship on a long voyage as they seem to do. "You will see the albatross as we get down south," continued the officer, "a bird worth watching, the largest of the gull family, frequently measuring across its outspread wings twelve feet from tip to tip." We resolved to be on the lookout for this king-bird, though rather doubting the mammoth proportions attributed to him.

By turning to a map of the Western Hemisphere it will be found that the Sandwich Islands are located far up in the northeastern part of the Pacific Ocean, whence a vessel laying her course for New Zealand steers south by west through a long tract of ocean, seemingly so full of islands that the inexperienced are apt to wonder how she can hold such a course and not run foul of some of the Polynesian groups. But so vast are the distances in Oceania, so mathematically exact are the rules of navigation, so well known are the prevailing winds and currents, that the passengers of a steamship may make the voyage and not sight even a headland between Honolulu and Auckland, — a distance of more than four thousand miles. This is the course we pursued, first steering for the Hawaiian group, and thence for the north headlands of New Zealand, *via* Tutuila, of the Samoan Islands.

It was Magellan, the Portuguese navigator, who first discovered this great ocean, sailing through the strait which bears his name. In the month of November, 1520, he finally came into the waters of the new sea upon which he was the first to sail, and which he named Mar Pacifico. It may have been "pacific" in his day, or may have seemed so to him after experiencing some rough weather on the other side of the continent of America, but we have seen it more turbulent than the Atlantic, especially where it approaches the Antarctic circle. Magellan did not long survive to enjoy the fame and profit of his discovery, as about a twelvemonth later he was killed in an unfortunate skirmish with the savages of some of the Pacific islands. He is often compared with his great contemporary Columbus, whose experience in the West Indies was undoubtedly the incentive for Magellan on his voyages of discovery.

Sea-life is conducive to idleness, and the saline atmosphere is narcotic. Lying in his berth the voyager gazes listlessly at the yellow iron-mould on the towels, the greasy moreen curtains, the restless hanging-lamp, and the damp, begrimed carpet, while he inhales the unpleasant bilge-scented atmosphere which penetrates everything. The jerking motion of the ship shaken incessantly by the propeller, causes the letters of the printed regulations tacked upon the door to run together in unintelligible lines, until at last he grows dizzy with the ceaseless motion imparted to everything. Finally, with a sudden burst of energy the deck is reached, where there is pretty sure to be something suggestive to occupy the mind and vary the wearisome monotony. The wonderful blue of the sea by day, and its fire-like phosphorescence by night, are always interesting. The Mediterranean between Malta and Gibraltar is proverbially blue, but the Pacific seemed to us more so. At times it lay as if in a trance, a perfect calm, the ship's keel gliding as it were over a burnished metallic field, or a flood of molten sapphire. The familiar jelly-fish often appeared above the liquid depths, contracting and expanding its soft, flat body, and thus progressing through the still waters, its half-transparent form emitting opaline colors under the warm rays of the sun. The many-armed, vaulting cuttle-fish was seen now and again leaping out of the water as though pursued by some aquatic enemy, though its general habit is not to frequent the surface by daylight. Specimens of the deep-sea star-fish with its five arms of equal length were abundant. Those which we met here were of a reddish and purple color combined, but we have seen them in shallower waters of a bright orange-yellow. While exhibiting but little apparent life, the star-fish can yet be quite aggressive when pressed by hunger and in search of food, having, as naturalists tell us, a mysterious way of causing the oyster to open its shell, whereupon the star-fish proceeds gradually to consume the body of the bivalve.

One frail, small rover of the quiet surface of the sea always interested us, — the tiny nautilus, with a transparent shell almost as frail as writing-paper. It was to be seen only in calm weather. If disturbed, it drew itself within its sheltering cover and sank slowly from sight. No wonder the ancient Greeks saw in its beautifully corrugated shell the graceful model of a galleon; and hence its name, derived from the Greek word which signifies a ship.

Every amusing suggestion, however trivial, is welcome, if it only serves to break the depressing monotony of the sea, — a sail, a shark, a new ocean bird, a school of porpoises. Two or three of our passengers had supplied themselves with microscopes, and they often dropped a gauze scoop-net over the ship's side, where it was permitted to trail for a few moments;

then drawing it on board they amused themselves by subjecting the contents to a microscopic examination. The results were often very curious. On one occasion a short bit of floating sea-weed was thus obtained, upon which was securely woven a cluster of what looked like tiny quinces in shape, though the color was jet black. They were called sea-grapes by the sailors, but we knew them to be a cluster of fishes' eggs. They proved to be those of the cuttle-fish, and were eighteen or twenty in number.

Amiable persons exhibit their natural traits of disposition at sea in strong contrast to those who are actuated by opposite qualities, — the latter, we are sorry to say, being nearly always in the majority. Enmities and friendships are formed with equal promptness and facility; but however desirable it may be, there is no escaping the forced companionship incident to life on shipboard, where ceremony is for the time being mostly banished. Customs become established which would be considered rather *outré* upon land. Ennui has made more persons reckless than has despair. Those individuals are comparatively few on such occasions who have sufficient mental resource profitably to occupy their minds, and those who have nothing to do quickly tire of themselves and of all about them. If it were not for the decided breaks in the routine of each day and evening afforded by the several meals, surely suicides at sea would be frequent. One inevitable conclusion is sure to be arrived at; namely, that a long sea-voyage is an infallible remedy for over-fastidiousness and sickly sentimentality.

When we had been at sea about a week there was observed floating upon the water a pale-gray, amber-like substance; it was not abundant, but to the watchful eye seemed peculiar, and was several times apparent. This our captain declared to be ambergris,— a substance originally found in the intestines of the sperm whale, and believed to be produced there only. Science declares it to be a diseased secretion of the animal, probably induced by indigestion,— just as the pearl is a diseased secretion of the Australian and Penang oysters. Ambergris is often found floating about the shores of the Coral Sea and throughout the region known as Australasia, having been ejected by the many whales frequenting these latitudes. On the west coast of New Zealand the natives may frequently be seen searching along the shore after a heavy gale, eagerly securing more or less of the article. The "Zealandia," on her previous voyage to that of which we are now writing, brought from Auckland to San Francisco three boxes of ambergris weighing about one hundred pounds each, the three boxes being invoiced at a valuation of thirty thousand dollars. It is rarely that so much is imported into this country in a twelvemonth. When first taken from the whale it is of a soft texture, and is quite offensive to the smell; but after a brief exposure to the air it rapidly hardens, and then emits a sweet, earthy odor, and is used for the manufacture of the choicest perfumery, being nearly as important for that purpose as the more costly musk.

The peculiar currents of the sea in these special regions, its vast extent and fabulous depths, the huge monsters and the tiny creatures occupying it, the speed of the ship, her exact tonnage and the trade in which she had been engaged since she was launched on the Clyde, — all these items became of vital importance to the voyagers, but their detail would seem prosy to the general reader. It was really surprising to see how earnest intelligent people become over matters which under ordinary circumstances and on shore would not have received a moment's consideration.

The distance which we expected to accomplish was referred to daily, and was thus formulated: From San Francisco to Honolulu is twenty-one hundred miles; from Honolulu to Auckland is thirty-eight hundred miles; from Auckland to Sydney is twelve hundred and eighty miles. The ship's run was daily recorded and posted up for the general satisfaction, the result being promptly deducted from the aggregated figures as above.

It was on the eighth day of the voyage that we made the Sandwich Islands. A glance at the map will show the reader that these volcanic upheavals lie on the bosom of the North Pacific, in a slight curve, and number thirteen in all. The total area combined does not exceed sixty-five hundred square miles, seven of them being mere islets, and six only are inhabited. The largest of the group is Hawaii, situated the farthest south, being in round numbers a hundred miles long by eighty broad, and with the natives gives its name to the whole group, as they are here officially called the Hawaiian Islands, — though Captain Cook, on their first being discovered, about a hundred years ago, gave them the name of the Sandwich Islands, after the then first Lord of the English Admiralty, and by this latter name they are generally known on the maps and in geographies.

The chain of islands which form the group are but a series of volcanic peaks rising abruptly from a depth of three miles below the sea-level to as great a height above it, being, so to speak, natural chimneys from the tops of which vast internal fires in former ages have found vent.

We made the island of Oahu, passing along the windward shores of Maui and Molokai in the early gray of a soft June morning, and doubling the lofty promontory known as Diamond Head, which rears its precipitous front seven hundred feet above the sea. We ran along the coast while the sun rose and beautified the mountain-tops, the green slopes, gulches, and fern-clad hills sparkling with streamlets. The dawn was lovely in its aspect, fresh and sweet. A gentle land-breeze brought us the dewy fragrance of the flowers which had been distilled from a wilderness of bloom during the tropical night. The uncertain light melted slowly away as a dainty flush appeared in the east. A few transparent clouds hung over the verdant isle, clouds so fleecy and ermine-like that they might have been the mantles of angels. It was entrancing thus to be gliding noiselessly over a perfectly calm sea, with so many attendant elements of beauty. We stood quite alone in the bow of the ship, wondering how the passengers below could court the thrall of sleep at such a moment.

As we drew nearer and nearer to the shore, sugar plantations, cocoanut groves, and verdant pastures came clearly into view, dotted here and there with the low primitive dwellings of the natives, and occasionally ornamented by the picturesque, vine-covered cottages of American and European residents. As the city of Honolulu was approached, it seemed to be half buried in a cloud of luxuriant foliage. Blessed with frequent rains, drought is not known here, and the verdure is perennial.

The sudden change of the color of the ocean was very noticeable as we steamed at half speed through a narrow gap of the coral reef which forms a natural breakwater to the harbor. We passed the lighthouse which stands on the inner edge of the reef, — a structure not over thirty feet in height, consequently not visible from a ship's deck more than ten miles away. The captain informed us that it was the only light between this island and the coast of New Zealand, in the far South Pacific. The channel through the reef to safe anchorage is carefully buoyed on either side, and at night a safety-lantern is placed upon each of these little floating beacons, so that a steamer can easily steer her course in safety, come when she may.

Though the volcanic origin of the land is plain, it is not the sole cause of these reefs and islands appearing thus in mid-ocean. Upon the flanks of the upheaval the coral insect with tireless industry rears its amazing structure, until it reaches the surface of the waves as a reef, more or less contiguous to the shore, and to which ages finally serve to join it. The tiny creature delegated by Providence to build these reefs dies on exposure to air, — its work being then done. The far-reaching antiquity of the islands is established by these very coralline formations, which could only have attained their present elevation just below the surface by the growth of thousands of years. As already intimated, the land rises so abruptly from the bottom of the sea that the water retains its dark-blue tint to within a short distance of the shore, where it assumes a light-blue and bottle-green hue, with other magic colors striking in their effect viewed beneath the clear morning light and embossed with the rays of the glowing sun.

We were soon safely moored inside the harbor, where there is an average depth of sixteen fathoms, and room for a hundred large vessels to find anchorage at the same time. The wharves are spacious and most substantially built, with ample depth alongside. Honolulu, which is situated on the south side of the island, is the commercial port of the whole group, — the half-way house, as it were, between North

America and Asia, California and the New World of Australasia.

The streets of the Anglo-Hawaiian capital are clean and all admirably macadamized, the material employed for the purpose being coral, black lava, stone, and sand. At night the thoroughfares are rendered nearly as light as by day, through the liberal use of gas. One of the first things to attract our attention after landing was a huge steam-rolling machine at work upon the road-bed of one of the streets leading to the wharves. The city, with its twenty thousand inhabitants more or less, has all the belongings of modern civilization, such as churches, charitable institutions, hospitals, schools, gas, electric lights, and the telephone; yet it was forced upon the mind how brief the period that had transpired since this was nearly a wilderness, peopled by a race of cannibals, whose idolatrous superstitions involved frequent human sacrifices. To-day nearly all the rising generation can read and write, and the entire race are professed Christians. One fact especially indicative of progress came to our knowledge; namely, that the government expends fifty thousand dollars annually upon the local schools. Could a stronger contrast be found than the aspect presented by Honolulu when Captain Cook discovered these islands, in 1778, and that of the Honolulu of 1888? In imagination we find ourself trying to look forward to the close of another century, and surmising what may then be the condition of these isolated spots of earth.

The original paganism of this people was of the most brutal type, revelling in human gore. We were told of rows of stone altars on which a hundred victims are known to have been sacrificed at one time, the altars still standing as memorials of the wretched idolatrous worship of the past. Such scenes were of frequent occurrence among the aborigines, surrounded by a climate which was nearly perfect, and by a profuseness and bounty of vegetation that made the support of life a mere holiday existence. They poured out human blood like water upon the altars erected to their idols, and fattened upon human flesh. It is strange indeed that some of the most lovely parts of the world should have been peopled by cannibals. We speak in the past tense; but all travellers in savage, half-civilized lands know that there are many waste places of the earth which are to-day the abode of the anthropophagi.

In those early days the several islands of the Hawaiian group had each a separate king. Bitter wars were frequent among them, and the savages of the Pacific islands always ate their prisoners taken in battle. King Kamehameha finally subjected the several isles to his sway, and founded the government which has lasted to our day.

Many of the streets of Honolulu present a grateful shade along the sidewalks, being lined by choice ornamental trees, of which the cocoanut, palm, bread-fruit, candle-nut, and some others are indigenous; but many have been introduced from abroad and become thoroughly domesticated. The tall mango-tree with its rich, glossy leaves, the branches bending under the weight of its delicious fruit, was seen growing everywhere, though it is not a native of these islands. It was impossible not to observe with acute interest the great variety of fruit-trees, most of whose pendulous branches were heavy with luscious products. Among them were the feathery tamarind, the orange, lime, alligator-pear, citron-fig, date, palm, rose-apple, and some others whose names we did not learn. Of all the flowering trees the brilliant *Ponciana regia* was most conspicuous and attractive, with its cloud of scarlet blossoms, each cluster as large as a Florida orange.

Some of the thoroughfares, especially that known as King's Street, are lined by pretty, low-built cottages, standing a hundred feet and more back from the roadway, with broad, inviting verandas, the whole front festooned and nearly hidden by tropical and semi-tropical plants in full bloom. This delightful aspect was supplemented by lovely flower-beds, and groups of ornamental trees in the gardens, with here and there an isolated Norfolk Island pine, forcing its strong individuality of shape and foliage upon the observation. A China rose-tree full of crimson flowers was noticed, and in a garden near the palace we saw a peach-tree, with one side full of rosy blossoms, while the other was decked with ripening fruit. How this was achieved we did not stop to inquire, pausing only long enough to admire the novel and anomalous effect. The gardens of Honolulu do not lack for water, a never-failing supply of the precious liquid being brought from the neighboring mountains in large iron pipes, and introduced into each city dwelling; moreover, we were told by the residents that they have only to sink a well ten or twelve feet deep anywhere on the plateau occupied by the city, when an abundance of water can always be secured. It was delightful to think that this lovely floral display to be seen all about us, around the native shanties as well as in the grounds of the better classes, was not confined to any one season, but that the various months of the year were severally beautified with roses, lilies, and the thousand and one gems of Flora's kingdom grown out-of-doors.

The race-course of Honolulu is situated four or five miles from the city proper, and is reached by a hard, well-kept, level road passing, it seemed, through one continuous tropical garden. Here was presented to us a gay and interesting picture of strong local color. The course occupies ample grounds laid out and fenced in the usual circular style of a one-mile track. The racing was conducted by the Jockey Club of the city, who certainly introduced on this occasion some remarkably well-bred animals. However they may have become possessed of the money, the natives, high and low, seemed to have plenty of loose cash to bet with, and the silver dollars were rapidly passed from hand to hand as each trial came to an issue. It was all conducted upon the cash principle; no accounts seemed to be kept, but settlements were made then and there, between the races. The scene was enlivened with music furnished by the king's native band, composed of twenty-eight colored men led by a German conductor. This band is certainly under remarkable discipline and very scientific instruction, and few similar organizations of white men in America can be truthfully said to excel them. They were uniformed in pure white linen ornamented with brass buttons, bearing the national Hawaiian arms, and wore snow-white helmets tipped with spikes of glittering brass of the German army pattern.

King Kalakana, who is very fond of racing and always assists at these exhibitions, greeted us cordially upon the grand stand, where he sat among the other spectators dressed in a suit of white linen and a plain straw hat. A few moments later, by invitation of his Majesty we stepped into an adjoining apartment, where he jauntily tossed off a goblet brimming with champagne, adding a few pleasant words of welcome. The trouble with him is that he is far too much inclined "to look upon the wine when it is red," though we were informed confidentially that his favorite tipple was gin. Notwithstanding that he is a man of more than ordinary intelligence, and even of a considerable degree of culture, morally speaking he has no traits of character which command respect, and is at times so much given to a sensual life as to outrage all kingly associations, incurring the disgust even of his most intimate associates. In person he is tall, well built, a little over six feet in height, of very dark complexion, and with crisp curly hair. He is remarkably superstitious, we were told, and consults pretended supernatural agents as to various State matters. This trait must have been born in him, and is matched by a similar spirit prevailing in the breast of every native. He is too selfish in disposition to be exercised by any real degree of patriotism, and "can be bought at a very low market value in connection with any private enterprise," to quote the words of a leading citizen with whom we conversed about the political condition of the islands. There are always plenty of adventurers ready to take advantage of such possible venality, and our informant told us that there were stories privately circulated, and undoubtedly true, which if publicly substantiated would result in his being dethroned. "Indeed," he added, "there is only a sort of phantom royalty maintained in Honolulu." These considerations did not tend to prepossess us much in the king's favor; and besides, it was impossible readily to forget that his direct ancestors slew, roasted, and ate Captain Cook.

This delectable monarch has just passed his fifty-second year, and as he may very properly be styled a fast liver, his career will hardly be a long one, more especially as the islands seem to be in a troubled political condition, so deep seated that a revolution is at all times imminent, while the proposed establishment of a republic is freely prognosticated and openly discussed. It is reported that the king has lately been detected in receiving heavy bribes for the granting of certain valuable and exclusive privileges; besides which, his personal life and habits being, as already intimated, extremely repulsive to a large portion of the people, he is growing daily more and more unpopular. It is well known that merchants and resident foreigners have been for some time taking serious steps for self-protection and the safe care of their property in the event of a popular uprising. The present king, it will be remembered, was elected to the throne by ballot upon the death of the former sovereign, who died about fourteen years ago, without leaving any regular heir to succeed him. The heir-apparent to the throne is the brother of the king, and is now thirty-three years of age.

CHAPTER II.

Ladies Riding Astride. — Passion for Flower Decorations. — A Sailor on a Bucking Horse. — A Weekly Gala-day. — Hawaiian Ladies' Costume. — A Famous Battle-ground. — The Native's Staff of Life. — Ubiquitous John Chinaman. — Largest Apple-orchard in the World. — Hawaiians as Cannibals. — An Active Volcano. — Colony of Lepers. — Unwelcome Visitors. — Our Political Relations with the Sandwich Islands.

THERE are not infrequently substantial reasons for customs which appear to us absurd at first blush. It was observed at the race-course of Honolulu that the women all rode man-fashion, — that is, astride of their horses; and being accustomed to the saddle from childhood they rode remarkably well. Even European and American ladies who become residents also adopt this fashion of riding, for the reason, as we were told, that side-saddles are not considered to be safe on the steep mountain roads. If one rides in any direction here mountains must be crossed. Every one rides on horseback, — men, women, and children. He must be a poor man indeed who does not own two or three horses of the pony, island breed. There are plenty of light American-built vehicles to be had for use about the city roads, but wheels will not answer upon the mountain paths. It should be mentioned, for the benefit of invalids as well as pleasure travellers, that there is an admirable public house in the centre of the town, built by the Government and leased to a competent landlord. It is kept on the American plan, and has all the modern comforts and conveniences, is lighted by gas, furnished with electric bells, and has accommodations for fifty guests.

The native women festoon themselves in an extraordinary manner with flowers on all gala occasions, while the men wear wreaths of the same about their straw hats, often adding braided leaves of laurel hung across the shoulder and chest. The white blossoms of the jasmine, fragrant as tuberoses, which they much resemble, are generally employed for this decorative purpose, being offered for sale about the streets and on the veranda of the hotel in long strings woven fresh from the vines. Upon the slightest excuse for doing so, all Honolulu blossoms like a rose. We landed on a Saturday, which is a regular gala-day with the natives, and indeed every one seems to join in making it a general holiday. It is pay-day on the plantations and in the town establishments, besides being the day on which the country people come to market with their produce. But all marketing, all buying and selling of goods is over by noon or an hour after, when the riot of pleasure-seeking begins. It was a ludicrous sight to observe the sailors who happened to be in port join in the Saturday carnival. To do so in proper style it was absolutely necessary for them to be on horseback; and a sailor in that situation always seems like a fish out of water. With his feet thrust as far into the stirrups as possible, his body bent well forward and with both hands firmly grasping the pommel of the saddle, he leaves the horse to go pretty much his own way, while he thumps hard and fast up and down in his uncertain seat, to the undisguised merriment of the natives and lookers-on generally.

One of these foremast hands had been furnished with a bucking horse, — we rather think designedly so. The animal was subject to periodical attacks of this vicious propensity, one of which fits took him directly opposite the Post-office, where we chanced to be standing. It was really astonishing to see how successfully the unaccustomed rider clung to the horse's back; a practised rider could not have kept his seat more determinedly. The struggle between horse and man lasted for some ten minutes, but was finally ended by Jack Tar being landed in the middle of the street face downward, to the infinite amusement of the crowd who had watched the progress of the struggle. Jack, nevertheless, remounted his Bucephalus, and rode away with his comrades, who had patiently awaited the issue, bestriding the animal as he would have done a topsail yard in a gale of wind.

Both sexes of the natives much affect bright colors upon their persons, such as scarlet turbans wound about their heads; and sky-blue scarfs and yellow gowns predominate, producing a very picturesque if somewhat anomalous effect. When the head is bare their jet-black hair is sleek and glistening with cocoanut oil. The women wear but one garment, usually of French calico, close at the throat and extending from the yoke to the ankles. The gown is quite free and flowing, not confined at the waist, the wearer being generally bare-legged and bare-footed, — thus adding to the diaphanous nature of the costume, which after all is well adapted to the climate. It was noticed that the foreign-born ladies often appeared in the same style of dress, adding slippers and hose. To be very fleshy is considered as adding a charm to the Hawaiian ladies; and however this is brought about, it certainly prevails, affording the individual possessor of such a plethoric condition evident satisfaction. As a people the Hawaiians are very courteous and respectful, rarely failing to greet the passing stranger with a pleasant smile and a softly articulated " oloha," equivalent to " my love to you." The drinking of kava, the native spirituous liquor, is no doubt conducive to the immoderate accumulation of flesh, or at least to a bloated condition of the body; but as a rule the natives are not intemperate drinkers, except perhaps on Saturdays, when, as we have already intimated, the town is half mad with all sorts of excesses.

One statue only was noticed in Honolulu, — a bronze figure representing Kamehameha I., which was decked with a gilded robe and helmet, producing a tawdry and vulgar effect. There are four bronze tablets in bas-relief upon the pedestal, representing emblematical scenes relating to the first discovery of the island by Captain Cook and of his early intercourse with the barbarous natives. The whole monument is crude and inartistic, but doubtless it was an expensive affair. This Kamehameha I. must have been anything but a nice sort of person. When the missionaries first came hither he was living with his five sisters as wives; and when told how outrageous this was in the light of Christianity, he compromised the matter by selecting his oldest sister as his favorite wife and discarding the rest. He died in 1819, at the age of eighty-three years, and was a polygamous old rascal or a patriotic Alexander, according to the standpoint from which he is judged. If we can credit the Hawaiian legends, he was a man who possessed great physical strength as well as skill in the use of weapons, and was undoubtedly brave. He was the father of his people in more than one sense, having as many children as the late Brigham Young.

A drive of three or four miles from the city brings one to what is called the "Pali," which signifies in English the precipice. The route thither is straight up the Nuuanu Valley over a very uneven and only half-passable road, rocks and stones disputing every foot of the way with the vehicle, until by a not very abrupt ascent a height of three thousand feet above sea-level is reached. The last part of the distance is accomplished on foot, and presently the visitor finds himself standing upon the very edge of an abrupt precipice at the head of the valley, affording one of the most remarkable views to be found in any part of the globe. Lying fifteen hundred feet below the brow of this cliff is an outspread area of thirty or forty square miles embracing hills marked by winding bridle-paths, level plains, small rolling prairies, groves of cocoanut, of bananas, and sugar-cane plantations, small herds of cattle on grazing ranches, and rice-fields extending to the verge of the ocean. This large area is bordered on either side by mountains of various heights, composed of lava-rock so formed as to give the appearance of having been cleft in two, the precipitous side left standing, and the other half lost in the ocean; coral reefs form the seaward boundary marked by a long, white, irregular line of surf breaking over them. As one regards this view from the top of the Pali, there arises on his immediate right a steep mountain four thousand feet heavenward, forming the highest point on the island of Oahu, recorded as being at the apex seven thousand feet above the level of the sea.

The valley of Nuuanu opens with a broad entrance at the end nearest to the city, but contracts gradually as one ascends, until at its head it is a narrow gap or mountain-pass through which is a bridle-path leading over the range to the country below. Through this pass the wind draws with such power and velocity as to compel the traveller to grasp securely the iron barrier which has been erected to enable one to approach the verge of the cliff in safety. This narrow opening forms the gate through which Honolulu gets its daily taste of the refreshing trade-winds.

In ascending this beautiful valley one is constantly charmed by the discovery of new tropical trees, luxurious creepers, and lovely wild-flowers. The strangers' burial-ground is passed just after crossing the Nuuanu stream, and close at hand is the Royal Mausoleum, — a stone structure in Gothic style, which contains the remains of all the Hawaiian kings, as well as those of many of the high chiefs who have died since the conquest. Some shaded bathing-pools are formed by the mountain streams lying half hidden in the dense foliage. Here one also passes the residence of ex-Queen Emma, widow of the late king, pleasantly located and flower-embowered, having within its grounds some notable examples of fine tropical trees from other lands. Its mistress was educated in England, and has here surrounded herself with many European comforts and elegancies. She may be seen almost daily driving out in a pony-carriage, to which a nice pair of showy though small island-bred horses are attached.

This valley is classic ground in the history of these islands, being the spot where the fierce and conquering invader, King Kamehameha I., fought his last decisive battle, the result of which confirmed him as sole monarch of the Hawaiian group. Here the natives of Oahu made their final stand, and fought desperately, resisting with clubs and spears the savage hordes led by Kamehameha. But they were defeated at last, and with their king, Kaiana, who led them in person, were driven over the abrupt and fatal cliff by hundreds, bravely ending the struggle for liberty with the sacrifice of their lives. The half-caste guide tells the stranger of this battle and its issue with a sad air and earnestness of feeling not akin to the humdrum stories of European guides, who recite their lesson by rote, like parrots.

No person should land at Honolulu and go away without visiting the Pali. It can easily be accomplished in three or four hours by vehicle, or if one is pressed for time it can be done more quickly, and to the author's mind much more agreeably, on horseback. In our eagerness to see and enjoy every aspect of the valley, breakfast had been forgotten, and it was already high noon, so that a preparation of wild bananas, bruised into a paste and stewed in cocoanut cream, was partaken of with much relish at a native hut. The dish was new to us, and was rendered still more acceptable by a cup of native coffee, which had not been adulterated by the cunning trader's art.

On the way to the valley, and indeed all about the environs of the city, one passes large patches, measuring an acre more or less, of submerged land, where is grown the Hawaiian staff of life, — the *taro*, a root which is cultivated in mud, and mostly under water, recalling the rice-fields as we have seen them in Japan and China. The article thus produced, when baked and pounded to a paste, forms a nutritious sort of dough, like uncooked flour, which is called *poi*, constituting the principal article of food with the natives, as potatoes do with the Irish or macaroni with the

Italians. The baked taro is powdered and mixed with water, after which it is left to ferment; and when this process has taken place it is ready for eating. It is then placed in a large bowl about which the natives squat on their hams, and thrusting their fingers into the blue liquid mass they adroitly convey a mouthful at a time to their lips and rapidly swallow it. It is served in various degrees of thickness; if very thin, it is called two-finger poi, because in order to convey sufficient for a mouthful to the lips two fingers must be used; but if thick, it is one-finger poi. As the lazzaroni of Naples pride themselves upon their expertness in conveying the cooked macaroni to their mouths and down their throats, so the Kanakas become experts in the transmission of poi to satisfy their hunger. These Sandwich Island natives eat a small species of fish resembling our smelts, quite raw, with their poi.

The environs of the city in any direction are composed of well-irrigated gardens, plantations of bananas, clusters of cocoanuts, figs, mangoes, melons, and various tropical fruits. The cocoanut-grove of Waikiki, about four miles from Honolulu, contains many of these prolific trees, and well repays a visit. Single cocoanut-trees are always graceful and interesting, with their tall wrinkled stems, but a small forest of them is a sight worth going miles to behold. The weight of the nutritious fruit supported in the branches can only be computed by the hundreds of tons.

Palolo Valley is some ten miles from Honolulu, and is best reached on horseback. Here the crater of an extinct volcano forms the principal object of interest. Leaving the horses at the head of the valley, the visitor climbs up a precipitous slope some five hundred feet to the oblong opening, which is now filled with a great variety of peculiar ferns, quite unlike any to be found elsewhere. Many blooming wild-flowers also beautified the spot whence the fiery lava poured forth its molten stream long ages ago. Nearly a hundred marked varieties of ferns can be gathered here in the briefest period of time by an expert botanist. On the way thither one passes through gulches, forests, and fields of the rankest tropical verdure, at times enjoying glimpses from the heights, of scenery indescribably grand and beautiful, like all that appertains to this picturesque island group, the puzzle of geologists and geographers. Though Oahu is very mountainous, like the rest of the Hawaiian islands, still none of these ranges reach the elevation of perpetual snow.

The delight and favorite amusement of the natives is to get into the saddle, galloping hither and thither in a break-neck fashion, without any fixed purpose as to destination. Some are seen riding bare-back, some with bridles, and some with only halters; but all are astride. The women and young girls are particularly conspicuous in their high-colored costumes flowing in the wind, and supplemented by streaming wreaths and strings of flowers, while they manage their horses with consummate skill and masculine energy.

Having observed among the natives a certain type of features and general aspect which struck us as decidedly European, and which if genuine would seem to be traceable far back to early generations, the idea was expressed to a resident American, who had an interesting explanation promptly ready for us. It seems, according to our friend's story, that the Spaniards are accredited in the legends of Oahu with having discovered these islands, and with several times visiting them as early as the year 1500, thus rendering the first visit of Captain Cook no new discovery. It is further held that Spanish galleons on their way to and from Manila in the sixteenth century stopped at these islands for water and fresh fruits. Of course all this is but legendary, and based on the faintest shadow of proof. Furthermore, according to these traditions, a couple of Spanish ships from Mexico were wrecked on the Hawaiian islands about the year 1525, having, as was the custom in those days, a numerous crew as well as some passengers, who mixed with and married native women. Naturally the descendants of such unions have inherited a certain distinctiveness of features and complexion which is still traceable. We give this report as we heard it, though it may be all a myth.

The ubiquitous Chinamen are found here as gardeners, laborers, house-servants, fruit-dealers, and poi-makers. What an overflow there has been of these Asiatics from the Flowery Land! Each one of this race arriving at these islands is now obliged to pay ten dollars as his landing fee, in default of which the vessel which brings him is compelled to take him away. This singular people, who are wonderfully industrious notwithstanding their many faults and effeminacies, are despised in these islands alike by the natives, the Americans, and the Europeans; and yet we were told that the Chinese increase annually, slowly but surely, and it is believed here that they are destined eventually to take the place of the aborigines. The aggregate number now resident upon the group is placed at ten thousand. It was manifest that many branches of small trade were already monopolized by them, as one sees to be the case at Penang, Singapore, and other Pacific islands. On Nuuanu Street every shop is occupied by a Chinaman, dealing in such articles as his own countrymen and the natives are likely to purchase. It certainly does appear as though the native race would in the near future be obliterated, and their place be filled by the Anglo-Saxons and the Chinese, — the representative people of the East and the West. The taro-patches of the Hawaiians, will ere long become the rice-fields of the Mongolians and the places that now know the aborigines will know them no more forever.

The pertinacity which enables these Asiatics to get a foothold and maintain themselves in various countries in the face of such universal oppression and unpopularity, is a constant source of surprise to one who has seen them established and prospering in so many foreign lands. Nothing seems to discourage a Chinaman; he encounters rebuffs, insults, oppression, taxation, with entire equanimity, toiling on, suffering in silence, accumulating and hoarding his dollars with the fixed purpose of finally returning to his distant home. He is sober, painstaking, patient, and provided you do not have too much of him, is by no means a bad servant, laborer, or mechanic.

The general fish-market, situated at the northern extremity of Queen's Street, affords a most interesting exhibition of the marine products of these shores. Here all was life, bustle, color, and oddity, vividly recalling a similar scene in another hemisphere, at Havana. The berries, fish, and fruit which one purchases are delivered in a broad, fresh green leaf which forms the wrapper. This is much nicer, as well as more appropriate, than is the use of rough, ill-smelling brown paper. Here we saw devil-fish, dolphins, bonitos, flying-fish, ocean mullet, crabs, and a great variety of sea-mosses which the natives dry and eat with their poi. Among the rest a plenty of gold and silver fish were noticed, such as are kept in glass globes as pets with us. Here they are larger, and so plentiful that the natives catch and eat them as they would any other of the finny tribe. Some of the fishes displayed here are spotted like a leopard, and some are striped like a tiger, — dark brown lines on a buff ground. Besides these there was an abundance of rose-colored medusa. The variety and beauty of colors exhibited by the fishes of the tropics is quite confusing when they are arrayed side by side upon a white marble counter fresh from their native element. The natives eat very little meat, but keep in excellent physical condition upon poi and fish, supplemented by the abundant natural fruits which a bountiful Providence so liberally supplies. Chief among these is the banana, which seems to grow larger and finer here than elsewhere, being permitted to ripen on the parent stem. Like oranges which are allowed to mature in the same manner, the flavor is far superior to those ripened off the trees.

The steep conical hill which overlooks the city presenting its dull, brick-red façade when viewed from nearly any direction is a ceaseless reminder of the volcanic origin of the place. It contains a large extinct crater, and is called on account of its peculiar formation the Punch Bowl. Its apex is about five hundred feet above the level of the harbor. At the top one looks down into a large concave, — a scooped-out, bowl-like cavity, partially filled with a débris of stones and cinders over and about which vegetation has freely grown, the earth being mixed with decomposed lava. A few goats were browsing over this sleeping crater, which has been enacting the part of Rip Van Winkle for a score or more of centuries. We enjoyed a perfect view from the summit, which was high enough to form an admirable picture of land and sea combined. On the side which overlooks

Honolulu are the remains of an old fort, which commands the Hawaiian capital.

Speaking of fruits, we were informed that on the neighboring island of Maui, one of the most spacious and mountainous of the group, is the largest apple-orchard in the world. The natives call this fruit *ohias*. The forest of apple-trees stretches from sea to sea far up the mountains. The trees vary from forty to fifty feet in height, yielding their harvest from July to September, during which period they are laden with a fair-sized, wild, white apple, which is not unpalatable to the taste, though not equal to the cultivated fruit. This orchard is estimated to cover an area of over ten miles wide and nearly twice as long. The trees, we were told, will average over twenty-five barrels of apples each. No commercial and little domestic use is made of them, but the fruit ripens, falls off the trees, and there decays annually. One peculiarity of the product is that when ripe the apples will keep sound but for a few days, as is the case with ripe bananas. The natives eat them to a moderate extent, but make no great account of them. We took the liberty of suggesting the possible advantage of a cider-mill, but our informant said, with a shrug of the shoulders, that there was not sufficient local enterprise to start the business.

The six inhabited islands of the Hawaiian group are Kauai, Oahu, Molokai, Lanai, Maui, and Hawaii, the last containing the largest active volcano on the globe; namely, that of Kilauea, to visit which many persons cross the Atlantic and Pacific oceans, besides the continent of America, which lies between the two. Oahu, of which Honolulu is the capital, was chosen as the principal harbor because it is the only one presenting all the marine necessities, such as sufficient depth of water, space, and a secure anchorage for ships. In the olden days of Hawaiian history, Lahaina, on the island of Maui, was the city of the king, and the recognized capital. This was in the palmy days of the whale fishery. It has a sheltered roadstead, but will not compare with the present capital in this respect. The settlement is now going to ruin, the palace tumbling to pieces by wear and tear of the elements, and all the surroundings are a picture of decay. Should the Panama canal ever be completed, it would prove to be of immense advantage to these islands, as they lie on the direct course which a great share of navigation must follow. The aggregate population of the group is now about sixty thousand, of whom some thirty-eight thousand are natives. History tells us that Captain Cook estimated these islands to contain over three hundred thousand inhabitants when he discovered them. Perhaps this was an exaggeration, though it is a fact that they are capable of sustaining a population of even much greater density than this estimate would indicate. Until within fifty or sixty years the natives of the several islands made war upon one another, principally for the purpose of securing prisoners, whom they roasted and devoured. Indeed, cannibalism has existed in some of the islands even to a more modern date than that referred to. Of latter years the natives have shown a hearty desire to affiliate and intermarry with Europeans and Americans, discarding their idolatrous worship and professing Christianity; but those who read well-meant missionary reports can hardly realize how little this profession of Christianity generally signifies among semi-barbarous races. The manners, customs, and dress of the whites have been very generally adopted, so far as external appearances go; but as in the case of all other aboriginals who inhabit the Pacific isles, large or small, wherever the white man appears in numbers, the black disappears.

The crater of Kilauea on the island of Hawaii is still in a semi-active condition. Twice within our memory it has burst forth briefly but with enormous power, and at this writing it sends forth ceaseless vapor, smoke, and sulphurous gases, with occasional bursts of stones, lava, and crude metallic substances. The fiery opening is four thousand feet above the base of the mountain, the orifice having an estimated diameter of eight miles; that is to say, it is that distance across the opening. The height above sea-level is placed at six thousand feet.

One would surely think that such an enormous orifice on the earth's surface ought to be sufficient to relieve all the smouldering subterraneous fires and explosive gases confined beneath the crust of the habitable globe, saying nothing of Vesuvius, Etna, and a dozen other active volcanoes. In the year 1840 an eruption took place from the crater of Mauna Loa on the same island, which lasted nearly thirty days, and was of such body that the flood of lava ejected, running a destructive course of fifty miles, reached the sea, and added one quarter of a mile of territory to the area of Hawaii, raising also several hills of two hundred feet in height near the shore. Three subsequent eruptions occurred from this mountain, a few years intervening between them, the latest of which was in 1868. Were it not for this and other volcanic vents in the group, these islands in mid-ocean would doubtless be suddenly swallowed up by some great convulsion of the restless subterranean forces.

Some portions of the coast of Hawaii are indented by large and curious caves, which are the homes of thousands of sea-birds; but very little is known about them, as they have never been explored. It is natural, considering its active volcanoes, that earthquakes should be more common on this island than upon any other of the group. The population lives almost entirely near the coast; but where this people first came from not even cunning scientists pretend to know.

Leprosy is still prevalent among the natives, the victims of which dreadful disease are promptly isolated upon the island of Molokai, where there are now about a thousand sufferers confined. The island is in formation so mountainous that the natives call it *Kaaina pali*,— a land of precipices. Some portions can only be reached by water, and that in fair weather, the mountains being impassable. That portion occupied by the unfortunate lepers is a plain naturally cut off from the rest of the island by the pali of Kalae. Fully realizing the necessities of their case these people submit to their isolation without a murmur, and seem, as we were informed, comparatively content. A ration of five pounds of meat and twenty pounds of vegetables is issued to each person weekly, besides which they have garden-plats that they cultivate for such fruits, vegetables, and flowers as they choose. The supply of food furnished to them gratuitously is so much better than any Hawaiian gets under ordinary circumstances, that many persons are actually willing to make themselves lepers and be taken into this death-stricken community, in order to share its abundant provisions. There is here a little church wherein all the lepers congregate on Sundays, to listen to the preaching of a leper minister, and a day-school where the leper children are taught by a native schoolmaster afflicted with the same disease. We heard of a Roman Catholic priest who has devoted his life to these poor unfortunate outcasts, and who lives with them to comfort and aid them in their trials, though he is not himself a leper. This is indeed heroism, to brave the horrors of such an exile in the fulfilment of what he conceives to be his religious duty. If we knew the priest's name we would record it in this connection.

Like tropical regions generally, Honolulu does not lack for annoying insects and disagreeable as well as poisonous reptiles. That the mosquito reigns here goes without saying, and exhaustive measures are taken in every domestic establishment to afford protection against the ubiquitous pest. Our steamer, on the passage toward America, took on board five hundred packages of bananas, each bunch wrapped up in a covering of banana-leaf husks. The night after we sailed for San Francisco quite a commotion was created among the lady passengers, reinforced by the gentlemen, on the finding of huge roaches, scorpions, centipedes, and elephantine spiders meandering in and about the berths and the cabins. That the sensation experienced on awaking from sleep to feel a damp, slimy creature creeping slowly over one's face is excessively disagreeable, may be readily supposed. These reptiles and insects were brought on board in surprising numbers in the fruit packages, where they were securely hidden until they chose to come forth. The chief engineer of the ship prepared a number of bottles with proof spirit, in which a lot of these scorpions and centipedes were preserved, and which were secured by passengers curious in such matters. A young child was bitten by one of the mammoth spiders, causing its arm to swell up alarmingly, but the doctor treated the wound promptly with ammonia, and gave the little sufferer some internal medicine which seemed to act as an antidote to the poison.

We must not close these notes touching the Hawaiian group without a few words relating to our intimate national relation therewith, which at the present time is assuming special political importance.

The relation of the United States with the Hawaiians is in a somewhat peculiar state at the present writing. For ten years past there has existed a reciprocity treaty between us by which their sugar crop is admitted free of duty into the States, and a certain liberal concession on their part is made as to admitting the products of this country into the islands. The operation of this treaty has been to stimulate the production of sugar in the islands from about thirty thousand tons per annum to one hundred thousand tons and over, all of which comes to this country except a small amount used for domestic consumption. The incidental trade with us which has grown out of the treaty is very large, especially in machinery of several kinds, mills, engines, horses, hay, and grain. It has virtually brought the people of the Sandwich Islands under the wing of this Government, and concentrated her foreign trade almost entirely upon this country. The youth of the islands, of both sexes and in large numbers, are sent for educational purposes to our institutions. Forty of such persons were passengers on the "Zealandia" on the outward voyage, going home for a vacation trip. The luxuries as well as most of the necessities of the Hawaiians are now purchased in our markets. All of this business, or certainly nine tenths of it, is the natural outgrowth of the treaty referred to. There is no other foreign port in the world where the American flag is so often seen as in that of Honolulu, the carrying of this great amount of sugar being mostly done in American vessels. While England and Germany are watching for chances to "annex" coaling-stations, and small groups of islands in the Pacific, we virtually have the most admirable one in our own hands, — a fact which should not be lost sight of. Therefore when it is proposed, as it has been and will be again, to abrogate the treaty of 1877, let our statesmen carefully inform themselves of the entire bearing of so serious a matter. We have but casually enumerated a few of the items which bear more especially upon the subject, but perhaps it is enough to awaken intelligent interest therein.

Three quarters of all the money invested in the sugar-raising business of the Sandwich Islands is furnished by American capitalists who draw their annual dividends therefrom. The late revolution was a bloodless one, brought about by the conservative and intelligent element of the islands, composed largely of Americans. In order to retain his seat upon the throne, the king was obliged to grant some liberal concessions as to the laws of the realm and his own powers, still leaving him, however, with all the authority which should rest in the hands of a constitutional monarch of the nineteenth century. The very fact of this concession being promptly granted by the king is sufficient evidence of its most reasonable character.

Once more it was Saturday, the gala-day of the Hawaiians, when we bade adieu a second time to Honolulu; and the tableau which then fixed itself upon the mind will long remain. The brief stay had been full of interest and enjoyment; it was, indeed, only too brief.

Our good ship the "Alamada" got up steam in the early morning and was under way by nine o'clock, steering through the coral reef seaward. The king graciously sent his military band to play for us some parting airs, while a thousand spectators consisting of mingled races and equally of both sexes, gorgeously wreathed in flowers, thronged the capacious pier. It was high tide, so that the "Alamada" loomed up high above the heads of the motley assembly. In the middle foreground lay the tropical city enshrined in palms, cocoas, and flower-bedecked trees, beyond which the picturesque valley of Nuuanu formed a long perspective reaching into the volcanic hills. To the right and left the mountain range extended for miles, forming a series of valleys, gulches, and abrupt precipices, with here and there a plateau of table-land, all clothed in exquisite verdure. The shore was dotted by native huts, cocoanut-groves, and banana-orchards, adding infinite variety to the whole scene.

We had taken on board as passengers some native residents, whose friends had come to bid them good-by with all the earnest demonstrations of a tropical race. Amid the waving of handkerchiefs and the reiterated farewells came the hoarse command from the bridge to cast off the shore lines. Then the grand old flag — the Stars and Stripes — was run up at the peak, and the waiting band played "Hail Columbia," followed by "Home, Sweet Home," responded to by many moistened eyes and quickened pulsations of the heart. As we glided away our forecastle gun barked forth a sharp, ringing farewell which was echoed back a score of times by the mountain gorges.

CHAPTER III.

The Samoan Islands. — A Unique Race of Savages. — Diving for Money. — A Genuine Samoan Mermaid. — German Aggressiveness. — A South-Sea Nunnery. — A Terrible Disease. — Christianity *vs.* Paganism. — Under the Southern Cross. — Grandeur of the Heavens at Sea. — Landing at Auckland. — A Stormy Ocean. — The Famous Harbor of Sydney. — England and her Australian Colony. — The Modern Eldorado. — Early Settlers.

IN our course southward we made the islands known as the Samoan, or Navigator's group, and stopped to land the American and European mails at Tutuila, which is about two thousand three hundred miles from Honolulu. The six islands which form this group of the South Pacific lie between the Society and Feejee groups, three of them being among the largest in Polynesia. Their names are Savaii, Upolu, Tutuila, Manua, Manono, and Apolima. Savaii has a circumference of a hundred and forty miles, and is literally covered with forests of tropical trees from shore to mountain-top. Upolu measures nearly fifty miles from east to west, and is the most fertile and populous of the group. Apolima is the most remarkable for its cones and craters, giving unmistakable evidence of former volcanic action, by clearly-defined vents and fire-shafts among its hills. There are few rivers on these islands, but Upolu and Savaii have several crystal lakes among their mountains. Gales, cyclones, and earthquakes occur quite often enough to vary the monotony. We have said that there are six of these islands; there are also others, scarcely more than islets, however. The highest land in the group is on Savaii, — a lofty peak in the middle of the island, the top of which is nearly always hidden in clouds.

Tutuila was the island which was first sighted, and as it lay sleeping upon the bosom of the southern ocean it presented a beautiful picture of tropical verdure, — an oasis in the great desert of waters. And yet it did not present a very inviting aspect by its wave-lashed and rock-bound shore. It was calm weather, — that is, comparatively so; but there is always a long swell in these latitudes, which when it meets the impediment of shore or reefs is sure to express its anger by a wild display of force.

The island is remarkably mountainous, but the foliage rose to its lofty sky-line, and came down to where the breakers chafed the coast with tremendous fury. There was the azure of the sky, the deep green of the vegetation, the light blue-green of the shoal water, and the snow-white spray tossed high in air, to vary the richness of the coloring, which was finer than that of Oahu. We were told of a safe landing-place in a sheltered cove, and made out the slender spire of a wooden church, but could not see any opening in the long line of dashing spray which leaped twenty feet high as each successive swell broke upon the rocks. Just behind them the palm-groves, bananas, and cocoanut-trees formed a dense breastwork, flanked here and there by low native huts, grass-thatched and brown. In no other region does the cocoanut-tree thrive in greater luxuriance and fruitfulness than here; and were it not that the natives are so lacking in enterprise, this product alone might be made a very large source of profit. The deep green foliage of the bread-fruit all along the shore indicated the abundance of this natural food-supply of the islanders. Together with the yam and taro it forms their main support. The last named is called the daily bread of the Samoans, just as the poi forms the main sustenance of the Hawaiians.

The Samoans are fine-looking specimens of the savage races of the South Pacific. The men are broad-shouldered and athletic, the women by no means ugly, and certainly graceful. They have very little if any of the flat nose and protruding lips of the African race. Their complexion is a light brown, "the livery of the burnished sun," the women exhibiting a warm rosy hue upon their smooth, well-rounded faces. The bodies of both sexes are more or less elaborately tattooed in blue.

If tattooing constituted costume, of which in fact it takes the place here, the Samoans would be gorgeously clad, as they certainly excel in this respect the Maoris of New Zealand. This sort of savage ornamentation with the latter people is more confined to the face, which the Samoans neglect only to be more elaborate upon the limbs and body. It is really surprising to what pain and inconvenience the barbaric races of the Pacific Islands put themselves in order to gratify their vanity and conform to local fashion. The process of tattooing is a slow agony; but the laws of fashion are as imperious in the Cannibal Islands as upon the Parisian boulevards. The tedious and painful operation of tattooing is performed by professionals, who make a paying business of it. The skin is punctured by an instrument made of bone, or by spines of the shaddock-tree, while the dye injected is usually obtained by boiling the candle-nut. Among some of the Pacific tribes tattooing is considered religiously binding; by others it is adopted purely for fancy's sake.

The men wear their hair twisted up in little spiral horns, reminding one of the natives of the coast who meet the steamers at the mouth of the Red Sea, and who exhibit the same aptness in diving for silver coins. The women wear their hair rather short, and are given to dressing their heads and necks with flowers, — a similar fancy to that already described as connected with the Hawaiians. The missionaries have taught the women when they are on shore to wear a small strip of cloth with a hole in the centre for putting over the head, and which hanging down back and front partially covers the otherwise exposed bosom. About the loins they wear a breech-cloth like the men, and sometimes a short skirt reaching half-way to the knees. We were told that the women are fond, on all gala occasions, of painting their faces with any pigment that is obtainable. Our observation of both sexes was obtained chiefly as they came off in their boats to the ship, which they always do in scores; and those we saw were nearly in a state of nature. The yellow and abundant hair of the men must be colored by some process known only to themselves; for though they wear nothing to protect their heads, the sun could not so bleach it. At one time our decks were crowded with these savages, offering for sale curious shells, fruits, native-made ornaments, especially necklaces formed of a dried scarlet berry.

Apia, the capital town of Upolu and the metropolis of the group, presents an inviting prospect from the sea, and the whole island in its general conformation is the most notable of them all. The foot-hills lie quite back from the shore, rising one green elevation behind another, until the great central mountain range is reached, which has an elevation of some four thousand feet above the level of the surrounding waters. All of these hills and the top of the highest elevation are clothed in ever green vegetation, flanked here and there by exposed and abrupt cliffs, bare, rugged, and grand, standing like giant sentinels defying the power of the elements. In the distance, upon a mountain side, is seen a thin silver thread, sparkling in the sun's rays, stretching downward from the heights, which we were told would prove to be a clear, never-failing cascade of water could we approach near enough to discover its real character. It forms the source of a small river, which courses its way to the sea. Many a ship comes hither and anchors, to fill her water-casks from this crystal spring. The town, including its two meeting houses and many European cottages, was half-hidden by the trees, while the water between the ship and the shore was alive with small native boats full of naked islanders, men and women, ready to sell carved clubs, spears, and canes of native wood.

Of the many boats that came off to meet our ship two contained some remarkable swimmers and divers. The most expert among them all was a young woman, who by her rapid movements in the water managed to secure fully half of the sixpences and shillings which were thrown overboard for the divers, though there were numerous competitors of the other sex. She always came to the surface smiling, with the silver between her teeth; and after shaking her head like a Newfoundland dog, and wiping the brine hastily from her eyes, she was quite ready for another plunge, having in the mean time stowed the silver coin away securely in her cheek, as monkeys do nuts and candy. The water alongside the ship was probably thirty or forty fathoms deep, but no piece of money got half-way to the bottom before it was overtaken and secured by a native diver. Though all were as nearly nude as was admissible in the presence of civilized people, they evinced not the least consciousness of personal exposure. And after all, when we paused to think of the matter, it was they who were naturally covered and we who were artificially clothed.

A bunch of fresh, glowing, scarlet hibiscus was observed in one of the boats lying quite neglected, being evidently considered of too little value to offer for sale, but which we secured for a sixpence. This flower grows in wild luxuriance in the Samoan Islands, and forms the most common ornament worn in the hair of the women. The men pass much time in dressing their hair in the little spiral columns as already described, while the women cut theirs short, leaving only sufficient length in which to affix the flower-stems.

When articles of food, such as cake, meats, or candy, were given to the natives they invariably smelt of them before tasting, and if they proved palatable they expressed their satisfaction by a smile and a grunt, more animal than human. They had some few words of English, of which they made incessant use. Their unconscious manners and thoughtless by-play somehow recalled that of the monkey tribe, even to the way they curled their lower limbs under them in the boats, or when sitting upon our deck. Some of the spears and war-clubs which they offered for sale showed much delicacy and skill, both in the design and carving.

The German Government has for a considerable time carried matters with an arbitrary hand in these islands, showing a covert but determined purpose, shamefully oppressing the native race, of whom there are about thirty-five thousand, appropriating their lands, and under various pretences robbing them in every possible manner. While we were there four German ironclads lay off Apia, having come with the purpose of gaining possession of Samoa either by diplomacy or gunpowder. The pretext made use of was oppression of German citizens on the part of the native government! Unfortunately the natives were in a state of partial anarchy, quarrelling among themselves, there being two parties desiring to control the throne. The Germans incited a revolution among them a year ago, favoring one of these aspirants in order to take advantage of such a condition of affairs as would grow out of a pronounced revolution. An Englishman who took passage on our ship at the islands was full of indignation at the arrogance of the Germans, and infused a similar feeling among us by relating in detail the course pursued by these interlopers during the past twelvemonth, especially at Apia. The natives, as this gentleman represented them, are generally an inoffensive, frugal people, having few vices, most of which have been taught them by the whites. They are remarkably slow to anger, and bear the oppression of these foreign invaders very humbly.

There are some cotton plantations on the islands conducted by American and English enterprise. Cocoanut oil and arrowroot are also exported, being gathered by enterprising foreigners who employ the natives. The group contains a little less than three thousand square miles of territory. Statistics show that even here in their comparative isolation, the native race is rapidly dying out, there being now twenty thousand less than were estimated to exist on the several islands so late as 1848, when a census was taken as correctly as was possible among a savage and superstitious people. There are not more than three hundred foreigners all told, and these consist about equally of Americans, English, and Germans.

From the seemingly careless manner of life which prevails among the native race, one would hardly infer that any fixed form of government exists among the Samoans, but the contrary is the fact. They have a paternal system of government, which is scrupulously upheld by the several tribes, all the villages being united by the same customs and language, and amenable to the same code of traditional laws. The usages and customs of the fathers have an unfailing influence over their descendants, and though free intercourse with the whites has led to the adoption of certain foreign rules and laws of trade and land-tenure, yet these are feeble in effect compared with the force of those of early, native origin.

Apia, already referred to, is the residence of the several foreign consuls. It has a small but safe harbor, and in the olden times was a famous resort for American whalers. Prominent in the picture of the town as seen from the water is a Roman Catholic cathedral of stone, with a graceful spire, behind which upon a hillside is the comfortable house of the bishop. There are a number of Catholic priests upon these islands, and we were told that near to Apia is a convent of Samoan nuns, which struck us as the height of absurdity. Upolu claims the distinction of containing the only nunnery in the South Pacific. Grogshops have as usual followed close upon the footsteps of the missionaries, and even Apia contains six of them in full blast.

We had as fellow-passengers a family of English missionaries to land at Tutuila, who were on their return to the islands after a brief visit to their European home. This family had already lived five years among the Samoans, and were returning hither to complete their term of ten years under the direction of the London Missionary Society. Much interesting information was gathered from them concerning the manners and customs of the people of the group. As a race, it appears that they are quite distinct from other Polynesian tribes, and are far behind many of them in point of civilization. They seemed to us to be half amphibious, full of mirth and irresponsibility as we saw them in their naked simplicity, quite as much at home in the water as in their canoes. We were told that the children learned to swim before they could fairly walk, — which seemed almost incredible. They are mostly professed Christians, whatever that may signify to them, — though we very much doubt if a dozen could give the meaning of the term. One real and undoubted benefit which these missionaries impart to the natives is that they are teaching them to read, write, and speak English in regularly organized schools; so that there will be few of the rising generation who will not possess this important knowledge at least.

The health of the people on these islands is represented to be most excellent, owing to the perfection of the climate; but there is one prominent drawback to the locality in the presence and prevalence of elephantiasis among the natives, from which hideous disease the foreign residents are not exempt. It requires time to develop it in the system, and it does not attack persons until after a residence of eight or ten years. There is no known cure for the disease, unless one leaves the region where it is developed, and even then it requires a surgical operation to remove the enormous protuberance which usually forms upon the lower part of the body or the limbs. We saw some photographs taken from life of sufferers through elephantiasis, which exhibited swellings upon the limbs and body half as large as the individual's body itself. Nowhere else in the world do malformations caused by this peculiar disease assume such tremendous proportions as here in Samoa. Quinine is freely used to check the development of the affliction, as it is known to prevail most in low-lying and marshy neighborhoods; and yet what we term malaria is absolutely unknown among these islands. A German resident took passage in our ship on his way home to Berlin, who had lived some dozen years at Apia. The disease had begun its development in his ankles, one of which was swollen as large as his thigh. The local physician had advised his departure at once, and that a surgical operation should be performed in another climate. Singular to say, these protuberances can almost always be safely severed from the body by a skilful surgical operation, enormous though they be; nor are they liable to return if the patient keeps away from the climatic influences which caused them.

"The Samoans have no authentic information in any form concerning the past," said our intelligent friend the missionary. "It is to them quite as unknown as the future. They possess traditions, but such as are only fragmentary and unreliable, probably the inventions of their designing priests. Their origin and history are in fact clouded in utter obscurity." Their language seems to be an offshoot of the Malay, and does not resemble especially the Hawaiian or Maori languages, which are almost identical with each other. This seems rather strange, as their ocean home is situated in a direct line between the two, which should indicate, one would think, a similar origin of the races. "They live under an iron bondage of superstition, which seems inherent in their nature," said our informant, "and which no attempt at Christian enlightenment appears to dispel."

One instance was related to us relative to their blind simplicity, but which at the same time evinced a degree of shrewdness. A chief, old and decrepit, who realized that he was near his end, after attending the missionary services on a certain Sabbath afternoon, returned to his cabin where he was soon after found going through all the barbaric ceremonies of his ancient faith before a wooden image, beating time on a rude tom-tom, and performing other strange rites. The missionary, who had come to bring him some medicine for a chronic trouble from which he suffered, expressed his surprise that he should be thus engaged in idolatrous worship after so recently participating in the Christian ceremonies. "Ah!" said the old savage, "me fish with two hook. I catchee fish. Fish no like one hook, he bite other hook." It was naïvely expressed, but signified that by accepting both creeds,—that of the Samoan priests and that of the missionaries,—he would have two chances instead of one of getting to the better world, toward which even South Sea Islanders hopefully turn their eyes.

On the occasion of our second visit to the Samoans,—that is, on the return voyage coming north,—we had more opportunity to study the race; but the shrill whistle of the steamer finally warned our visitors away from the vessel,—a signal which they well understood and generally heeded. The Government boat having put her mail on board, there was nothing further to detain us. When we were once more fairly under way, it was found that one of the natives had been left on board bargaining with the passengers in the cabin below. He coolly tied up the silver he had received for his wares in a knot of his breech-cloth, stepped to the ship's side, and plunged headlong into the sea. Rising quickly to the surface he struck out for Tutuila, a league and more away, with no more seeming hesitation than we would feel in beginning a walk of a like distance upon the land. Once he was seen to turn upon his back and float for a moment leisurely upon the surface, but soon resumed his swimming position again, heading steadily for the land.

At that moment the cry came from forward, "There she blows!" the usual signal at sea for a whale in sight, and all eyes were turned to watch the gambols of a large whale and her calf, half a mile to windward. It will be remembered that these were once famous whaling latitudes, but this adventurous industry has now become almost a thing of the past in these regions. In the mean time the Leviathan and its giant baby were lashing the sea and sending up small mountains of spray, the calf occasionally leaping quite out of the water in its redundant sportiveness. When we finally turned toward the swimming native again, in the opposite direction, his shock of yellow hair was quite lost to view amid the vivid sunlight which blazed over the quivering sea.

After the Samoan group, we passed through or near the Society Islands, encircled by coral reefs, but kept steadily on our course south-southwest, making thirteen knots an hour, and hastening out of the heat of the tropics into a cooler and more comfortable region.

In no other part of the world has the author seen a clearer atmosphere or a grander display of the heavens at night than was enjoyed in the regions through which we were now sailing. Hours were passed in watching the luminous sky, where new and brilliant constellations were serenely gazing down upon us. Venus, the evening star, shone so clear and bright as to cast a long wake upon the wrinkled surface of the sea. There are but about fifteen hundred stars which can be counted from a ship's deck by the naked eye, — a fact which but few persons realize. With an opera-glass or telescope, however, the number can be much increased. We are told that astronomers, by means of their greatly improved facilities, have counted twenty millions of stars. This may be true, and yet it seems almost incredible. We have seen an observer, not familiar with the location of the Southern Cross, examine the heavens long and patiently before being able to find this famous cluster of the Southern Hemisphere, — a visual obtuseness not uncommon among persons who seldom watch the heavens by night. Few give much thought to the stars. Some hastily glance at them and pronounce them beautiful; others regard them with more patient admiration; but not one in a thousand seriously and carefully studies them. A good way of readily finding the Cross is to remember that there are two prominent stars in Centaurus that point directly to it. The one farthest from the Cross is regarded as the fixed star nearest to the earth, but its distance from us is twenty thousand times that of the sun. Stellar distances especially can be realized only by comparison. For instance: were it possible for a person to journey to the sun in a single day of twenty-four hours, basing the time upon a corresponding calculation of speed, it would require fifty-five years to reach this nearest star!

Probably not one half of those who have sailed beneath its tranquil and impressive beauty are aware, that in the middle of the Southern Cross there is a brilliant cluster of stars, which though not visible to the naked eye, are brought out with a strong telescope, — shining like new gems in a beautiful necklace of pearls. In these far-southern waters we saw for the first time what are called the Magellan Clouds. They lie between Canopus, Acherner, and the South Pole. These two light clouds — or what seem to be such, seen in a perfectly clear sky — are nothing more nor less than visible nebulæ, or star-clusters, at such vast distances from the earth as to have by combination this effect upon the human vision.

At sea the stars assume perhaps a greater importance in our estimation than on land, because from them is obtained latitude and longitude, on the principles of terrestrial measurement; and thus by their aid the mariner determines his bearing in the great waste of ocean. Forty or fifty centuries ago the Chaldean shepherds were accustomed to gaze upon these shining orbs in worshipful admiration, but with no idea of their vast system. They were to them "the words of God, the Scriptures of the skies." It has been left to our later days to formulate the methods of their constant and endless procession. All the principal stars are now well known and their limits clearly defined upon charts, so that we can easily acquire a knowledge of them. The inhabitants of North America have the constellation of Ursa Major as also the North Star always with them; they never wholly disappear below the horizon. When the mariner sailing north of the equator has determined the position of this group of seven stars, two of which are known as "the pointers" indicating the North Star, he can designate all points of the compass unerringly. But in the South Sea, where we are writing these lines, a little north of New Zealand, they are not visible. Other constellations however, whose relative positions are as fixed in the Southern Hemisphere, become equally sure guides to the watchful navigator.

How suggestive are these "altar-fires of heaven," particularly when seen from the deck of a ship, alone and at midnight, surrounded by infinite space, thousands of miles from land and home! Generations of men succeed one another in rapid succession, nations rise and fade away, whole races are obliterated from existence, pyramids moulder into dust with thousands of years upon their heads; but the stars fade not; they are the same, unchanged, unchanging, through all the centuries, uninfluenced by the fall of empires or the wreck of human hopes and beliefs.

On the night of the 20th of June the hundred and eightieth meridian was crossed, and the 21st of June was dropped into the sea, so to speak. We had no Tuesday that week; Wednesday followed Monday,— a natural experience in going round the world, which has often been explained. We had been losing time daily in sailing south and west, until this change of date became necessary to regulate the ship's time in accordance with that of Greenwich. An ungeographical Englishman whom we had on board our steamer refused to alter the time of his watch from the first, saying that he only knew that it would come right of itself when he got back to London, which was true enough, though he could not explain why.

Twenty-one days from San Francisco the light at Tiri-tiri Point, on the coast of New Zealand, was sighted, twenty miles distant from Auckland. We entered the harbor early in the morning, and were soon moored at the Union Company's wharf, at the foot of Queen Street. Here the ship not only had freight to discharge, but two or three hundred tons of coal to take on board; so we enjoyed a whole day wherein to stroll about the city, and in the evening we witnessed the "Pirates of Penzance" at Abbott's Opera House. The play was admirably performed by an itinerant company, which regularly makes the rounds of the colonial cities of both Australia and New Zealand.

The outer and inner harbors of Auckland are very beautiful, having picturesque headlands, dominated by volcanic mountains and extinct craters, — indeed the city stands upon the lava vomited from the bowels of Mount Eden. The first land made on coming from the Samoan group was great Barrier Island, which separates the ocean eastward from the Hauraki Gulf, upon which Auckland is situated.

As we shall return in future chapters to this interesting country, no more need be said of its northern metropolis in this connection.

Early on the morning after our arrival the "Zealandia" was again under way, steering north-north-east, until the most northerly point of New Zealand was doubled, then an exact due-west course sped the good ship on her way to Sydney, Australia, twelve hundred and eighty miles distant. It is a stormy ocean that lies between these two countries, and it is useless to disguise the fact that the voyager who crosses it must make up his mind to great and unavoidable discomfort. Any one pursuing the course indicated in these pages, however, will have become pretty well seasoned before entering upon this stage of the long journey. The famous English man-of-war "Challenger" essayed this voyage between Sydney and Auckland twice before she accomplished it, finally fighting her way through the boisterous waves and adverse currents with the united power of sails and steam.

We approached the coast of Australia in tempestuous weather and at night, the "Zealandia" stoutly ploughing her way through a heavy head-sea, while half a gale of wind blew in our faces, and hailstones nearly as large as marbles cumbered the deck. The ship seemed to evince almost human instinct, pausing for an instant now and again, and trembling in every seam as huge waves blocked the way; then, bending down determinedly to the work of forcing a path through the opposing billows, she forged ahead, with the bows at one moment lifted high in air, and the next half buried in the sea. A few days previous we were in the burning latitudes of the Samoans, now we were on the verge of freezing. This temperature was perhaps exceptional, and indeed after landing we were satisfied that it was so. The storm gradually abated during the night, and the clouds rapidly cleared away, racing madly across the sky like retreating cavalry. While we were still fifty miles off the shore, which was hidden in night and distance, the first officer of the ship, knowing that we would thank him for doing so, awoke us from sleep, and as soon as we joined him on deck he pointed out a glow on the far-away horizon, which he said was caused by the light-house on Sydney Heads. Having carefully watched the ship's reckoning, we knew her position very nearly, and looking at him in surprise, we asked, —

"Is it possible to make out a light-house at sea from such a distance as your reckoning shows you to be from land?"

"Certainly," he replied, "for there is Hornby Light."

"It seems impossible," we exclaimed.

"Perhaps I should qualify the remark," said he.

"In what way?" we asked.

"I do not mean that we actually see the light itself, but we clearly see its reflection upon the horizon."

"Still," we rejoined, "it seems incredible."

"You must remember," said he, "that this is an electric light, placed on the top of a very lofty cliff;

and also that the light-house itself is many feet in height."

"Seeing is believing," was all we could say.

But we had not before supposed that a light under any circumstances could be made out at such a distance on the sea. Hornby Light occupies one of the most important headlands on the entire coast of Australia, and great care is taken to maintain its efficiency.

After a sea-voyage of nearly a month's duration, the sight of land was indeed welcome. One could not but feel a burning impatience once more to tread the solid earth. This was no isolated volcanic island lying half submerged amid a broad expanse of turbulent seas; it was literally *terra firma*, the visible portion of a whole continent. A steamer of two or three hundred tons brings the pilot off the shore in these vexed and boisterous seas. The struggle to board us was one requiring coolness and courage, nor was it accomplished without considerable risk.

Six hours after sighting the distant light of Sydney Heads we were running in between the two bold, frowning, giant cliffs which form the entrance of this remarkable harbor. The ship was on half speed. Botany Bay was passed, — a now lovely retreat, retaining nothing of its ill-repute but the name. It is seven miles below the capital, and now forms a pleasure resort for the citizens of Sydney. Wooloomaloo Bay, McQuade's Point, Garden Island, and the forts were passed one after the other, as we slowly forged ahead through the channel. Some surprise was felt at the indifferent nature of the visible defences of Sydney harbor, assuming that defensive means are required at all; but it seems that there are torpedoes, booms, and submarine appliances all ready to be sunk should such defences be called for by any hostile demonstration.

To eyes weary of the monotony of the sea the aspect of the famous harbor with its lake-like expanse, its many green islands with handsome residences scattered over them, its graceful promontories and the abundance of semi-tropical vegetation, all together formed one of the loveliest pictures imaginable, heightened as these attractive surroundings were by the dewy freshness and glow of the early morning sun.

The wharf at which we landed was not in the busiest maritime district, but seemed to be situated in the centre of the town as it were, our tall masts taking their place among the multitude of church spires and weather-vanes which crowd together here. The usual custom-house ceremonies were encountered, which in this instance were not of an annoying character, and we soon began to realize that we were upon the soil of this great island-continent which possesses an area of nearly three millions of square miles. So far as we can learn, it was a land entirely unknown to the ancients, though it is more than probable that the Chinese navigators knew of the existence of North Australia at a very early period. Still, until about a century ago it presented only a picture of primeval desolation. The hard work of the pioneer has been done, and civilization has rapidly changed the whole aspect of the great south lands. To-day the continent is bordered by thrifty seaports connected by railroads, coasting-steamers, turnpikes, and electric telegraphs. It is occupied by an intelligent European population numbering between three and four millions, possessing such elements of political and social prosperity as place them in an honorable position in the line of progressive nations.

The first railroad in Australia was begun in 1850, but at this writing there are ten thousand miles of railroad in successful operation, owned by the several local governments. So favorable is the climate, that nearly the whole country might be turned into a botanical garden. Indeed, Australia would seem to be better entitled to the name of Eldorado, so talked of in the sixteenth century, than was that imaginary land of untold wealth so confidently believed by the adventurous Spaniards to exist somewhere between the Orinoco and the Amazon.

This new home of the British race in the South Pacific, surrounded by accessible seas and inviting harbors, inspired us at once with vivid interest. We say "new," and yet geologically speaking it is one of the oldest portions of the earth's surface, containing a flora and fauna of more permanent character than that of the European continent; for while a great part of Europe has been submerged and elevated, crumpled up as it were into mountain chains, Australia has been undisturbed. It is remarkable that in a division of the globe of such colossal proportions there was found no larger quadruped than the kangaroo, and that only man was a predacious animal. He, alas! was more ferocious than the lynx, the leopard, or the hyena; for these animals prey not upon each other, while the aborigines of Australia devoured their own species.

What America was to Spain in the proud days of that nation's glory, Australia has already been to England; and that, too, without the crime of wholesale murder and the spilling of rivers of blood, as was the case in the days of Cortez and Pizarro. The wealth poured into the lap of England by these faraway colonies belittles all the riches which the Spaniard realized by the famous conquests of Mexico and Peru. Here is an empire won without war, a new world called into existence by moral forces, an Eldorado captured without the sword. Here Nature has spread her favors broadcast over a land only one fifth smaller than the whole continent of Europe, granting every needed resource wherewith ultimately to form a great, independent, and prosperous nation; where labor is already more liberally rewarded, and life more easily sustained, than in any other country except America.

Among the most prominent advantages which at first strike the observation of the stranger in Australia are those of an extended shore-line indented with many noble harbors, a semi-tropical climate beneath bright Italian skies, a virgin soil of unequalled fertility, and a liberal form of government; while the hills, valleys, and plains abound in mineral wealth of gold, silver, iron, copper, and coal, inexhaustible in quantity and unsurpassed in quality. To the black diamonds of her coal-fields Australia will owe more of her future progress than to her auriferous products. They already have conduced to the grand success of various branches of manufactures, as may be seen in the many enterprises springing up in the neighborhood of Sydney. The coal-fields extend all along the seaboard from Brisbane to Sydney. Those at Newcastle are of vast proportions, having a daily out-put which gives employment to a large fleet of steamships and sailing-vessels. This coal is mined and put on shipboard, as we were told, at a cost of eleven shillings per ton. It is of excellent quality, admirable for manufacturing purposes, and very good, though somewhat dirty, for steamship use. Near these Newcastle coal-mines are ample deposits of iron ore of excellent quality, — two products whose close proximity to each other is of great importance in the economical production of manufactured iron and steel. Only immigration is now needed to develop these grand resources, and that requisite is being supplied by a numerical growth surpassed alone by that on the Pacific coast of the United States.

It is difficult to believe, while observing the present population, wealth, power, and prosperity of the country at large, characterized by such grand and conspicuous elements of empire, that it has been settled for so brief a period, and that its pioneers consisted of the overflow of English jails and prisons. The authentic record of life in the colonies of Australia during the first few years of their existence is mainly an account of the control of lawless men by the strong and cruel arm of military despotism, often exercised under the most unfavorable circumstances. Situated more than twelve thousand miles away from their base of supplies, famine was often imminent, and the unavoidable sufferings of officers and men, of officials and prisoners, were at times indescribably severe. The earliest shipment of criminals hither was in 1787, consisting of six transports with about eight hundred convicts, two hundred of whom were women. These were disembarked at Port Jackson, in Sydney harbor; so that the first settlement of New South Wales was strictly a penal one.

CHAPTER IV.

Interesting Statistical Facts. — Emigration. — Heavy Indebtedness. — Curious Contrasts. — New South Wales. — A Populous City. — A Splendid Harbor. — The Yacht "Sunbeam." — Street Scenes. — Gin Palaces. — Public Gardens of Sydney. — A Noble Institution of Learning. — Art Gallery. — Public Libraries. — Pleasure Trip to Parametta. — Attractive Drives. — A Sad Catastrophe in Sydney Harbor.

BEFORE proceeding to take the reader from city to city, and to depict their several peculiarities, a few statistics gathered by the author on the spot will afford as tangible evidence of the growth and present commercial standing of the colonies of Australasia as anything which could be adduced.

The annual revenue raised by these colonies aggregates a larger sum than that realized by Sweden, Norway, Switzerland, Denmark, and Greece united. Five hundred million dollars are annually paid for imports; and exports to a like amount are sent from the country. Up to the present writing Australia has realized from her auriferous soil over three hundred and thirty million pounds sterling. Her territory gives grazing at the present time to over seventy-five million sheep. This is more than double the whole number of sheep in the United States. When it is remembered that the population of this country is sixty millions, and that Australia has not much over three millions, the force of this comparison becomes obvious. The amount of wool exported to the mother country is twenty-eight times as much as England has received in the same period from the continent of Europe. The combined exports and imports of the United Kingdom of Great Britain are shown to be a little over one hundred dollars per annum for each unit of the population; in Australia the aggregate is a trifle over two hundred dollars per head. The four principal capitals of Australia contain over eight hundred thousand inhabitants. The railroads of the country have already cost over two hundred million dollars, and are being extended annually. New South Wales has in proportion to its population a greater length of railroad than any other country in the world, while there are some thirty thousand miles of telegraph line in the length and breadth of the land. In ten years, between 1870 and 1880, New Zealand doubled her population, having now some six hundred thousand; and the Australian colonies increased at nearly as rapid a rate, while the monthly immigration still going on gives constant and profitable employment to one of the best equipped steamship lines upon the ocean.

The steady and natural increase of population in Great Britain, taken in connection with the circumscribed limits of her territory, demands an outlet for the annual emigration of a large percentage of her people. There are no better lands for those who are thus induced, or compelled, to seek another field wherein to create a new home than Australia and New Zealand. There are several considerations that lead to this conviction. First, such immigrants will still be under the fostering care of their native government; second, the colonial authorities offer great inducements to immigrants, such as grants of land together with free transportation from the old to the new country; and third, there is here a climate far more desirable and healthful than that of England, Ireland, or Scotland. While the necessary cost of living is less, wages are higher, and many luxuries can be enjoyed which at home would not be considered within the reach of persons of moderate means. Bread, the staff of life, and meat, its strong supporter, are both very much cheaper in the colonies than in any part of Great Britain. These considerations enforce the conclusion that Australasia is the natural resort of emigrants from the British Isles, and that it will continue to attract thence a steady flow of population. Canada for the emigrant presents not a moiety of the inducements of these South Sea lands, nor can we understand what possible reason can lead British subjects to select it above the favored country of which we are treating.

While we were discussing the economical and political condition of the colonies with a government official at Sydney, he took occasion to express regret at the large debt of the colonies. We are glad to know, however, that these debts of the several divisions of

Australia and New Zealand do not represent the cost of useless wars or expenditures for vain glory; on the contrary, the money has been invested in railroads and other necessary and substantial improvements, which form an ample security or mortgage for the same, and which is yearly increasing in value. Probably some of these enterprises have been premature, but their ultimate value is beyond all doubt.

Australia is divided into five provincial governments, — New South Wales, Victoria, Queensland, South Australia, and West Australia. The island of Tasmania forms another province, and is separated from Victoria by Bass Strait, the two being within half a day's sail of each other. Sydney is the capital of New South Wales; Melbourne, of Victoria; Adelaide, of South Australia; Brisbane, of Queensland; Perth, of West Australia; and Hobart, of Tasmania. It may be remarked incidentally that South Australia might more properly be designated by some other title, as it is not South Australia at all. Victoria lies south of it, and so does a large portion of West Australia. The governments of these several divisions are modelled upon that of New South Wales, the parent colony of them all.

Though we are by no means attempting to write a history or make a geography of these great southlands, still an enumeration of certain important facts is not inappropriate, and will serve to make matters more clear to the general reader as he accompanies us through the following pages.

We have said that the several governments of these colonies are modelled upon that of New South Wales, which has a constitution and two Houses of Parliament. The first, or Legislative Council, is composed of a limited number of members nominated by the Crown, and who hold office for life; the second, or Legislative Assembly, is composed of members elected from the various constituencies, who are chosen by ballot. All acts before becoming law must receive the approval of the Queen of England, though this is said to be practically a mere form. There is a resident Governor in each colony, also appointed by the Queen. Educational facilities, especially as regards primary schools, are abundant, attendance upon which is compulsory. Where children reside at some considerable distance from school, free passes are given to them on the railroads to facilitate compliance with the legal requirement.

One of the first thoughts that dawned upon us after we had time fully to realize this state of affairs in these Antipodes was that as compared with our own country this is a land of curious contradictions. Here the eagles are white and the swans black; the emu, a bird nearly as large as the ostrich, cannot fly, but runs like a horse. The principal quadruped here, the kangaroo, is elsewhere unknown; and though he has four legs, he runs upon two. When the days are longest with us in America, they are shortest here. To reach the Tropics Australians go due north, while we go due south. With us the seed, or stone, of the cherry forms the centre of the fruit; in Australia the stone grows on the outside. The foliage of the trees in America spreads out horizontally; in this south-land the leaves hang vertically. When it is day with us, it is night with them. Here Christmas comes in midsummer; with us, in mid-winter. Bituminous and anthracite coal are with us only one color, — black, black as Erebus; but they have white bituminous coal here, white as chalk. We are thousands of miles north of the equator; they are thousands of miles south of it. The deciduous trees with us shed their leaves in winter; with them they are evergreen, shedding their bark and not their leaves, — the gardens of Alcinous being not more perennial than the length and breadth of this favored land.

In proceeding with our subject it is proper to begin with New South Wales, at whose capital we landed, this colony being also the oldest if not the wealthiest province of the entire country. Not only her mineral wealth and great agricultural facilities, but her commanding position and numerous admirable harbors will ever enable her to maintain precedence among her prosperous and wealthy sister colonies. As originally founded, New South Wales embraced the whole eastern seaboard of Australia; but in 1851 the southern part was formed into the province of Victoria, and in 1859 the northern part was divided into a separate colony, called Queensland, still leaving her an extensive sea-coast of eight hundred miles in length. When we say that New South Wales is twice as large as California, it will be realized that she is not greatly circumscribed in territory. The present population, in the absence of actual statistics, may be safely stated to amount in round numbers to one million.

Sydney, often called by her citizens the Queen of the Pacific, is built upon two ridges of land of considerable elevation, the valley between being occupied by the busiest portion of the population and containing the best shops in every department of trade. There are many fine large business and public edifices of stone, but these are only too often flanked by buildings of a very low and awkward construction, one story in height. There is no consecutive purpose or uniformity in the street architecture, a wild irregularity prevailing. George Street, which is the main business thoroughfare, is two miles in length, and contains many stores or shops furnished as well as the average of those in Vienna and Paris. These are really fine business edifices, having massive French plate-glass windows and being in all particulars admirably appointed.

The peculiar conformation of the town makes the lateral streets precipitous, so that a large portion of the city is composed of hilly avenues, to surmount which there is a constant struggle going on with loaded teams. Like the old streets of Boston, those of Sydney were the growth of chance, and were not originally laid out after a system, as in Melbourne, Adelaide, or Brisbane. Our Washington Street was originally a cow-path, while the present site of George

Street in Sydney was at first a meandering bullock-track. The names of the streets are historic in their suggestions. George Street was named after George the Third, during whose reign the colony was founded. Pitt Street is named after the Earl of Chatham; Castlereagh, Bathurst, Erskine, and other streets recall familiar names of English statesmen. The higher thoroughfares, those upon the ridges, overlook the inner harbor and shipping, affording a constantly varying maritime picture. Thus from nearly opposite our hotel, on the day of our arrival, we saw lying upon the waters of the bay four large German men-of-war (the same which afterward visited and terrorized the simple natives of the Samoan Islands), and also an iron-clad belonging to Japan fully equal in nautical appearance to the German craft. All were dressed from their hulls to their topmast heads with tiny flags in gayest colors, as it happened to be Coronation day. A little nearer the heart of the town, in what is known as Farm Cove, Lord Brassey's famous yacht, the "Sunbeam," rode quietly at anchor, whose keel has cut the waters of all the notable harbors of the world, and whose significant name the late lamented Lady Brassey has rendered a household word by her delightful pen. The snow-white hull and graceful rig of the yacht was not unfamiliar to the author, who saw it six years ago at Port Said, and who then met its late mistress at Cairo, in Egypt. Excursion steamers, ferry-boats, men-of-war launches, racing-cutters, and a hundred small sailing-craft added life and interest to this impressive picture of Sydney harbor, as seen from the higher streets of the town.

The much-lauded bay is indeed charming, as the most indifferent spectator must admit; yet it did not strike us as so much more beautiful than others that we have visited in various countries. It is better, however, not to challenge the ire of all Sydney by speaking irreverently of the harbor, since the faithful worship of its alleged incomparable beauty is with the citizens a species of religion. It has the advantage of being but slightly affected by the tides, and in consequence has no shoals to spoil the view with their muddy aspect at various times each day, or to emit noxious fumes under the rays of a burning sun. Eight or nine fathoms of water in nearly any part of the bay make it accessible to ships of heaviest draught. It is seven miles from the entrance at the Heads up to the city proper. This capacious basin, with its countless nooks and windings, has a shore line of two hundred and fifty miles, the whole of which is so well protected and land-locked that in all weather it is as glassy and smooth as the Lake of Geneva.

The main thoroughfares of Sydney are not kept in a very cleanly condition, — a statement which even the residents must indorse; but the streets are full of the busy life which appertains to a great metropolis. Cabs and private vehicles dash hither and thither; heavily-laden drays grind their broad wheels over the rough pavements; pedestrians crowd the sidewalks; messenger boys, mounted upon wiry little horses, gallop on their several errands, some of them dressed in scarlet coats, signifying that they are in Government service; newspaper hawkers, boot-blacks, bearers of advertising placards, itinerant fruit-venders, Chinamen with vegetables in baskets slung on a pole across their shoulders, pass and repass one in rapid succession; omnibuses rattle furiously over the pavements, while the "going, going, gone," of the open sham auction-rooms rings upon the ear. Now and then one meets a beggar, blind or decrepit; but such are not numerous, and generally palliate their vocation as well as evade the law by offering some trifling articles for sale, such as pencils, shoestrings, or matches. In European cities, where professional beggary is so often resorted to as a regular occupation, one hardens his heart and passes these people heedlessly by; but here in Sydney he drops a trifle in the hat. Every street-corner has its bar-room, about whose doors are congregated a disreputable crowd of bloated faces and bleared eyes, among whom are seen only too many of the youth of the town, beginners in vicious habits, besides numerous idle but able-bodied representatives of the laboring classes. No part of London even is more numerously supplied with gin palaces and low tap-rooms than Sydney. The sad sight of intoxicated women staggering along the public way shocked the sensibilities, though this unfortunate exhibition was far less common than we have seen it in Liverpool and Glasgow. The demi-monde are fully represented upon the streets,— one of the sad but inevitable concomitants of a great city. Let us add, in all fairness, that this objectionable feature is certainly no more conspicuous here than in Chicago or New York, — a fact which is mentioned not to draw a comparison, but in order faithfully to depict the every-day aspect of a colonial capital.

Turning from these multiform scenes of human life, often ludicrous, but oftener painfully sad, we sought the Botanical Gardens; and after that at Calcutta, and the superb gardens of Kandy in Ceylon, this of Sydney is the next finest we remember to have seen. In round numbers these gardens embrace fifty acres of land, laid out in terraces and irregular elevations, so that many of the broad paths overlook portions of the city and harbor. The grounds extend on a gentle incline to the shores of the beautiful bay, forming a semicircle round what is known as Farm Cove, a picturesque indentation of the harbor. The several main paths are liberally ornamented with statuary representing Flora, Ceres, Commerce, Science, etc. One special charm of these delightful grounds is the fact that they are accessible by a walk of about five minutes from the centre of the city. It is not necessary to organize an excursion in order to reach them, as is the case with many similar resorts elsewhere, such as Sydenham in London, Central Park in New York, or the Bois de Boulogne, Paris. Here semi-arctic and semi-tropical plants and trees were found growing together, and all parts of the globe seemed to be liberally represented. The hardy Scotch fir and the delicate palm of the tropics jostle each other; the india-rubber tree and the laurel are close friends; the California pine and the Florida orange thrive side by side; so with the silver fern-tree of New Zealand and the guava of Cuba. China, Japan, India, Africa, Egypt, and South America, all have furnished representative trees and shrubs for these comprehensive gardens, and here they have become acclimatized. A thrifty cluster of the Indian bamboo, that king of the grasses, was seen here forty feet high, close by a specimen of the native Australian musk-tree, which attains a height of nearly twenty feet and exhales from leaf and bark a peculiarly sweet odor, though not at all like what its name would seem to indicate; it has broad, laurel-like leaves and bears a pale yellow blossom. There was pointed out to us a sheoak-tree, which it is said emits a curious wailing sound during the quietest state of the atmosphere, when there is not a breath of wind to move the branches or the leaves. This tree is almost universally found growing near the sea, and is said to have borrowed the murmur of the conch-shell. No reasonable cause is assigned for its mournful song, which has proved to be the inspiring theme of many a local poet.

Near the very centre of the gardens three Norfolk Island pines attracted particular attention because of their remarkable development. The head gardener told us that they were planted here about 1820, and they are certainly the noblest examples of their kind we have seen. The oldest one, perfect in form and foliage, is ninety-five feet high, and three feet from the ground measures fourteen feet nine inches in circumference; the other two are even taller, but measure one foot less in circumference. The density of foliage, uniformity of shape, and general perfection of these beautiful pines exceed anything of the kind to be found elsewhere.

In walking to the Garden by the way of Bridge Street, there was observed, just opposite the buildings containing the Educational Bureau, a dual tree of great size and beauty. The effect was that of one immense tree, but there were really two trunks which furnished this mountain of foliage. They were Moreton Bay Fig-trees, and were full of green fruit. This tree, the fruit of which we believe is useless, has a singular habit which recalls that of the banyan-tree; namely, that of forming many aerial roots which hang downward from the branches, though they do not grow long enough to reach the earth and produce new stock like the banyan, — which is known, by the way, as the Indian fig-tree.

Within the Botanical Gardens the flowers were as attractive and in as great variety as the trees. Fuchsias, roses, camellias in great variety, pansies of the double species, a whole army of brilliant tulips, and many other plants were in gorgeous bloom, though this was in July, which, it must be remembered, is winter in Sydney. The collection of camellias was remarkable both for the size to which they grew and for the abundance of the blossoms. Over three hundred were counted on one tree, as white as untrodden snow, all being of perfect form and freshness; there were others double, single, striped, and scarlet, all thrifty and lovely, but none of them quite equal to the myriad-decked one in white. The azaleas, double scarlet geraniums, violets, heliotropes, and daphnes were dazzling in color and confusing in their abundance. Nestling among the mounds of rock-work were succulent plants, orchids, cacti, ferns, and other pleasing forms of delicate vegetation. Flowers bloom in every month of the year in this region, out of doors, and are rarely troubled by frost.

As we came out of the Public Garden after this first visit, the last rays of the setting sun threw tremulous shadows over the foliage and the pale faces of the marble statues. The softening colors of the western sky were reflected clearly in the unruffled arm of the bay close at hand, tinging its waters with purple and golden hues. It was a scene and moment to put one at peace with all the world. The atmosphere was intoxicatingly fragrant just at this bedtime hour of the flowers, filling one here, within pistol-shot of the crowded, boisterous life of the town, with sensuous delight.

Sydney has two or three moderate-sized but very attractive arcades, — one especially worthy of note leading from George Street near the City Hall, in which are many fine shops, refreshment saloons, and cafés, with flower and fruit stores. These areas being under glass — that is, roofed over at the top of the buildings — are a favorite resort for ladies and promenaders generally. On entering these arcades one steps from deafening and confusing noise into a quiet atmosphere, with most agreeable surroundings. Not far away on George Street is the general vegetable and fruit market, where poultry and flowers are also sold. The articles are displayed with an artistic eye for color and appropriate effect. Young women are employed to sell the fruit and flowers, whose pleasant and by no means obtrusive importunity with visitors makes many purchasers. George Street is fragrant on a sunny afternoon with button-hole bouquets, purchased of these flower-girls, who evince admirable taste in the graceful and effective manner of arranging their floral gems. The display of fruit is remarkable, and the article is as cheap as it is tempting; so that those who in England or in many parts of America would not feel able to afford to indulge in oranges, apples, pears, and bananas, not forgetting the appetizing fruit of the passion-plant, here make of these a wholesome addition to their daily food-supply. Sydney is only rivalled in this respect by San Francisco, which city cannot be surpassed in the cheapness or quality of its fruit from tropical and semi-tropical regions within its own borders.

Many floral establishments solely devoted to the sale of plants and cut-flowers were observed in different sections of the city with very beautiful displays in their large plate-glass windows. It is only a liberal population of refined taste which will support these attractive establishments; their manifest thrift tells its own story.

If in these notes we speak most frequently of the common classes, depicting scenes illustrative of humble and every-day life among the masses, it is because such are the most representative; but the reader may be sure that there is another class happily existing in Sydney, and in all of these Pacific colonies, where the author met with and shared the hospitality of many cultured people, who exhibited a degree of refinement unsurpassed in the best of our own home circles. Some writers choose to dilate upon their intercourse with such people, giving the names of officials and the initials of private individuals from whom they received entertainment; but it seems to us better to avoid such personal mention, in which the reader can feel very little interest.

The University of Sydney, admirably situated about a mile from the business portion of the city, not far from the Alfred Hospital, is the first that was founded in the Southern Hemisphere. In its immediate neighborhood are the affiliated colleges of St. Paul, St. Andrew, and St. John, belonging respectively to the Church of England, the Presbyterian denomination, and the Roman Catholics. Religious instruction is given at these colleges, but not in the University. This edifice is of Gothic architecture, built of freestone, and is situated in spacious elevated grounds overlooking Victoria Park and the city, being enclosed by a high iron fence. Within this enclosure, which is several acres in extent, the land is terraced and ornamented with choice trees and flowers. The façade of the main building is over four hundred feet in length. On one side is a fine large stone building just finished, which is designed for a Medical School; and on the other is a spacious structure appropriated to the purpose of a museum, where we found some thousands of classified objects of special interest as antiquities. The object of the University is to afford a liberal education to all orders and denominations without distinction. Graduates rank in the same order as those of similar British home institutions. This University was originally founded by Government, but from time to time it has been the recipient of rich endowments from private sources, until it has become nearly self-supporting. The great hall of this building deserves particular mention. It is a remarkable apartment finished elaborately in the Elizabethan style, and is lighted by ten large stained-glass windows. In these were observed representations of the sovereigns of England, from William the Conqueror to Queen Victoria. Several of these windows are the gifts of wealthy patrons. The room is about a hundred and fifty feet in length and fifty wide, with a ceiling reaching to the roof, being at least seventy feet in height, finished in Gothic style and forming a marvel of carpentry, carving and painting. The citizens of Sydney may well be proud of this admirably appointed University.

The Art Gallery is a low one-story iron building

in the grounds of the park known as the Domain, and it well repaid a visit of a few hours, though it is at present only the nucleus of a future collection. It contains some excellent modern pictures by popular artists, English and French. One fine example by Louis Buvelot, an Australian artist, is full of merit. There are many excellent models of classic sculpture, including the group of the Laocoön. Some choice water-colors interested us, and there were some meritorious pieces of sculpture by native artists. One or two unselfish and devoted friends of art in Sydney have given the most of their time and much of their pecuniary means for years to promoting the interests of this collection, which under their fostering care has already reached a high intrinsic value, and is full of promise of future permanence and still greater excellence.

On the way back to our hotel from visiting the Art Gallery we stopped at the Free Public Library, which contains over one hundred thousand volumes arranged after a most admirable system. Not only do the immediate residents of the city and its environs enjoy the advantages of this collection, but the books are sent all over New South Wales, upon application from local authorities, in boxes containing one hundred volumes each, free of transportation. To secure this privilege in any instance, it is only necessary for the town authorities to sign a bond, making themselves responsible for the return of the books within a given period, or agreeing to pay for any that are lost.

This system of distribution, we were told, worked admirably, involving no loss and no more wear and tear than any other consistent use of the books, while the benefits of the library are thus extended to half a million of people.

Another circulating library, known as Maddock's Select Library, was found in George Street, after the style of Mudie's in London, or Loring's in Boston, the object of which was to supply its patrons with the best books and serial publications as soon as published. Besides the periodical literature of the day, this establishment contains thousands of standard books, which are constantly lent for a moderate sum to the reading public. This library, we were told, has been established for twenty years, and has really become a city institution. It is only upon visiting places which do not possess such convenient literary resorts that one can properly estimate their public value and importance.

Walking about the wharves in the early morning we one day saw and awaited the mooring of the incoming boat from Parametta. It was crowded with merchants' clerks, shop-keepers, and business people generally who are employed in the city during the day, but who return to their suburban homes to sleep. Among these were women from the shores of the river and harbor, with baskets of cut-flowers for the Sydney market. They were all neatly dressed, bright-looking girls and women, as rosy as their lovely wares. Some of them had two long light frames of wire which they carried in each hand, and in the openings of which were double rows of flowers, enabling each girl to carry a score and more of bouquets. These were glowing with morning freshness imparted by "some sweet mystery of the dew," and were composed of camellias in three or four colors, lilies of the valley, blue violets, and tea-roses, with sheltering borders of maiden's-hair fern and other varieties of green. All these were of out-door growth. Truly, flowers are appreciated, cultivated, and loved all over the world; even here in Eldorado they delight the eye with their beauty and the senses with their fragrance.

A brief day devoted to a trip from Sydney to the town of Parametta will well repay the visitor; and to vary the scene one should go thither by steamboat and return by the Sydney and Bathurst Railroad. This excursion gives one a better idea of the harbor in detail than can be acquired in any other manner. The comfortable little passenger-boat skirts the shore and winds among the small islands, stopping at many of them to land or to take up passengers. These islands are dotted with villas and cottages, each having a two-story veranda, generally decked with vines, and all overlooking the bay. The boat passes under a picturesque iron bridge painted white, which crosses an arm of the sea. Skilled oarsmen are constantly pulling up and down the Parametta River in their long, pointed, egg-shell boats, for here is the famous boat-race course. Verdant and well-wooded lawns of exquisite green sweep grandly down to the water's edge. Orange and lemon trees, with here and there a group of bananas and other tropical plants, bend gracefully over the tide. Now and again the Australian ivy beautifies the shore, creeping over the quaint little cottages and bursting out at times in clouds of yellow blossoms on rocky promontories and gently swelling knolls. One recognizes also the scarlet nasturtium and beds of soft blue violets intermingling with fragrant jonquils. The lily of the valley, forgetting that it is winter here, opens its bell-like blossom of snowy-white and fills the whole air with dainty sweetness. The green and striped aloe grows wild in clusters affording variety and beauty of effect to all around. There were here and there clusters also of the yellow-leaved wattle, producing by its foliage almost the exact effect of blossoms; and as the river is ascended, an abundance of the water-loving mangrove is seen bordering the banks, like willows in New England. And if one turns for a moment from the enchantment near at hand, far away over the plains and undulating country, mingling with the very clouds, are seen the Blue Mountains. All faraway mountains present an aspect of blue, but those of New South Wales are indeed cerulean.

A quiet aspect of stupid respectability, if we may be permitted the term, environed the town of Parametta. It is a dull place, and fully merits its expressive nickname of Sleepy Hollow. One is half inclined to look for a coating of blue mould over the streets and houses. While driving in the neighborhood, where everything seemed so purely English, one felt the sight of the many orange-trees in full bearing, or the flitting about of small paroquets, to be a sort of incongruity. The early colonists, as we were told, tried to raise wheat hereabout, but the soil was ill adapted to that cereal, though for raising oranges and semi-tropical fruits Parametta has since become quite famous.

The town is just fifteen miles from Sydney, and has in its environs some beautiful drives. Rocky Hall, the residence of a hospitable and wealthy citizen, not far from the town of Parametta, contains in its spacious grounds an orchard with a marvellous variety of growing fruits. The proprietor, Mr. James Pye, is good authority on all subjects relating to horticulture. The salubrious character of the climate has enabled this gentleman to produce in abundance thriving specimens of nearly every known fruit either tropical or hardy, added to which he has a large and choice variety of flowers.

We are reminded in this connection of one of the pleasantest drives in Sydney, not to be forgotten by the visiting stranger, — that along the shores of Port Jackson. Here, within a few minutes' walk of the heart of a populous city, we have rippling waters, waving foliage, frequent gardens, vine-clad cottages, a yellow pebbly shore, and a bay full of maritime beauties, — all combining to form a lovely panorama full of local color and of infinite variety.

But even the beautiful aspect of Sydney harbor has

its drawbacks. With a single oarsman we crossed the bay from Port Jackson shore, and as we glided quietly over the water and looked down into the depths alongside, we saw more than one hideous man-eating shark of the dreaded white species, stealthily in search of human prey. Though they feed on other fish, the white sharks seem to prefer human flesh to all other, and will remain patiently for days at a time in the same spot, watching for a chance to satisfy this terrible appetite. Sad accidents from this source are not infrequent, two young lads from an overturned boat having been seized and eaten by these voracious creatures just one week previous to our arrival in Sydney. The instance here referred to was particularly afflicting as we heard it described. The father of one of the boys was the horrified witness of the scene, without being able to render his son the least assistance.

The sharks which frequent the coast of Norway, the catching of which forms a regular industry there, are what are termed the mackerel shark, because they feed mostly upon that fish. The size of this kind averages from six to eight feet in length; but those which frequent the coast of Australia will measure from ten to twelve feet, and have enormous mouths furnished with four or five rows of long sharp teeth. They are well called the tigers of the sea.

CHAPTER V.

A Zigzag Railway.— Wonderful Series of Caves. — Immense Sheep-Runs. — Sheep-Shearing. — Central Australia. — City Characteristics. — Fine Architectural Development. — Steam Tramways. — Labor Unions. — Colonial Federation. — The Tariff. — Loyalty to England. — Spirit of Local Rivalry. — The St. Giles of Sydney. — City Clubs. — The Laughing Jackass. — Public Parks. — Gold Mines.

THERE is one special excursion which should not be neglected by travellers to Sydney; namely, a visit to what are called the Fish River Caves at Tarana. No person would neglect them who could anticipate the novel experience to be enjoyed by such a visit, which need occupy but four days' time. We had not even heard of these singular wonders of Nature's handiwork before coming hither. The short journey to the caves takes one through a delightful though wild and mountainous region, replete with grand natural scenery. The route leads through the Emu Plains and over the Blue Mountains by the Zigzag Railroad, from whose various elevations lovely far-reaching views are enjoyed of the district left behind and the gleaming Nepean River winding gracefully through it. This range of mountains reaches a height of three thousand four hundred feet, intersected by precipitous ravines fifteen hundred feet in depth, and by gulches scarcely excelled in our own Rocky Mountains. One is reminded here most forcibly of the precipitous zigzag road at Darjeling, in India, which ascends toward the Himalayan range, and which is nearly as remarkable as this example of Australian engineering. We were told that this Zigzag Railroad of five miles more or less in length cost three million dollars, and saw no reason to doubt it. In working out some of the levels from the face of the precipitous and rocky sides of the mountain, laborers were suspended by ropes from holding-ground far above their heads, and very many of the cuttings were accomplished under equally trying circumstances. As a piece of daring and successful engineering there is nothing to equal it in the Southern Hemisphere.

The subterranean temples and halls of limestone which constitute these remarkable Fish River Caves are of vast extent, filled with many intricate windings, galleries, and irregular passages, in which one would inevitably be lost without an experienced and faithful guide. The many apartments are known by special names, and there are several singularly perfect archways whose exact proportions no architect could improve. These caves present some of the most beautiful stalactites we have ever seen, and in many prominent features they are considered to be unique. Whole days of examination would not exhaust their variety. One of the caves is of cathedral dimensions, having a height of five hundred feet and a length and breadth according well with its altitude. Another of the apartments is appropriately designated as the

Menagerie, on account of the peculiar shapes produced by the crystal-like formations, from which the imagination can easily create various animals.

When lighted, these subterranean palaces form a gorgeous spectacle. One peculiar division is called the Bell Tower, being a small chamber in which are five or six stalactites hanging near together, and which when struck give out rich metallic tones similar to a chime of bells. For extent, variety, and beauty combined, these buried halls and chambers have no equal so far as our experience goes, though they recall the grotto of Adelsberg, near Trieste, which exhibits some similar features, and also the subterranean caverns in the environs of Matanzas, Cuba. In these Fish River Caves the fantastic shapes assumed by the limestone formations are infinite in variety, as well as weird and singular in their groupings. But perhaps they excel most particularly in their beautiful coloring, in many instances presenting great brilliancy of lustre, which causes the individual stalactites to seem like ponderous opals.

A magnesium wire is introduced by the guide for the pleasure of the visitor, and when the caves are thus illumined the most fairy-like effect is produced. It is as if one suddenly stood within the charmed palace of Aladdin, the gauze-like fountains reflecting the light upon one another like a series of mirrors, and the whole sparkling like rubies, emeralds, and diamonds. The effect then becomes fantastic, unreal, theatrical. From some of the intricate windings the distant music of waterfalls strikes pleasantly on the ear, and crystal streams reflect the light in azure hues. When the guide extinguishes for a moment his powerful light, gloom and darkness surround the visitor, stimulating the imagination to vivid activity. These might be the caves of Erebus leading to Hades, and where is Charon to ferry us across the Styx? May not that distant sound of falling water be the voice of Lethe, that river of oblivion "whereof whoso drinks straightway his former sense and being forgets"? Some of these natural temples have domes rivalling St. Peter's and St. Paul's. How many there are of these caves, running for miles into the mountains, no one can say, as they have never been fully explored; but every year some new grotto is discovered and added to the number already recorded.

Caves of limestone formation are produced in many parts of the world, and the simplest knowledge of chemistry coupled with a little careful observation shows us clearly how they have been created. The conditions must first be those of an underlying bed of limestone nearly horizontal in its layers, over which a forest or wooded surface has grown. The falling rain washes the decaying leaves, and in doing so borrows from them certain chemical properties, charged with which the water sinks into the limestone beds. The carbon acquired by the water combines with and dissolves the lime and other components of the rock, which then escape as gases through the interstices of the earth. Thus openings are at first formed, which are slowly increased in size by the same process during the passing ages, until vast and curious caves are created. When underground channels have been begun, coursing streams of water assist the chemical action and wear away the rock by simple friction. With these facts in mind, the Fish River Caves cease to be miraculous formations, as some have imagined them, and are only marvels, — giving us tangible evidence of the many thousands of years which must have transpired during their creation.

In the broad space of country lying between the coast and the Alpine range, of which the Blue Mountains form a part, there are many sheep-runs of large proportions, upon which are sheep in almost fabulous numbers. The land here seems especially adapted in its natural condition to the raising and sustenance of these profitable animals, though it is also susceptible of a much higher degree of improvement and cultivation. Our observation was confined mainly to the country nearest the borders of New South Wales and Victoria. Here one man, a thrifty Scotchman from "Auld Reekie," with whom we became acquainted, was the owner of over one hundred and twenty thousand sheep, and several other men had more than half that number each. Forty or fifty thousand belonging to one person is not considered at all remarkable in this great South-Land of Australia. When it is remembered that each one of these animals must be sheared annually, the enormous labor involved in caring for such a stock begins to be realized.

In the clipping season, bands of men sometimes numbering forty or fifty, go from one run to another to shear the sheep, and become very expert at the business, realizing a handsome sum of money at the close of each season. Some of these men invest their money in flocks, and thus gradually become possessed of runs of their own. Several such instances were named to us. Such "a neighbor" (any one within ten miles is called "a neighbor") "began as a clipper two or three years ago, and now he owns his twenty thousand sheep." The annual natural increase is fully seventy-five per cent per annum. Some clippers are not so careful of their means, but after the season is finished they hie away to Sydney, Melbourne, or some other populous centre, where they drink and gamble away their money much faster than they earned it.

A smart professional shearer will clip one hundred sheep in a day of ten hours. The highest price paid for such service is five dollars a day, or rather five dollars per each hundred animals sheared. These men often work over hours during the season, for which they are paid at the same rate, and are always found in board and lodging by the owner of the run by whom they are employed. Machinery to do the clipping is being introduced, though not rapidly, as only a few more animals can be sheared per day by machinery than by hand, — a process similar in its operation to that of horse-clipping. The great advantage, however, of machinery is the perfect uniformity of cut obtained, — a result which the most experienced shearer cannot insure. The operator often cuts the sheep more or less severely in the rapidity of the hand process; but this is impossible where the machine is used, though it leaves the animal with a shorter fleece all over its body, and consequently gives a yield of three or four ounces more of wool from each. To feed and properly sustain such vast numbers of sheep requires ample space; but there is enough of that, and to spare.

Australia in its greatest breadth, between Shark's Bay on the west and Sandy Cape on the eastern shore, measures twenty-four hundred miles; and from north to south — that is, from Cape York to Cape Otway — it is probably over seventeen hundred miles in extent. A very large portion of the country, especially in the interior and northwestern sections, still remains unexplored. The occupied and improved portions of the country skirt the sea-coast on the southern and eastern sides, which are covered with cities, towns, villages, and hamlets where nine tenths of the population live. The country occupied for sheep-runs and cattle-ranches is very sparsely inhabited. The reason for this is obvious, since the owner of a hundred thousand sheep requires between two and three hundred thousand acres to feed them properly. The relative proportion as to sheep and land, as given to us, is to allow two and a third acres to each animal. Of course there is land which would support these animals in proportion of say one sheep to the acre; but the average is as above.

Those who are engaged in agriculture have pushed their homes back inland as far as the soil and the water-courses will avail them. The latter element must be especially regarded, as the country is unfortunately liable to severe droughts. Thus district after district has been reclaimed from the wilderness and turned into fertile grazing lands. There is no bound to this gradual progress of land cultivation; slow but sure, it will only cease when the western coast bordering on the Indian Ocean, now mostly a wilderness, shall be reached.

A sort of patriarchal simplicity has until lately governed these pioneers of agriculture. Any unmarked and unoccupied land has been freely appropriated to their use. But as a higher grade of husbandry has advanced, more stringent laws have been enforced and cheerfully acquiesced in; so that at present there is very little near the coast suitable for grazing which is not under registry with the Crown officers. Squatting is therefore no longer a happy-go-lucky venture, but that which the pioneer has he pays for, — a small sum to be sure, but it renders his claim safe from any chance infringement. The want of such well-defined rules in the earlier days led to many a bitter quarrel, which not infrequently ended in a fatal manner. Adventurous men, who always go armed, are generally quick to quarrel, and reckless in the use of weapons.

The central portion of Australia is described as being one vast extent of alluvial plains, interspersed with sandy ridges, dry lakes (or land depressions), and occasional hills. Many portions have a very rich black soil, bearing what are called nigall-trees, which yield a transparent gum in large quantities, in all respects resembling gum-arabic, being perfectly soluble in water. This gum the natives eat freely; and it is very palatable, though its nutritive qualities are quite doubtful. The natives eat this gum to allay the pangs of hunger, but it is not believed that human life could long be sustained upon it. On some of these central plains there is a natural grass of the most nutritious quality, which grows profusely. The Europeans call it blue-grass, of which sheep and cattle are very fond. Large tracts are liable to inundation from floods during the brief rainy season. The soil consists of a rich plastic formation. Wild carrots and wild flax abound; the former are especially sought for by sheep, while the bolls of the latter are considered fattening for all stock. Sheep will patiently dig with their forefeet to get at the carrots, and devour them eagerly, though they are very bitter to the taste. Another peculiarity of the country, as it was described to us, is the entire absence of all stones; not one is to be found except at the foot of some of the hills, which are often twenty miles apart. It is believed that this part of the territory is at a certain depth underlaid by an abundance of fresh water, which would be perfectly accessible by means of artesian wells.

If a suitable and efficient system of irrigation could be adopted it would bring into use at once an enormous territory as large as half-a-dozen of our largest

Western States, which is now little better than a dry desert, where in summer the grass becomes hay dried upon the roots, but which in winter, when the rain falls, puts on an inviting aspect of rich verdure.

The great dividing mountain chain of Australia is near the coast-line in the south and east, averaging perhaps a hundred miles or more from the sea. Nearly all the gold which the land has produced has come from the valleys and hillsides of this range. The gold diggings of New South Wales have proved to be very rich in some sections; but unlike those of Queensland and Victoria, — the former six hundred miles north of Sydney, and the latter six hundred miles south of it, — the precious metal is here found mostly in alluvial deposits. A true fissure vein of gold-bearing quartz, as we were informed, has never been found in New South Wales. As a source of pecuniary and lasting income, her coal mines are far more valuable than all the rest of her mineral deposits combined.

Sydney holds high rank as a British colonial city, and deservedly so, having special reason for pride in the complete system of her charitable and educational organizations, her noble public buildings, and the general character of her leading citizens. Land in the town and its vicinity is held at prices averaging as high as in Boston or New York, and the wealth of the people is represented to be very great in the aggregate.

The City Hall, now in course of enlargement, is an

admirable structure of stone, grand in its architecture and most substantially constructed. When finished it will equal the Hôtel de Ville of Paris in size, and to our taste surpass it architecturally. It is of the composite order, with bold reliefs and pillared front, its whole effect being in strong contrast to that of St. Andrew's Cathedral in George Street, which is close at hand. The latter is in pure Gothic of the pointed style, and although it is comparatively small, it will rank favorably in its decorations and internal arrangements with any of the lately-built English cathedrals. The view from the open cupola of the City Hall, at a height of about one hundred and fifty feet above the level of George Street, is unusually comprehensive, taking in not only the immediate city on all sides, but also the environs, including the several divisions of the harbor. To the westward, fifteen miles away, lies Parametta, while eastward the heaving breast of the restless Pacific Ocean dies away in the far horizon. From this eyrie one looks down upon the Cathedral, which is a very costly edifice, and was thirty-one years in building, — the funds being frequently exhausted, and money for the purpose difficult to raise. But it now stands as a fine Christian monument of choice design, thoroughly and artistically carried out.

The Post-Office is a very large stone structure surmounted by a tall square tower, rather out of proportion. This building extends over a whole square, or rather fronts upon three streets, embracing ample room for every department of the postal service, including that of the telegraph. The whole building is surrounded on the three sides by lofty pillars of stone, forming a corridor open to the streets, admirably conceived so that the attendant public are at all times under shelter.

Among the other prominent public buildings are the Treasury, the Land Office, and the Colonial Secretary's Office, each four or five stories in height, built of stone, and situated near the shore of the harbor. This is the immediate neighborhood of the Circular Quay at the head of Sydney Cove. This quay has a length of over three thousand feet, and is available for the mooring of the largest steamers that navigate the ocean. Numerous steamships of five thousand tons and upward lay here on the occasion of our visit.

The erection of new buildings is always an evidence of thrift and general prosperity. Much building was observed to be in progress here, mostly large stone edifices designed for business purposes, remarkable for their architectural pretension and the solidity of the mason-work. All this activity gave us the impression of being in the midst of a prosperous, progressive people.

The contrast presented by Sunday compared with the rest of the week was remarkable, the day being one of perfect repose so far as all outward appearances went. The bar-rooms were all closed and every branch of business suspended. The Public Gardens,

Public Library, and Art Gallery, however, were all open.

The tramways of Sydney are operated by steam-power, noisy, smoke-dispensing locomotives being in constant use on the main thoroughfares where tramways are laid. Two or more passenger-cars are run coupled together, stopping at certain designated points for passengers, say at the end of every other block, and nowhere between stations either to take up or set down passengers. Flag-men are placed at what are considered to be extra-hazardous crossings, and we were told that accidents seldom occur, except through the carelessness of the passengers; but that there was constant and imminent risk caused by these steam-cars was perfectly manifest. A woman was run over and fatally injured, so that she died on the same day in the hospital, while we were in the city. Of course it was represented to have been the victim's own fault; but we beg leave to differ from this decision, and to ascribe the blame to those who first permitted the introduction of so dangerous a motor into the crowded streets of a large city.

Labor combinations, labor "unions," as they are called, have proved very disastrous in Sydney to all concerned, but more especially to the laboring classes themselves. General enterprise in several departments of mechanical labor is seriously impeded. Men well inclined and able to work for fair wages are not permitted to do so, the "unions" terrorizing them into obedience to their ill-conceived and arbitrary rules, though wages are about double what they are in England, and as high as in this country. The consequence is that the street-corners and bar-rooms are crowded with idlers and vicious men, half driven to despair by their own folly, who somehow find money for beer and rum if not for bread for their suffering families. There is ample and remunerative employment for all independent men, but those who prefer to be led by others rather than to think and act for themselves must pay the penalty. The laborer of to-day if thrifty, industrious, and sober becomes the employer of to-morrow, and as soon as a man is possessed of land or other real property he begins to complain of the want of hands to carry on the same, and to look upon the whole subject of labor and capital in a more reasonable light. That the real interests of both are entirely mutual is perfectly obvious to the intelligent mind, and those designing agitators who strive to array one against the other are emissaries of ill-omen.

Laborers were asking for work from the Government officials when we were in Sydney, and demanding high wages with circumscribed hours. Such were told that there was employment for all who would seek it inland, upon the farms and plantations, where indeed the great drawback was the want of able hands; but the naturally idle and dissipated will always crowd to populous centres. Agriculture is taking its place as the main industry of the country, and if people who are now asking for aid from the Government in these colonies would go inland and seek occupation, independent of all hampering "union" connections, they would promote their own interest and the best good of their adopted country.

Respectable female help is especially needed here, for which the best wages are paid; and when we read of the somewhat startling cry of London women of the humbler class, "Give us work and pay which will feed and clothe us," it seems as if the need might be easily supplied here, to the mutual advantage of these women and the colonists. Already in these colonies there are well-organized means by which worthy and deserving persons can reach Australia or New Zealand free of cost to themselves so far as passage is concerned, so desirous are the colonists to induce emigration from England of a class of men and women who will become of general use in the community. The explanation of this incongruity between want of occupation and the dearth of laborers of either sex is, that the sensational cry which we have quoted comes mostly if not entirely from a class whose habits and lives are not such as to make them desirable in the colonies, or indeed anywhere else. For the most part, undoubtedly, it is the dissolute, drinking, thieving classes of London and other large cities who loudly utter these demands, spurred on to do so by reckless socialists and conspiring anarchists.

For the worthy and industrious poor, above all others, Australia and New Zealand offer unequalled inducements in the way of a new home. The climate is admirable, not liable to extremes, and constantly reminding one of the south of France or the shores of the Mediterranean. Statistics exhibiting the death-rates of the several colonies were a surprise to us, showing that Australia, New Zealand, and Tasmania were healthier even than London, which is well known to be remarkable in this respect. Owing to the purity and elasticity of the atmosphere, which is proven to contain an unusual amount of ozone, the same degree of heat is not realized so much as it is elsewhere. The thermometer while we were in Sydney showed a mean of 60° Fahrenheit in the shade, in the month of June, which answers to our month of December in America. The death-rate of the New England cities is perhaps safely put at twenty-one per thousand, while that of Australia is shown to be seventeen per thousand, — a statement equally applicable to New Zealand and Tasmania. So far as we could learn by careful inquiry, malarial fevers are there quite unknown.

While in Sydney, we heard much relative to the proposed federation of the several colonies; that is, the adoption of one parliament for and a recognized union of all the provinces, following as a model the general idea of the Canadian organization. At present each section of the country — namely, Queensland, New South Wales, Victoria, South Australia, West Australia, and Tasmania — is under a separate government, carried on without any unity of interest as regards the whole. Indeed the bitterest rivalry seemed to exist between them, a petty jealousy being fostered which is entirely unworthy of an intelligent and liberal people. Doubtless the world at large can see that the best interests of Australia would be served by a consummation of this purpose of federation, but it is not universally popular among the colonists. New South Wales, we were told, decidedly holds back from such a plan, her individual interest inclining her to maintain isolation; but, so far as one might judge, the other colonies favor it. It has been said that New South Wales is more loyal to the Queen than are her own English subjects at home; and as shrewd judges surmise that a complete federation of these colonies would ultimately lead to a declaration of independence of the mother country, they partly oppose the idea upon this ground. Undoubtedly it would be a step in that direction.

Many nationalities are represented in Australia and New Zealand, but the majority are English, Scotch, and Irish. The officials of New South Wales, especially, look to England for many favors which a separation would cut them off from; among these are honorary titles and appointments under the Crown. The constitution under which these colonies are living is such as to entitle them to be called democracies. In many respects they are more liberal and advanced than is England herself. Church and State, for instance, are kept quite distinct from each other. As to the legislative powers of the colonies, the home government has not even a veto which can be said to be of any real account. When such dissent on the part of the Queen is expressed (which is rare), there is a certain legal way of avoiding its force, — a resort to which the colonists have not failed to betake themselves at times.

Here as elsewhere there are two parties in the general politics of the country, — one loyal to the last degree to the British throne, the other ready at the first opportunity to cut loose from the home government, which is so many thousands of miles away. The most important question relating to federation seems to be that of the tariff. While New South Wales favors a low and simple tariff, Victoria insists upon "protection" in the fullest sense of that much-abused term. Queensland is more liberal, and favors free-trade. This question therefore becomes an important factor in the proposed federation; and could it be settled, no doubt a general union would soon follow. It is clearly in accordance with the logic of events that in the near future not only will federation take place throughout these colonies, making them one just as these United States are one, but their independence of the mother country will naturally follow. That great English writer on political economy, John Stuart Mill, says: "Countries separated by half the globe do not present the natural conditions for being under one government, or even members of one federation. If they had sufficiently the same interests, they have not and never can have a sufficient habit of taking counsel together. They are

not part of the same public; they do not discuss and
deliberate in the same arena but apart, and have only
a most imperfect knowledge of what passes in the
minds of one another." It would seem as if Mr. Mill
had these colonies of the South Pacific in view when
he expressed these ideas. The pride of empire is all-
powerful, but the growth and extent of nations, as
shown in the history of the Babylonian, Assyrian,
and Roman Empires, are governed by principles
beyond their individual control. When men have
builded too high the structure topples over. The
more dominion is extended the more vulnerable it
becomes. There is also, as Mr. Mill intimates, a vital
distinction between continuous or contiguous empire
and empire dispersed and separated by thousands of
miles of ocean.

If there were not such a persistent spirit of rivalry
existing between the several colonies of Australia,
the different railroad gauges which have been pur-
posely established could not be maintained for a single
month. Such obvious folly seemed inexcusable to a
stranger. Victoria has the broad gauge of five feet
three inches; New South Wales has a gauge of four
feet eight inches; while in Queensland the narrow
gauge of three feet six inches is adopted. Freight or
passengers going over the railroads from Brisbane to
Adelaide must change cars twice, and from Sydney
to Melbourne — only six hundred miles — freight and
passengers must change cars at Albury. It was not
very clear to the writer why this spirit of jealousy

should exist at all, much less why it should be so universally indulged in. At Sydney, Melbourne is vilified most recklessly; its simplest enterprises are decried: no good can come out of Nazareth! Melbourne, on her part, returns the compliment with interest; and so it is also with Adelaide. This feeling operates as a serious and ever-present drawback to colonial progress in nearly every direction.

Were Australia to become independent of the mother country, and its divided interests consolidated, the benefit to be derived therefrom seemed to us to be unquestionable. One occasionally heard the saying, "Australia for the Australians," in the same sense as the Irish demand "Ireland for the Irish." It is a favorite phrase used by the agitators in addressing the masses. The only possible danger of this country becoming involved in a foreign war arises from her being a dependency of England; and it is doubtful how long these colonists will remain contented to be exposed to such a serious emergency, in the issues of which they could have no direct interest.

The proposal for federation, as it was explained to us, contemplates uniting far-away New Zealand with the other colonies, — a purpose which seems to be without any good reason to recommend it. New Zealand and Australia are as far apart as Africa and South America, or as Turkey is from England. The sea which separates them is without islands, is turbulent, torn by Antarctic currents and swept by raging storms at nearly all seasons. Even in what is called fine weather there is a ceaseless swell heaving the bosom of this sea very trying to endure, and which it is only safe to encounter in large, well-equipped vessels. In ethnological respects as well as in scenery and climate the countries are diametrically opposite. The Maoris and the native Australians — the aborigines of the two countries — are as different as white men are from negroes, there being no actual resemblance except that both are of bronzed hue. New Zealand has a damp, windy, but not cold climate, with a never-failing supply of water; Australia is a dry, arid land often suffering from drought. The first is characterized by deep cool shades, the latter by heat and glare, and by inland plains which in their present condition might not inappropriately be compared to an African desert for sterility and temperature.

Nearly every city has its "St. Giles." In Sydney the quarter which might be thus appropriately designated is known as "the Rocks." Here the backsliders most do congregate, and here are located rookeries devoted to their temporary lodgment. The police rarely penetrate here unless in the special pursuit of a criminal, as it forms a sort of neutral ground between crime and justice. This city contains at least as many whitewashed rogues as other cities of its size, — men and women who cunningly keep within the pale of the law, or who may have served out one or more sentences of imprisonment, and are legally clear from the clutches of justice. Such characters, if they do not openly resort to "the Rocks," are very apt to have some secret connection therewith. The daily habitués are persons whose lives are filled with constant misdeeds, who gain their bread by criminal acts, and whose career is characterized by recklessness and excess. Sailors are often enticed hither, and after being plied with drugged liquor are robbed. We do not remember to have seen anywhere more petrified rascality to the square inch than was evinced in the features of the men and women of "the Rocks." No enterprise, it seemed, could be too wicked for them to engage in. Gold-digging is not as a rule conducive to morality; indeed it is apt to lead directly in the opposite course. Thus it is that toilers after the glittering metal having acquired a goodly sum are apt to toss aside the pick and shovel for what is termed a "lark," and wending their way to town bring up finally at "the Rocks," where a miner and his gold are almost sure rapidly to part company. If he shows resistance, a knife or a revolver may be the fatal resort.

Clubs are as much of an institution in the colonies as they are in London; indeed, an Englishman at home or abroad without his club is never quite himself. In Sydney and Melbourne the club takes the character of a private hotel where members, and strangers introduced by them, lodge and take their meals. We were officially informed in both of these cities that our name had been recorded as entitled to all the conveniences of more than one of these organizations; but further than the prompt recognition of the courtesy and kindness of these committees we did not avail ourself of the privileges tendered. To be sure one is introduced at these clubs to the best society of the place, but the only trouble encountered by the author in this respect was that he could only with difficulty escape the profuse hospitality and cordial attention pressed upon him by the colonials. Our journey into the South Pacific was a long one; we had but a few months in which to traverse the length and breadth of these great islands; time therefore was precious, and self-abnegation a duty in order to fulfil a comprehensive programme.

The first time the author made the acquaintance of the "laughing jackass" was in the bird, fruit, and flower market on George Street. His sarcastic notes were afterward often encountered in his wild state and among his open-air haunts. Not to make special mention of him would be to omit reference to one of the most curious creatures the traveller meets with in his wanderings about the country. Mischievous, sly, droll, insulting, without a particle of shyness, what a bird it is! His plumage is mottled, white and black; he has very little tail, but is provided with a great gawky head, a well-rounded body, and is a little larger than the domestic pigeon. His eyes are preternaturally big, and gaze coolly at you as though they would pierce you through. He laughs almost exactly like a human being, with a touch of bird malice added; and though it is harsh, his merriment is ludicrously contagious, for no one can avoid laughing both at and with him. It is a riotous tumult of laughter. He is as intelligent as the mino-bird, and can be taught to talk better than a parrot, — at least so we were told, — and, sad to say, shows a manifest delight in profanity. The bushmen consider him to be a sort of barometer foretelling the weather; for when it is about to rain the jackass becomes miserable, dejected, and sleepy, sitting upon a branch of a tree with his feathers all awry and his head hidden under his wing, — a very picture of melancholy. Of all birds he seems most like a caricature of his own species. Though he is of the kingfisher tribe, he does not seem to pay much attention to fishes, his favorite food being small snakes. These he seizes just back of the head, and flying rapidly aloft drops them upon stony ground, thus breaking their delicate spine. This process is repeated until life becomes extinct in the victim, when the jackass proceeds leisurely to devour the body piecemeal. As he is thus considered to perform an important service to the settlers, who are much troubled with snakes, he enjoys complete immunity from trap and gun.

Sydney fully illustrates the commendable passion which all the colonies of Australasia evince for the establishment of public parks. If this is a weakness it is a grand one, which we heartily wish was epidemic in this country. Nothing is more conducive to health, beauty, and good morals than these beautiful places in and about populous cities and towns. Every capital or considerable town in Australia, New Zealand, or Tasmania is thus beautified and improved; but Sydney and Melbourne have endeavored in this respect especially to rival each other. Sydney being the oldest settlement has had more time to perfect a grand system of gardens and reserved lands which are not surpassed by any European capital. First there is Hyde Park, situated in the centre of the town; next the Domain, as it is called, containing one hundred and forty acres on the north side of the metropolis, ornamented by broad paths and noble shade-trees; close at hand are the beautiful Botanical Gardens of forty acres in extent, which we have already described. Added to these there is the Prince Alfred Park of twenty acres, and the Belmore Park of ten acres. Virtually forming a part of this same system of reserved lands is a tract of six hundred acres known as Moor Park, lying on the southeast side, adjoining which is the popular metropolitan race-course. This list of parks speaks for itself, representing an amount of open, ornamental space which would serve a city of three millions, while Sydney has but about that number of hundred thousands. No one thing is more indicative of opulence, liberality of sentiment, and regard for the public good than such grand free resorts.

Being in the vicinity, a flying visit was made to the township of Bingera, situated in a northwest direction from Sydney on the Gwydir River, at a distance of three hundred and fifty miles from the capital. It possesses more than passing interest, as it has, besides some valuable and paying "diggings" of gold near at hand, something still more attractive to adventurous spirits,— namely, diamond mines. These are being industriously worked and with paying results, though no very large amount of profit has yet been realized. Nearly a thousand small diamonds have been found here and sent to market. Though they are not large, they are remarkable for purity of color and excellence of quality. This is a rich mineral district, abounding specially in copper and tin; but there are not over a thousand people at Bingera, even including the floating population attracted by the diamond-fields.

The most famous of the gold mines here is the "Upper Bingera," which has proved very profitable to its owners, and is about sixteen miles from Bingera. Another somewhat famous mine of this neighborhood is known as the "Bobby Whitlow;" and still a third which deserves mention as being nearly as prolific is called "The Boro." All these mines have been more or less freely worked and partially abandoned for more promising fields, but they are by no means exhausted.

It may very reasonably be doubted whether Australia would have risen into notice, or have been so promptly peopled by Englishmen, had it not been that hordes of convicts were shipped thither from Great Britain in the early days of its discovery. Though this transportation of criminals thither was long ago abolished, and this element of reproach has been nearly lived down, "there is still unfortunately a convict flavor permeating some classes," — we use the very words of a respectable citizen with whom we were conversing upon the subject. Some of the rich men of to-day came out from England as prisoners; and the heads of some families, whose descendants are now reasonably esteemed and respected, were once ticket-of-leave men. But in sheer justice it should be remembered that persons in those days were very often transported by the courts of the old country for crimes of the most petty character.

CHAPTER VI.

The Capital of Queensland. — Public Gardens. — Gold Mines and Gold Mining. — Pleasant Excursion. — Inducements to Emigrants. — Coolie Principle of Labor. — Agricultural Products. — Sugar Plantations. — Australian Aborigines. — Cannibalism. — Civil Wars. — Indian Legends. — Fire-arms and Fire-water. — Missionary Efforts. — A Brief Romance. — The Boomerang. — The Various Tribes. — Antiquity of these Lands.

BRISBANE, the capital of Queensland, which was originally known as Moreton Bay District, lies about five hundred miles north of Sydney, and is reached most readily by coasting steamers; though the railroad long since begun, has been nearly completed between the two cities, and may possibly be open by the time these notes are printed. It has a population, if we include the immediate suburbs, of fully fifty thousand. Until 1860 it was an appendage of New South Wales, but was in that year formed into an independent colony and named Queensland, after the reigning queen of great Britain. The site of the city is a diversified surface, with the river whose name it bears winding gracefully through it about twenty-five miles from its mouth; though in a direct line it would be but half that distance to its debouchment into Moreton Bay, one of the largest bays on the coast of Australia. It was discovered by Captain

Cook in 1770, and is formed by two long sandy islands running north and south, named respectively Standbroke and Moreton Islands, enclosing between them and the mainland a spacious sheet of water more than thirty miles long and six or eight wide, beautified by several small and fertile islands. On approaching Brisbane by the sea one is puzzled at first to find where the mouth of the river can be, so completely is it hidden by mangrove swamps which skirt the coast hereabout for many miles. A pleasant little watering-place is located close at hand named Sandgate, which is connected by hourly stages with the city. Several small rivers, all of which however are more or less navigable, empty into Moreton Bay, showing that the district of Brisbane is well watered.

It is less than fifty years since Brisbane was opened to free settlers, having been previously only a penal station of the English government. But of this taint here the same may be said as of Sydney or Hobart in Tasmania, — scarcely a trace remains.

The principal streets run north and south, and are half a mile long, being crossed at right angles by smaller ones. All of these thoroughfares were originally laid out too narrow for the purpose designed. Here one remarks the same system of verandas reaching from end to end of the streets, and stretching over the sidewalks to the edgestones before the shops, which is observed in all the other cities and large towns of Australia and New Zealand. For a city of its size it is unusually well supplied with churches and places of public worship, of which there are forty-one, embracing all sects of professed Christians. Queen Street is the main thoroughfare and is lined with handsome stores and beautiful edifices, for there is no lack of architectural pretension either in the public or private buildings. Like all of its sister cities in these colonies, Brisbane has an elaborate Botanical Garden, in which the people take great interest; it certainly seemed to approach very nearly that of Sydney not only in spaciousness, but in general excellence, — the climate here favoring even a more extensive out-door display of tropical and delicate vegetation than can be obtained farther south. The fine examples of the great india-rubber tree found here were nearly equal to those we have seen in their native forests, where the great anaconda-like roots are often as much above as below the surface.

Contiguous to these grounds and forming a conspicuous object in the landscape is the Parliament Building, a grand structure of cut-stone brought from neighboring quarries. This building has been a very expensive affair, and probably antedates by half a century the absolute requirements of the colony. Still, one pauses to ask himself if it is possible that only a few years ago the present site of Brisbane was a waste of dense jungle, a reeking swamp, a barren hillside. And if it has accomplished so much in the way of growth and material progress in so short a time, what may not be hoped for it in the near future?

There are besides the Botanical Gardens three other "reserves," as they are universally denominated in Australia; namely, Queen's Park, Victoria Park, and Bowen Park, each laid out in the most liberal spirit and in anticipation of a population which the city will undoubtedly realize within a few years from the present time. The ample water-supply of the town has also been partially anticipatory; but what an immense advantage it is to Brisbane! The sparkling liquid is brought by an excellent system of pipes from the hills near Enaggera Creek, seven miles distant from the city. Here a large reservoir has been created by throwing a dam across a narrow part of a deep gully, and thus a large body of water securely preserved. This water is both palatable and wholesome. An intelligent spirit of enterprise is evinced by the citizens, and everything goes to show that this is destined to be a populous and prosperous centre. As to the climate, it is simply perfect, the mean temperature being set down at 69°.

Ipswich, about twenty-five miles from the city, on the road to the Darling Downs, has a population of ten thousand. Gympie, a gold-mining town a hundred miles north, has about the same number of inhabitants. Maryborough, on the banks of the Mary River, is another thriving town equally populous; and Rockhampton, near the mouth of the Fitzroy River, is a town of similar size and importance. Charter's Towers, Croyden, and Table-Top are each productive gold centres; and there are many others which might be named, as showing the populous and important character to which Queensland has already attained. Of the gold-producing localities, Charter's Towers is perhaps the best developed and the richest. The particular " claim " at this point, known by the name of the " Day-Dawn," is thought to be the most valuable, and has turned out a very large aggregate of gold. Through the country, inside of the coast-range, there runs a broad belt of gold-bearing quartz more or less near the surface, but which requires organized capital to improve it effectually. At first the localities are worked by a few hands for the surface yield, and the excavation is continued as far down as can be done without elaborate hoisting apparatus. Then the claim is apt to be abandoned, or left to be eventually improved and worked by machinery aided by wealthy organizations.

To the west of this mineral belt are situated the endless rolling downs and prairies of the province, covered with herbage suitable for the support of countless herds and flocks, and where some fourteen millions of sheep are now yielding meat and wool for export, and where some four millions of cattle are also herded. The real greatness of the country is to be found in this agricultural capacity, this pastoral interest. Gold will attract adventurers, but the substantial permanent population will be found west of the auriferous range of mountains.

The pursuit of gold-mining has been called the triumph of hope over experience, since notwithstanding the rich rewards so often attendant on this pursuit, by it more seekers mar than make their fortune; and when once a man has engaged in it, he seems to become utterly unfit for any other occupation. Nevertheless, so great is the infatuation pertaining to gold-mining, that when one seeker, broken down by ill-success, ill-health, and perhaps the contracting of bad habits, is finally forced to abandon the pursuit, his place is quickly taken by fresh recruits, over-credulous and ever increasing in numbers.

We spoke particularly of Charter's Towers as being a remarkable mine in its productiveness. We mean comparatively so, as those at Gympie are also of great promise. The "Lady Mary" claim in this district is known all over Australia for its profitable yield. The Mount Morgan mine near Rockhampton, on a branch of the river Dee, is thought by some to be the richest gold mine in the world; nor should it be supposed that the auriferous fields in Queensland have all been discovered. It is the same here as among our own rich gold and silver leads. Take those of Montana for instance; no one who knows anything about that Territory believes that one lead has been found out of one hundred that are in the hills awaiting the prospecter's pick: yet Montana has sent within the last year,— 1887,— the extraordinary sum of thirty-five million dollars in gold and silver to the mint.

An extremely pleasant trip may be enjoyed up the Brisbane River and Bremer Creek, on which latter stream Ipswich is situated. It is twice as far by water as by land, but the sail is delightful. The visitor often gets a charming view of the city from the river, while at the same time passing suburban residences, flourishing farms, banana-groves, cotton-fields, sugar-plantations, orange-orchards, and the varied scenery which borders the river's course. If one has time for but a single excursion from the capital of Queensland, let him go to Ipswich by the river. We would also advise him not to miss the trip from Sydney to the town of Parametta up the river of the same name.

The unreasonably high rates demanded as wages, we were told, had the effect of crippling many industries at Brisbane, and especially of hindering the successful development of agriculture, farmers in many instances being unable even to harvest their crops. This is a natural sequence of the mining attractions of the country. Queensland is probably as rich as any portion of Australia in other mineral deposits as well as in gold, abounding in copper, silver, tin, and coal, so that mining, first and foremost, absorbs the attention of large numbers at the expense of other enterprises. The immediate need of this province is more population and more laborers. We were told that liberal inducements were held out to acceptable people to come hither from the old country, but just what these inducements were it was not so easy to ascertain.

It is for the common interest both of England and her South Sea colonies that the rough, rude men who throng to the gold-diggings of those colonies should be in a measure counterbalanced by an influx of well-disposed and intelligent people, with such domestic associations as will insure their responsible and good citizenship. Families, where they can be induced to emigrate, should be offered the most liberal inducements, especially if they are persons possessing a knowledge of farming, — these would be a most valuable addition to the colony. Government can well afford to give to such desirable emigrants a free passage, and land on which to settle without a cent of first cost to them. The high rates of passage and the price charged for land in these colonies have together acted as prohibitory measures to new settlers going thither. There are millions of acres of good land in Australia and New Zealand which lie idle, and will continue to do so for a century to come, unless proper persons are induced by liberal terms to go and occupy them. There is a certain class in England and Great Britain generally to whom the agents of the colonies can well afford to be liberal and open-handed, and there are others upon whom all such liberality would be worse than thrown away. To cause a steady emigration from the old country the conditions must be made at first entirely for the benefit of the new-comer, and in the end his presence will redound to the permanent good of the colonies.

The cultivation of wheat is growing more and more general in Queensland, but the staple productions may be said to be wool and sugar. Coffee, tobacco, and cotton are also grown, but only to a limited extent, though the acreage devoted to the latter is said to be annually increasing. The laborers upon the plantations, and indeed the colored laborers both in town and country, are composed largely of South Sea Islanders, imported hither from both the near and far islands on the very objectionable Coolie principle which so long prevailed in Cuba. These laborers are engaged to serve a certain period, — say five years, — for which time the employer contracts to pay them six pounds sterling per annum, feeding and housing them in the mean time; and at the expiration of the term agreed upon he promises to return them to their island homes free of all cost to themselves. Of course this system is open to unlimited abuse, as was proved in the West Indies and elsewhere, resolving itself into a species of actual slavery. Besides which, under the guise of securing contract labor it has been proved that natives were forcibly abducted from their homes by unprincipled sea-captains, who realized a large amount of money per head for passage and for procuring the stolen islanders. One instance of this sort was related to us in detail, where a small coasting-vessel brought a large number of natives from an outlying island of the Feejee group, whence they were forcibly abducted, and treated with as much cruelty as formerly characterized the slave trade between Africa and Cuba. Even when imported under the fairest scheme that could be conceived, the ignorant "Kanacks," as they are called, cannot enforce their rights, and rarely ever see their homes again after having once left them. The contracts entered into between employers and these men are little more than a farce on the part of the principals, and are probably never consummated. It is gratifying to know that this iniquitous system of Coolie labor is becoming a thing of the past. Freely expressed public opinion has nearly abolished it, although its evil results are by no means yet outgrown.

It is clearly apparent to any observant person that the pastoral and agricultural interests are paramount to all others in Australia. This is amply proved by the published statistics of the past five years. Few persons not especially interested to inquire have any idea of the large amount of fresh meat shipped thither in refrigerator steamers, or of the aggregate amount of wool and flour exported thence to England, India, and China. The tenure upon which farm-lands are held in Queensland, as already intimated, seemed to us to be not a little confusing. In order to make men good citizens their land should be to them a freehold; that is, the title should be solely vested in themselves. The laws relating to this matter differ in the several colonies.

The semi-tropical climate of Queensland permits of the cultivation (as we have already stated) of pine-apples, cotton, arrow-root, bananas, coffee, mangoes, and the like. The cotton is of the long and best staple. The planters here already compete with those of the West Indies in the product of the sugar-cane, three varieties of which are especially adapted to this climate; namely, the Burbon, the purple Java, and the yellow Otaheitan. It must not be forgotten that two thirds of this colony is within the tropics, stretching northward until it is separated from the Equator by eleven degrees only. Three tons of sugar to the acre is no uncommon yield upon the plantations of Queensland, and this too where the machinery used in the grinding and reducing is of a poor character. Were more modern methods adopted, the aggregate result would not only be much increased in quantity, but also in quality. The machinery used for this purpose in the Sandwich Islands — all brought from the United States — is infinitely better adapted to the purpose, besides being actually more economical in the long run. Some of the Queensland planters have taken pride in demonstrating that intelligent white labor is possible, and more profitable, all things considered, than any other. There is one characteristic of sugar-raising here which we should not omit to mention; namely, that several crops can be realized from one planting. The first crop is called the "plant" crop, and those that follow are known as "ratoon" crops, the latter continuing several years. In the West Indies and some other countries a first and second crop are realized from one planting; but the third year requires new planting.

This division of Australia is more than five times as large as the United Kingdom of Great Britain, possessing a world of undeveloped resources of the most promising character. When the great central railroad shall be built,— and it is believed that it will soon be under way,— an immense impulse will be given to Queensland. The sun here shines with a more tropical ardor and a more genial warmth than in New South Wales; the trees are of more varied shapes and of richer growth,— similar, in fact, to those of Central America. The palm takes the place of the eucalyptus to a certain extent, and the woods teem with the bunya-bunya,— a very desirable and ornamental tree, which belongs to the pine family. Here also abound the tulip-tree, rosewood, sandal-wood, and satin-wood, with other choice varieties not found farther south. The tulip-tree and the sour gourd recall the vegetation of equatorial Africa, which many of the natural products here very closely resemble.

We have spoken of the bunya-bunya tree. When it is full-grown it towers two hundred feet in the air; but when young, it throws out branches all about its base close to the earth and to a distance of several yards. Above these, smaller branches rise in regular gradation to the top, forming a perfect cone of dense foliage. At maturity it produces annually upon its apex a large cluster of fruit, which is nutritious and palatable, being eagerly consumed by both the natives and the whites. This product is similar to the chestnut in taste and appearance, each tree producing a bushel or more at a time. The bunya-bunya has a sort of mysterious significance with the "black fellows" as the aborigines are called, and no one is permitted to cut down one of these trees. The laws of the colony also forbid its destruction.

The aborigines are oftener met here than at the south, as they prefer to live in the more temperate climate, and where they can have the country more to themselves. They are all nomads, and probably do not number over twenty-five or thirty thousand, slowly but surely decreasing numerically before the advance of the whites. Even when first discovered they were but a handful of people, as it were, scattered over an immense continent. They have still no distinct notion of the building of houses in which to live, or at least they adopt none, though they have the example of the whites ever before them. As a rule they are hideously ugly, with flat noses, wide nostrils, and deep-sunken eyes wide apart. A bark covering, much ruder than anything which would content an American Indian, forms their only shelter, and they often burrow under the lee side of an overhanging rock. Unlike the Maoris of New Zealand, they have no settled abode, and are more nomadic than the Bedouins of the Desert. The skill of this people in tracking game or human beings is nearly equal to that of the blood-hound. In the early days of penal servitude they were specially employed by the authorities for this purpose, and have been known to conduct a pursuit after an escaping convict for a hundred miles without once losing his trail, and finally leading to his capture. In the more modern conflicts between the Bushrangers and the authorities they proved of great value, not as fighters, but as trackers.

Missionary effort among these Australian tribes seems to have been pretty much abandoned, and by intelligent people is considered to have been a failure. Like all savage races, they are full of superstitions. They pay little attention to marriage obligations, but buy and sell wives according to their fancy, the women acquiescing with quiet indifference. We were told of one practice among them so ridiculous that we doubted it when first we heard of it. Ocular demonstration, however, proved its reality. It appears that when a youth arrives at such an age that he aspires to be a man, so to speak, — to own property or to marry, — he is put through some cabalistic rites the nature of which they will not divulge. The initiation ceremony ends, however, by the aspirant having one of his front teeth knocked out, or broken off close to the gum. This is accomplished by means of a sharp blow from a stone shaped for the purpose. After this deforming process is accomplished, the youth is pronounced to be eligible to all the rights and privileges of the elders of his tribe. Any of these aborigines, therefore, whom you meet is sure to be minus a front tooth. By the bye, it is all important that this tooth-smashing business should be performed at the full of the moon, and it is followed by what is termed a grand " corrobberee," or feast. In old times, — not long ago, — the menu on such occasions was incomplete unless the principal dish consisted of human flesh; but if this practice still prevails, as many believe to be the case, it is indulged in secretly. We were informed that the only way of accounting for the lack of numbers among the children of the aborigines is on the theory that infanticide is still practised by the native tribes.

These savages are as fond of disfiguring themselves with yellow and red pigments as are our Western aborigines. The tribes in the northwestern part of Queensland are at constant enmity among themselves, and being naturally fond of quarrelling, like our Indians, they improve every opportunity to do so, frequently attacking and killing one another for the most trivial causes. Each tribe has its territory carefully marked off, and any infringement by another tribe is sure to end in bloodshed. It would seem as though everything conspired to wipe them from off the face of the earth. It is a remarkable fact that consumption causes the death of a considerable percentage of the tribes annually. They believe its victims to have become bewitched, having had an evil eye cast upon them; the result is that they redouble the incantations which they consider to be necessary to remove all illness.

The Australian blacks have a plenty of legends of the most barbaric character, but by no means void of poetic features. They believe that the earth was created by a being of supreme attributes, whom they call Nourelle, and who lives in the sky surrounded by children born without the intervention of woman.

They entertain the idea that because the sun gives heat it needs fuel, and that when it descends below the horizon it procures a fresh supply for its fires. The stars are supposed to be the dwellings of departed chiefs. The serpent is believed to contain the spirit of a real devil. To eat the kidney of an enemy, it is thought, imparts to the one who swallows it the strength of the dead man. Any number above five these blacks express by saying, "It is as the leaves," — not to be counted. The white man's locomotive is an imprisoned fire-devil, kept under control by water. The lightning is the angry expression of some outraged god.

One singular tradition which this people have is to the following effect: In the beginning there was no death. The first created men and women were told not to go near a certain tree, in which lived a sacred bat. The woman one day approached the tree, whereupon the bat flew away; and after that came death. One would be glad to know if this fable antedates that more familiar and not dissimilar one of the Garden of Eden.

The period of the total extinction of this race cannot be far distant. Queensland is the only province where the Australian aborigines are still an element worth taking into account. Statistics show that they are dying at the rate of ten per cent per annum! The author asked an intelligent citizen of Brisbane what could be the cause of such mortality. "Oh," said he, in an airy way, "fire-arms and fire-water are doing the business for these black fellows." A remarkably comprehensive temperance lecture embraced in a single line, formulated by an old chief of these natives, occurs to us in this connection. He was one of the Brisbane tribe, and on a certain occasion said to a Government agent: "One drink is too much; two is not half enough." To taste was to drink to excess; abstinence with these people as with many white men is easy enough, but temperance in the use of spirits impossible.

The natives will accept work from the whites when driven to do so by want of food. Some of them work well and are liberally paid for it; but to insure this, liquor must be carefully kept from them. A single glass demoralizes, a second draught intoxicates. A drinking native is of no use to himself or any one else; and if he can get the means he rapidly drinks himself to death. The women are undersize as compared with the average of white people; but the males are athletic, excelling as axe-men and bullock-drivers, while on the sea-coast, when they work at all, they are good hands at the oar. Their hair is not curly like that of the Africans, but straight and silky like that of the Malays, and they have the long, attenuated limbs of the Hindu race.

As in all barbaric countries invaded by the whites, the native race fade rapidly away. Mr. Anthony Trollope depicted the true relative conditions of the races here when he said: "It was impossible to explain to the natives that a benevolent race of men had come to live among them, who were anxious to teach them all good things. Their kangaroos and fish were driven away, their land was taken from them, the strangers assumed to be masters, and the black man did not see the benevolence. The new-comers were Christians, and were ready enough to teach their religion if only the black man would learn it. The black man could not understand the religion, and did not want it, and to this day remains unimpressed by any of its influences. But the white man brought rum as well as religion, and the rum was impressive, though the religion was not." He adds significantly: "There was much spearing on one side and much shooting and hanging on the other."

The extent of the country is suggested by the fact, as given to us, that the natives in the far interior of the north, while they doubtless have heard of a white man have never yet seen one. Efforts have been freely made by philanthropic associations to ameliorate the condition of these blacks, but it seems impossible to turn them from their nomadic habits, — their instincts leading them to seek support as hunters, and after the manner of their forefathers, rather than by any more civilized pursuit. We were told of an instance of a young native lad of ten years, who was taken from his wild life by the mutual consent of all concerned, and brought to Brisbane to live with the whites and be educated. Great effort was made in his behalf, to render him in every respect comfortable and contented. He was placed at a suitable school, where he gradually developed an unusual degree of intelligence, showing much aptitude at learning, and becoming a favorite with both pupils and teachers. He lacked for nothing; was dressed like his associates and pleasantly domesticated. He remained several years among the whites apparently well satisfied with his surroundings, and great hopes came to be entertained that he would become thoroughly civilized, and exercise in manhood a strong influence for good among his native people. Finally at the age of nineteen he was suddenly missing, and no one could say what had become of him. After months of search, he was discovered to have returned secretly to his former home and associates, and was there found as naked and nomadic as the rest. No inducement could prevail upon him to return to a life among the whites.

There is a brief romance connected with the story of this youth which is not without interest. It appears that the young native, who was a fine specimen of his race, became warmly attached to the lovely daughter of the white family with whom he made his temporary home. The girl was about his own age, and it is believed that her refining influence over him was the secret of his remarkable studiousness and rapid progress in learning. After he was discovered among his own people, the young lady acknowledged that they had regarded each other with tenderest affection, and that the youth would long before have returned to his tribe but for her restraining influence. He regarded her with too much honest affection, however, to suggest even her going with him to share the hardships of his savage life, but told her that he grew hourly more restless and miserable, and that he *must* seek his native wilds. This girl was too sensible to argue against the manifest destiny of both their lives, and with a first and last kiss they separated forever. No one can say how it was with the savage youth, whose eyes had been opened to all there is of noble and good in civilization; but doubtless he was finally consoled by some dusky maiden of his tribe. As to her whom he left behind, her true woman heart was sorely tried; and after hiding her sorrow for some five years she died unmarried.

The most singular weapon possessed by these aborigines is one which originated with them, and is known as the boomerang,— of which every one has heard, but which perhaps few of our readers have seen. It is a weapon whose special peculiarities have caused it to pass into a synonym of anything which turns upon the person who uses it. It seems at first sight to be only a flat, crooked, or curved piece of polished wood, about twenty or twenty-four inches long (though these instruments vary in length), and three quarters of an inch in thickness. There is nothing particularly striking about this weapon until you see a native throw one; in doing which he carefully poises himself, makes a nice calculation as to the distance from him of the object he designs to hit, raises his arm above his head and brings it down with a sort of swoop, swiftly launching the curved wood from his hand. At first the boomerang skims along near the ground, then rises four or five feet, but only to sink again, and again to rise. As you carefully and curiously watch its course, and suppose it is just about to stop in its erratic career and drop to the ground, it suddenly ceases its forward flight and rapidly returns to the thrower. Sometimes in returning it takes a course similar to its outward gyrations; at other times it returns straight as an arrow, gently striking the thrower's body or falling to the ground at his feet. It is thought that no white man can exactly learn the trick of throwing this strange implement, and few ever attempt to throw one, — or rather we should say, few attempt it a second time; nor can the native himself explain how he does what we have described. "Me! I throw him, just so," — that is all the answer you can get from him. We were told that the most expert of the blacks will not only kill a bird at a considerable distance with the boomerang, but that they cause the bird to be brought back to them by the weapon. This last degree of expertness we certainly did not witness, nor do we exactly credit it; but we can vouch for the first, as we have described it.

The common weapons possessed by the aborigines when first discovered by the whites — besides the boomerang, which can inflict a severe if not fatal wound — were heavy war-clubs curiously carved, wooden spears tipped with flint, and many others made of sharpened stones. In throwing their wooden spears they were wonderfully expert,— an art which they still cultivate and willingly exhibit to strangers. A bullet from a rifle speeds not more surely to the bull's-eye than do these spears when thrown by the hand of a native; but the singular skill which can impart such magic to a weapon like the boomerang, might well be supposed to prove effective in launching a straight spear to its mark. All these weapons constructed by the Australian natives are elaborately finished, and so polished, indeed, as to surpass the effect of varnish, in every way showing great care and patient labor in their manufacture. But though possessed of such skill in the construction of weapons, they appear to have none in the building of houses. In no part of the world have we seen people so poorly lodged, for even the Digger Indians of California afford themselves some sort of secure shelter while these people have none.

Ethnologists tell us that these blacks belong to the Ethiopian race,— the lowest, probably, of all the human family. That they form a special type is very clear to any one who has been among them. The conviction forces itself upon one that they must be the remnant of some ancient and peculiar people, of whom we have no historic record. It is believed among well-informed persons in Brisbane (as we have already intimated) that cannibalism is still secretly practised among some of the tribes. Those living in northern Queensland are so isolated as to have adopted but few modern tools or domestic utensils, but they still have their stone knives and axes. As a people they are very far behind the Maoris in intelligence, and are ever ready to adopt the vices of the whites but not their virtues. Great care is taken to keep fire-arms away from them, which effort is by no means successful, as there are plenty of adventurous white men — themselves outlaws — who will sell arms and ammunition to the natives whenever it is for their own advantage to do so. These tribes are quite pugnacious, and are known to have killed many of the Chinese who have landed at the north, near Torres Strait, whom they doubtless devoured. The old Brisbane tribe, known to have numbered not many years ago some twelve hundred, is now absolutely extinct, not a word of its language even being spoken by a human being. Within a wide sweep of Sydney and Melbourne the aboriginal tribes have virtually died out.

As regards morality, or virtue, among the black women, they would seem to have no idea of the significance of such terms. We learned one curious fact relating to the burial of the dead among the natives, which is that they always place the body in the ground in an upright position. Their religion seems to be a sort of demon worship. "Good God take care himself; bad God [devil], — look sharp for him!" There is some cunning if not philosophy in this sort of reasoning. Like many other savage people, especially those inhabiting tropical regions, they have no idea of harvesting, or of storing food for future use. If they have enough to eat at the present hour, that is all-sufficient.

When Australia was first taken possession of by the whites it seems to have been, if the term is in any instance admissible, a God-forsaken land; certainly the most destitute of natural productions of any portion of the globe. We can well believe that before these blacks came hither, — perhaps a thousand years ago, — this land was untrodden by human beings, though scientists are by no means agreed upon this point. No species of grain was known to these natives; not a single fruit worthy of notice grew wild, and not an edible root of value was produced. The only game of any size was the kangaroo and a few species of birds. Now the trees, fruits, vegetables, and game of all regions have become domesticated here, and have all proved to be highly productive, whether transplanted from tropical or from semi-tropical regions. While we write these lines, one most palatable and peculiar product is recalled, namely, the passion-fruit. The gorgeous flowering species is familiar to us all, but the fruit-bearing vine grows in Australia to perfection. When ripe it is egg-shaped, and about the size of a hen's-egg, being eaten in much the same manner. The top is cut off, leaving the skin as a shell from which the luscious contents are eaten with a spoon. The flavor is a most agreeable sub-acid.

We have intimated that appearances lead to the

conviction that both Australia and New Zealand were uninhabited about ten centuries ago; and yet it would seem as though the South Pacific must have been peopled by races of a certain degree of civilization in the far past. On the Marshall and the Gilbert groups of islands, as well as on the Kingsmill and the Ladrones, there are prehistoric stone monuments which were never constructed by savages. On Lele, near Strong's Island, there are elaborate stone fortifications overgrown by tropical forests, the walls of which are twelve feet thick, underlaid by caverns, vaults, and secret passages. Here also is a quadrangular tower forty feet in height. The tradition of the present inhabitants is that a great city once existed on this site, of which they know nothing. Ruins are also found in the Navigator's Islands, the Marquesas, and even the Sandwich Islands, whose origin is as much a mystery to the present inhabitants as to the inquiring stranger. Was there once in the far-away past a great Malayan Empire existing in the Pacific Ocean? There is a Peruvian tradition that in the olden times strangers came from the great South Sea in ships to the west coast of America, for commercial intercourse with the civilized race which existed there.

In visiting these various by-paths of the globe, one realizes that there are problems as to the antiquity of our race the solution of which reaches far beyond any of the most ancient records of our present civilization. We have seen in the Boulak Museum at

Cairo objects of Egyptian make which were doubtless six thousand years old; and the Sphinx, situated ten miles away, where the city of Gizeh once stood, must antedate that period. But among these South Sea Islands are prehistoric ruins and monuments which are believed to antedate the Sphinx. The same may be said of the buried columns that have been overgrown by the forests of central Ceylon to the depth of a hundred feet. To our humble perception, so far from bringing man's origin more into accordance with the Darwinian theory, these facts widen the gap, and render it still more doubtful.

CHAPTER VII.

Morning in the Forest. — Flying Foxes. — A Startling Snake-story. — Geographical. — Want of Irrigation. — Droughts. — Immense Sheep-Runs. — Seeking a Shepherd Life. — Wonderful Gold Nuggets. — A "Welcome" Discovery. — Wool is King in Queensland. — The Chinese Population. — Education in Australia. — Peculiar Banking Business. — Waging War upon Kangaroos. — Journalism in Australia. — Proposed New Colony.

A DRIVE of a few miles inland from Brisbane carries one through pleasant villages and among farms, plantations of sugar-cane, orchards, and fields of pine-apples, beyond which one enters the forest. The banks of the rivers and creeks are generally covered with a dense semi-tropical growth of vegetation, while the forest stretches for many a mile into lonely districts. A great variety of trees are found here, some of primeval growth and large size, belonging to the blue-gum species; others, like sassafras, pine, and cedar, are fragrant and delight the senses, being surrounded by a thick undergrowth of marvellous luxuriance. The jungles in India or the islands of the Malacca Straits are not more dense than some of the wooded districts to be found in Queensland. These retired spots are filled with bird and insect life, but with few animals. Cockatoos and parrots, in gay colors and gaudy combinations, are the prevailing representatives of the feathered tribe. There are also numberless wild pigeons, in great variety, uttering a ceaseless, low, brooding note which seems to be in exact harmony with the sylvan surroundings. The bell-bird, cat-bird, and laughing jackass announce their presence in unmistakable utterances, all serving to keep the senses on the *qui vive*.

The early morning was the hour chosen for our visit to one of these forest glades, while the dew was yet upon the grass. Our companion — a resident full of enthusiasm and intelligence, and withal a good horseman — hurried us into the saddle to reach the woods betimes. "At noon," said he, "you might hear a leaf drop anywhere hereabout, for at that hour, bird, insect, reptile, even the flies and mosquitoes of the Queensland 'scrub,' take their siesta; but in the morning and the gloaming they vie with one another in their vocal demonstrations." The morning was cloudless; the advancing day was already tempered by the warmth of the sun, but in the shade of the trees there was a cool fragrance and only a dim cathedral light.

Flying foxes greatly abound in this vicinity as well as in other parts of the country, often appearing in surprising numbers, especially on moonlight nights. They prove most destructive to choice fruits, and are said to be an increasing nuisance. The leaves of the gum-tree seem to form their principal food; but at times they visit a cultivated section in such marvellous numbers as to sweep away every green leaf and tender shoot in the gardens and fields, like an army of locusts. The natives and Chinese eat them, but the more civilized inhabitants would as soon eat rats and mice. These flying foxes are unable to take flight from the ground, and when they are found there can easily be captured. Neither can they run rapidly, but waddle toward the nearest tree-trunk, which they ascend rapidly by means of their long, sharp claws, and from the branches of which they throw themselves into the air, where they skim about like a bird on the wing. They are rarely seen until evening, always performing their depredations by night. It is a remarkable fact that these peculiarly awkward creatures, whose legs seem utterly unavailable for ordinary service, unless it be for climbing, will carry large fruit, weighing nearly a pound, long distances to their nests. During the day they retire to secluded places in the woods, where they sleep hanging head downward from the branches by the natural hooks attached to their shoulders. As with common bats, which they resemble in some respects, secluded caves are a favorite resort of the flying foxes.

We are reminded in this connection of another remarkable animal found here, called the flying 'possum, — a creature which does not actually fly, but which "shoots" across a considerable space through the air, between tall trees or elevated objects like cliffs, by means of expanding a loose skin or membrane formed on both of its sides, and which connects the front legs with the hind ones. This creature, like the kangaroo, is indigenous, and only found in Australia.

We heard much said about the venomous nature of Australian snakes, and were cautioned especially to avoid the places known to be frequented by them. Doubtless there are plenty of snakes in Australia as in most other regions, poisonous ones also in the bush, and that they do sometimes fatally bite persons there can be no question; but we did not chance to see any, either of the venomous or harmless sort. There is one quality very commendable in the serpent tribe: as a rule, they show a disposition to get out of the way of human beings. If trampled upon, of course they will turn and bite or sting; but this is not to be set down to their discredit, but to the natural instinct of self-defence. One of the most venomous of all snakes is indigenous to our own country, — namely, the rattle-snake; but even he never fails to give ample warning of his presence before attacking any one. The habits of these Australian snakes are similar to those of their species wherever found; their usual resort is a hole in the ground under fallen leaves, or in the decaying trunk of a tree, and they live by preying upon frogs, mice, lizards, and birds. We were told of some instances of their power to charm small birds, — an old story to be sure, and one for which we must have ocular evidence before crediting it. New Zealand is happily free from the pest of snakes, — there being no more there than in Ireland.

Doubtless Providence had some legitimate purpose to subserve in creating tarantulas, poisonous spiders, and scorpions in Australia, but the "why and wherefore" is rather a conundrum.

We heard while in Sydney a singular snake-story, which we have every reason to believe to be true, the facts of which were said to have occurred not long before near the town of Parametta. In the family of a settler who resided some half a league from the town was an invalid daughter, of an extremely nervous temperament. She was sleeping one summer afternoon in a hammock swung between a couple of supporting standards in the shade of the piazza, when she was suddenly awakened by feeling something cold and moist clinging about her throat. She put up her hand to the spot and clasped the body of a snake just back of its head, and with a horrified cry wrenched with all her strength to tear it away. This was the first instinctive action of the moment, but so great was her terror that she speedily lost all consciousness of the situation. Her hand however still grasped the snake where she had first seized upon it, and with such a convulsive force that the creature was rendered powerless. The cry of the terrified girl brought the father from within the house, who instantly came to her relief; but in the fit which her fright had induced, her hand slowly contracted about the creature's throat with a force which awake she could not possibly have exerted, and before her fingers were unclasped by the aid of a bit of the hammock cord the reptile was completely strangled. Fortunately the creature had not bitten the girl before she seized it; and after that, it was unable to do so. It is said to have been four feet long and of a poisonous species.

Queensland is nearer to New Guinea on the north than Victoria is on the south to Tasmania. The depth of Torres Strait, which separates Queensland and New Guinea, is nowhere over nine fathoms. It is generally believed by those who make a study of such matters that these two countries were originally connected, and that the sea, aided perhaps by some volcanic action, finally separated them. After a current between them was once established, the land on each side would wear away rapidly. The distance across the Strait is to-day less than one hundred miles. Doubtless many of the island groups in this region were first formed in some such manner as we have indicated. By glancing at a map of the world the reader will observe that there are islands that extend almost uninterruptedly from the southeastern extremity of Asia nearly half-way across the Pacific. Oceania is the favorite word applied by geographers to this world of islands, especially as indicating Australia, New Zealand, Tasmania, and their immediate dependencies. Of this system Australia forms the great central feature. Some idea of the immensity of the Pacific Ocean may be realized when we see that there is nevertheless an unbroken waste of waters between these islands and the coast of America of some two thousand miles in width. These lands of

Oceania are surrounded by water not only of the widest expanse, but also — as has been proved by scientific soundings — of the greatest depth of any on the globe.

Queensland is as liable to serious droughts as the rest of Australia on the slopes of the mountain range of the interior. As we have already shown, nearer the coast the land is well watered. There are few lakes in the colony, — indeed, none worthy of the name; and the one river which is the Mississippi of the country, known as the Murray, — navigable for over a thousand miles of its course, — is not at all times to be relied upon. This is an evil which could easily be remedied by skilful engineering. This river has no proper outlet to the sea, but debouches into a shallow marsh called Lake Alexandrina. "Sir," said an individual to us at Sydney, with piscatorial dogmatic emphasis, "No country can be great without trout or salmon." As Australia has no available rivers for these fish to swim in, the inference as to her possible greatness was obvious.

We have said that the Murray is the Mississippi of Australia, but it is no more like that great Father of Waters than Tom Thumb is like Hercules. Like the Mississippi, however, it has a greater, or at least longer, tributary than itself. As the American river is the receptacle of the Missouri, so the Murray obtains its greatest volume by means of its principal branch and feeder, the Darling. This river extends over twelve degrees of latitude, and by its winding course would measure three thousand miles. It is mostly supplied by the snow-clad Australian Alps. The fitful nature of this watercourse may be judged by the fact that although it is often in places a torrent, and in others expands into lake-like proportions over low-lying country, at certain seasons it may be crossed on foot where it joins the Murray. Below this junction the latter river frequently expands to three hundred yards and more in width, with a depth of from ten to twenty feet. For fifteen hundred miles of its course it is called a navigable river, though it is not to be relied upon as such, — small river steamers being not infrequently caught upon shoals, where they are left high and dry for months together. So with regard to the Darling; notwithstanding its erratic character, it has often been ascended by light-draught steamers nearly a thousand miles above its junction with the Murray.

It is singular that in a country where irrigation is so much needed, and where enterprise is so general in all other directions, this matter does not receive more attention. To the stranger, irrigation seems to be the one thing lacking in this favored land. Canals tapping these rivers at points where they should first be dammed, would pay a twofold reward, — not only supplying water wherewith to quench the thirst of the half-exhausted land, but, being made navigable, they would convey to market the very crops they had already enabled the husbandman to raise. Where the country is thus irrigated, — as in India and Utah, — the crops are simply certain, rain or shine; and the transportation is also assured at a reasonable figure. Australia, with its rich virgin soil and dry climate, is just the place to repay tenfold all irrigating enterprise. We were told of certain points on the Murray River, where, by one properly constructed dam, water in abundance could be held and thrown back for a distance of thirty miles. It appears that in one year not long ago, when there was a great drought, over fifteen million sheep and horned cattle died of thirst in New South Wales and Queensland! This sounds almost incredible, but it was so recorded in the official reports of the colonies. And yet the means of conserving water by simple methods are, as we have seen, quite within the reach of government or private enterprise. In one year, by suitable arrangements, animal property alone might have been saved to the value of fifty million dollars. We were told of one extraordinary period of drought which extended over five years previous to 1870, which was followed by copious and excessive rains lasting for months, — "thus," as our agricultural informant pithily expressed it, "turning a blessing into a judgment."

Queensland, as we have shown, occupies the northeastern portion of the continent, and measures thirteen hundred miles in length from north to south, by eight hundred miles in width, containing a population at the present time of about three hundred and forty thousand. The climate of Brisbane is often compared to that of Madeira; it is entirely free from the hot winds which sometimes render Sydney, Melbourne, and Adelaide so extremely uncomfortable. The river which divides the city into north and south Brisbane is crossed by a grand iron bridge over a quarter of a mile in length, a portion of which swings upon a centre to admit of the passage of steamers and sailing-vessels, the river being navigable above the capital.

Political excitement runs high in Brisbane. We were told of scenes that occurred in the local parliament leading to bitter criminations between members, which would certainly have resulted in duels in most countries. Sometimes, however, a different spirit prevails, and a spicing of fun is introduced. On one occasion the bill of a firm of solicitors against the Government came up for discussion. The firm name was Little & Brown, and their account seemed to some of the members to be exorbitant. While the question of voting the money to pay this bill was before the house, there was also one pending for the protection of wild birds. At last a humorous member proposed that the account of the "lawyer-bird" should be included in the bill. His meaning was not at first apparent to the assembly, and the presiding officer asked him to explain what this bird was. His answer created an uproar of laughter among the members. "The bird I refer to," he said, "is little and brown; and it has a very long bill!"

The wide-spread plains of this part of Australia, so specially adapted for sheep-runs and cattle-ranches, are largely improved for that purpose; and it is estimated that there are over twelve millions of sheep upon them to-day. Wool is one of the most valuable raw materials known to commerce, and that shipped from Queensland has had a preference, owing to its adaptability to manufacturing purposes. Sheep-farming is here carried on upon a scale exceeding that of all other parts of the world. Single individuals hold even larger flocks than those of New South Wales. We have not seen an official statement of a year's clip for the whole country since that for 1883, which gave as the aggregate value of that year something over twenty million pounds sterling. Besides sheep, the plains also sustain large herds of horned cattle. One owner told us he had over fifteen thousand cattle on his ranch, and that some of his neighbors had a still larger number.

The coast portion of Queensland is the most desirable of all the colony. It is well wooded, and the climate is equable. The entire shore is studded with picturesque islands and has numerous excellent harbors. The three summer months — December, January, and February — are hot; but as plenty of rain falls at this season, tropical moisture and heat are agreeably combined. Cool southerly winds also prevail during this season, so that it is rarely oppressively hot. The famous Great Barrier Reef of Australia belongs entirely to this province, and is twelve hundred miles in length, extending along the coast from Port Brown to Torres Strait, the average distance from the shore being about sixty miles. Though the sea on the coast is made smoother by this giant reef, navigation in other respects is undoubtedly rendered precarious by it. Scientists think it indicates the former outline of the coast and continent, about one fifth of which is supposed to have sunk beneath the ocean.

Leaving out West Australia, which is at present so little developed, the country may be divided thus. Queensland is the best and most extensive pastoral section; in this respect New South Wales comes next. South Australia should be characterized for its grain-fields, and Victoria is richest in auriferous deposits; but there is gold enough in all the colonies to afford constant stimulus to mining enterprise, fresh discoveries in this line being made every few weeks.

Many young men belonging to the better classes of England's youth, filled with poetic ideas, come out here to seek employment on sheep-runs, having imbibed certain notions of a free out-of-door life, and the charm of a half-wild career in the open country. But the reality often amazes them. Some of these young men have been accustomed to a life of elegant leisure, soft beds, dainty food, and plenty of servants to do their bidding; but actuated by a desire to attain to a condition of independence of family control, a wish to pay their own way, to earn money by manly labor, or by some other of the thousand incentives that not infrequently sever family ties, they have resolved to seek a new field. In Australia they find freedom, but it is coupled with hard work. There is no chance for drones in the business of sheep-raising, or for those who would languish on downy beds of ease. The competitor in this field must be in the saddle at daybreak, must learn to ride all sorts of horses, and to catch and saddle the one he does ride; for all the horses are turned out to get their own feed at large, and are never stabled. They also get no grooming, except what their riders give them; they are not even shod, and are sometimes addicted to bucking, which will require all a man's knowledge of horsemanship to overcome. The ranch-man has ten hours a day in the saddle, and must often ride fast and far to round in his flocks. He must acquire the art of counting them, of judging correctly of their condition, of shearing, and often of killing them. For all this he may get five or six hundred dollars a year and his rations, with the advantage, however, of living in the open air, of having an unobstructed digestion and a ravenous appetite, and of sleeping the sleep which no opiate can produce. The life upon a sheep-run will be likely to make a man of him if he has the right material in him, with plenty of endurance and adaptability.

The idyllic notions of shepherd life which may at first have attracted him, and the real thing as encountered in the neighborhood of the Darling Downs of Queensland, are two quite different things. There are some who experience all this and with their first year's earnings purchase sheep and go on adding to their flock annually, until by natural increase and purchased additions they become master shepherds and owners of great numbers. When success is thus achieved, which is quite possible under ordinary good fortune, the profit that follows is almost fabulous.

In a country where there are such enormous sheep-runs and where owners count their herds by twenties of thousands, there must at times be a glut of meat, and at all times an endless supply of it on hand. The cattle-ranches, though not nearly so numerous, nor carrying such large numbers of animals, yet produce relatively an immense supply of meat, since one average steer is equal in weight to eight or ten sheep. Before the present method of shipping fresh meat to Europe was perfected, it was often the case that tens of thousands of sheep and horned cattle were boiled down simply to produce tallow; and this practice is even now resorted to, though to a more limited extent than heretofore. Tallow was and is very easily packed and shipped. There were at one time over forty boiling-down establishments in New South Wales alone, and statistics show that three hundred thousand sheep and some hundreds of bullocks were in one year converted into tallow by these establishments. The carcasses of the animals for any other purpose were absolutely wasted, while the poorer classes of England were denying themselves meat because of its high cost in their own country. It was a realizing sense of these facts which first led to the meat-canning process, which is still a thriving industry here, and afterward to the building of ship refrigerators, which make it possible to ship entire carcasses fresh to Europe, where they never fail to arrive in the best condition for the market.

The very name of Australia has a flavor of gold, and yet not one half of its auriferous diggings have been discovered, — every twelvemonth bringing to light new deposits of rich quartz, and fresh alluvial diggings. While the author was in Sydney, a gold nugget was found at Maitland Bar and brought to that city, for which the Commercial Bank of the metropolis paid the finder the handsome sum of seven thousand six hundred dollars. It soon after passed into the possession of the Government, and is now held by it for the purpose of being exhibited at the forthcoming centennial exhibition to be held at Melbourne. At the museum of this latter city we saw a cast which was taken of the largest nugget ever found in Australia. As it was perfectly gilded, it seemed in its large glass case as though it might be the real article. It weighed originally two thousand three hundred ounces, and was valued at forty-six thousand dollars. It is known by the name of the " Welcome Nugget." It seems that the finder had heretofore sought in vain to make a living at gold-digging, having worked long and patiently in search of the precious metal. Finally he had reached a condition of poverty and desperation which had led him that very day to resolve upon throwing up his claim (nobody would give him anything for it), and to seek work in the nearest city as a day-laborer; he would thus secure at least food and a shelter. It was in this frame of mind, weary and hungry, that he chanced upon this marvellous discovery; and hence he appropriately named it the "Welcome Nugget." These remarkable "finds," as the miners term them, happen once in a series of years; but in getting at the average success of gold-mining the larger number of those who have not been able to realize even a laborer's day-wages at the business, must be taken into the account. It is safe to accept the conclusion which every intelligent person in Australia, New Zealand, and California has arrived at; namely, that the cost of getting gold out of the earth is as much as its intrinsic value. To put it in other words: in the long run, the average laborer, working at any other calling for three dollars or even less per day, will realize more money in a twelvemonth than the average gold-miner in the same period. Nevertheless, gold-mining seems to be the active agent which Providence has employed to people the waste places of the earth. The Western States of America are ample proof of this.

In glancing at a printed record of the finding of golden nuggets, we see that among others one of pure gold was found in 1502, in Hayti, which weighed forty-six pounds troy. Another is mentioned as having been found in Bolivia in 1730, weighing fifty-five pounds troy. But the wonder of its time was found in the Ural Mountains in 1842, and weighed ninety-seven pounds troy. This specimen the author saw, two years ago, in the Museum of Mining at St. Petersburg. The largest single mass of pure gold found in the United States came from California, and, if our memory serves us correctly, weighed a little over twenty-six pounds troy. All these examples, however, have been placed in the shade by numerous nuggets that have been found in Victoria in later times. The "Welcome Nugget," already mentioned, came from Balarat, in Victoria. A nugget was also discovered here, which should be mentioned even in this by no means complete list. We refer to that found in 1857, called the "Blanche Berkeley," after the Governor's daughter, and which weighed one hundred and forty-five pounds troy.

Far-seeing political economists do not hesitate to pronounce the coal mines of New South Wales and Queensland of far more value than the gold mines of Victoria and South Australia; and they claim that these coal deposits are the most extensive in the world. The government of Queensland (and we believe the governments of the other colonies also) pays a gratuity of five hundred pounds sterling to the first discoverer of gold-diggings, provided the new place be twenty miles away from any previous discovery. The governments are not affected by the glamour of the gold; that is a secondary consideration with them, for they know that it is not the glittering metal itself which enriches the country, but the vitality imparted by its agency. Men are brought together from near and far in large numbers, and those are induced to work who have never worked before. All must live, and to enable them to do so there must be busy hands and brains occupied in other lines than that of actual mining. The consumption of many articles is stimulated, and fresh life infused into new and legitimate channels of trade.

Wool, not gold, is the real "King" in Queensland to-day. It is thought by many that by and by sugar may become the rival of wool in this section. Mackay, situated on the Pioneer River, is the chief centre of the sugar industry of the colony, which extends over a large acreage north of Cape Palmerston, and around the slope of Mount Bassett. Here the noise of the crushing-mills in the grinding season, and the busy whirl of the centrifugal machine greet the ear in all directions. So prolific is the soil here that the cane is said to grow like weeds, and without cultivation.

Brisbane, like the rest of Queensland, has not escaped the inroads of the Chinese; and here they are not favorites any more than elsewhere. This universal prejudice against the Asiatics is in many respects both reasonable and unreasonable. That the Chinaman never fails to introduce certain vicious habits wherever he appears, goes without saying; opium-smoking and gambling have become as natural to him as breathing. But he is frugal, energetic, industrious, and in some respects a very valuable member of a newly colonized country, filling a position which would otherwise be unoccupied. In Australia he is content to follow in the white man's footsteps, and utilize — as a miner, for instance — what is left by his predecessor. A Chinaman will obtain fair results and good wages by working over the "tailings" of the gold-fields, which are thrown aside as useless by the more impatient and ambitious English laborer. John is specially useful in many occupations, and is a natural gardener, raising the best of vegetables for market upon refuse grounds that no one else would think it worth while to cultivate. He reduces all fertilizing matter to liquid form, and industriously applies it by hand, destroying each insect pest with his fingers. No slug, caterpillar, or vicious parasite can escape his vigilance. He sacrifices himself entirely to the object in hand, and as long as there is sufficient light for him to see to work, he continues to toil : no eight-hour or ten-hour system answers for him. He is to-day essentially the market gardener of Australia and New Zealand; no one attempts to compete with him in this occupation. No European can bear the exposure to the sun or support his strength under the enervating heat as the Chinaman can do. And yet with all these qualities to recommend him, so undesirable is his presence held to be by the people, that a law has been passed by which each Chinaman landing in any of these colonies is obliged to pay the sum of fifty dollars " head money," as it is called ; and no women of the race are permitted to land at all. Here, as in California and elsewhere, the dead Chinaman is embalmed by a cheap process,—the body being finally enclosed in a lead coffin, which in turn is put into a wooden box, and exported to its native soil. The poorest Chinamen rarely fails to leave money enough behind him to accomplish this purpose, and the friends of the deceased consider it a religious duty to fulfil his last wishes.

Judging critically from what we saw of this race of people in the various parts of the colonies of Australasia, we should say that they are individually and collectively superior to the average European immigrants, in the general characteristics which go to make up a desirable citizen. In industrial habits they far excel the common immigrant from England and Ireland. If the Mongolians have some bad habits, the Europeans have ten to their one. It is mostly the pugnacious British, striking, never-satisfied laborer who complains of the presence of the Chinese, because he cannot compete with them in sobriety, industry, frugality, and faithfulness of service. The Chinese are naturally very hospitable, and no lonely shepherd or roving prospecter ever came to their cabins hungry, or in want of any special article, without receiving the needed aid gratuitously. John always marries when he can induce a European or American woman to have him for a husband, and there are many such instances all over the colonies. No one ever hears of a Chinaman abusing his wife;

indeed, they are remarkable for being good husbands. They take particular delight in seeing their wives well-dressed, especially on all gala occasions, and cheerfully and liberally contribute the means for this purpose. Chinamen are never seen here in a state of intoxication; and they thus form a noticeable exception among a population of such incessant drinkers as one sees everywhere in these countries. Australasia affords unlimited scope for Chinese industries, and we hardly know how the colonies could get on without them.

It is highly gratifying to see how thoroughly the cause of universal education is appreciated and supported in these colonies, as there can be no stronger evidence of legitimate progress than this fact furnishes. Brisbane is no exception to this remark. All education is secular in character, even the reading of the Bible being omitted in the primary and other schools. In New South Wales special Scriptural lessons are read; but in Victoria and South Australia Scriptural teachings can only be given out of the regular school hours, — and thus the various denominational prejudices are carefully respected. Victoria furnishes absolute free education. In the other colonies a very small fee is charged, which is apparently the best policy; since parents and children will naturally prize more highly that which costs them money, be the sum never so small, nor will they willingly neglect that for which they are required to pay.

The result of this educational zeal is obvious to any

one, tending as it does to raise the character of the colonies at home and their good reputation abroad. The general population forms already a reading community which supports a large number of excellent book-stores in each populous centre, besides public libraries, many newspapers, and well-conducted local magazines. Concerning the newspapers of Australasia, let us bear appreciative testimony to their general excellence, to the able and even scholarly manner in which they are edited, and to the remarkable liberality evinced in the collecting of news from all parts of the globe. The mechanical appearance and general make-up of the colonial newspapers is fully equal to that of the best American and English dailies. In Auckland, New Zealand, with a population of not more than sixty thousand, including the immediate suburbs, we saw one of Hoe's large, rapid, completing presses, printing the "New Zealand Daily Herald" at the rate of fifteen thousand copies an hour, folding and delivering it automatically ready for the carriers. The whole work was done by machinery, the roll of paper being suspended above the press after the latest improved style, so that no "feeders" even were required.

One is sure to remark the large number of banking establishments in every city and considerable town throughout Australasia. We were told that there are thirty joint-stock banking companies in the country, with some eight hundred branches more or less. These companies pay an annual dividend of from ten to fourteen per cent to their stockholders. The existence of so many successful banks in so circumscribed a community is a matter not quite clearly understood by the author, though upon inquiry it was found that the style of banking business done here differed materially from that transacted in populous cities of the Old World. For instance, the banks here advance money freely upon growing crops, wool on the sheep's back, and other similar securities that would hardly be considered as legitimate collateral in America. The usual rate of interest to borrowers upon what is considered fair security, is never less than ten per cent, — twelve and fifteen per cent being most common. The speculative nature of nearly all kinds of business in the colonies impairs general confidence, and people come to be unduly sharp, requiring even heavier rates than those already named where there is any chance of getting them. They simply illustrate the axiom, that a high rate of interest signifies a high degree of risk. In the mean time the banks flourish, occupying the largest and most costly business edifices that are to be seen in Sydney, Melbourne, Brisbane, or Adelaide.

We did not chance to see any specimens of that curious animal the kangaroo while we were in Queensland, but this marsupial is represented to be more numerous and more of a pest here than in any other part of the country. We were told of a certain sheep-run known as Peak Downs Station, where the proprietor had been obliged to wage a long-continued war against them, instituting annual hunts over the extensive district which he held. He was joined by his friends and neighbors in an annual raid upon the animals, which lasted not infrequently for ten consecutive days. He kept an account of the number of kangaroos destroyed upon his lands, which had reached the almost incredible aggregate of thirty-eight thousand in a few years. That special district absolutely swarmed with these animals until the means mentioned for their destruction were adopted. The kangaroo is very prolific in its wild state, and would, if allowed to multiply undisturbed, soon drive the sheep from their feeding-grounds. Its skin, when properly cured and dressed with the fur on, makes good rugs suitable for domestic use. Leather is also made from the skin, and when well tanned and carefully prepared is available for many purposes, although as a regular industry the skin of the kangaroo has never been made much use of in the form of leather; it is considered very desirable as a fur robe, or when made up into a garment.

The Darling Downs of Queensland, several times alluded to in these notes, consist of broad, undulating, grass-covered steppes, with a rich black soil admirably suited for agricultural purposes. They are easily reached from Brisbane by rail in a few hours, and at Warwick, the principal town of the Downs, good hotel accommodations may be found. Stanthorpe is the centre of the tin-mining industry of this region. For a number of years surface diggings only were attempted here, but later many deep shafts have been sunken and are now profitably worked. In this more legitimate form of mining a permanent industry has been established. There are so many prolific and excellent tin mines in the colonies that these special deposits are held to be of no extraordinary value.

It is proposed, as we were informed at Brisbane, to separate the north of Queensland from the south, at the twenty-second parallel of latitude, and to form the northern portion into a separate colony. This purpose seemed at one time to have very nearly reached consummation, but it has not been pressed for some unknown reason. As Queensland is larger than England, Ireland, Scotland, France, Belgium, Holland, and Denmark added together, there can be no want of territory for such a political division. It is only about thirty years since this province, as it now stands, was separated from New South Wales.

From Brisbane we returned to Sydney on the way to the southern cities; and here the journey was broken by a day's rest, as it is nearly twelve hundred miles from Brisbane to Melbourne.

CHAPTER VIII.

An Inland Journey. — The Capital of Victoria. — Grand Public Buildings. — Water-Supply of the City. — Public Parks and Gardens. — Street Scenes. — Dashing Liveries. — Tramways. — Extremes. — Melbourne Ladies. — Street Beggars. — Saturday Half-Holiday. — Public Arcades. — The City Free Library. — The Public Markets. — China-Town, Melbourne. — Victims of the Opium Habit.

MELBOURNE, the capital of Victoria, lies nearly six hundred miles southwest of Sydney. The journey from one city to the other by rail is rather a tedious one, as there is very little of interest upon the route to engage the attention of the traveller. Soon after leaving the latter city the road runs through a level country, which is sparsely inhabited, but quite heavily wooded with that wearying tree the eucalyptus, presenting hardly one feature of attractiveness to recommend it to the eye. It is always dressed in a sober, funereal garb, which by no effort of the imagination can one reasonably call green. Miles and miles were passed of houseless monotony, the land often denuded of trees, and showing only a low growth of wattle, or some small shrub of the eucalyptus family. Most of the settlers' cabins seen inland were mere shells, consisting of frames of wood covered on roof and sides with corrugated sheet-iron, unpainted; while others presented a still ruder appearance, being frames of wood covered loosely with bark, only one degree better than the bark shelters of the aborigines in northern Queensland. At some of the railroad stations a faint effort is made at the cultivation of flowers, and occasionally pretty effects are produced by planting California pines in groups or borders, mingled with some other species of imported trees, mostly of the conifer family, — their foliage, by its choice verdure, putting the native trees to shame, though they are known as evergreens : there are indeed no deciduous native trees in Australia. Here and there a small orchard of orange-trees was seen, the fruit in its deep-yellow glow standing out against the surrounding foliage in bold relief. The traveller meets with no more delightful experience than when approaching an orange-orchard in full bloom. For a mile before the place is reached, the fragrant atmosphere foretells the coming pleasure to the senses. This is oftenest realized in the West Indies, or in Florida. Here it was not the season of the bloom but of the fruit. A few gardens of tropical aspect, with groups of bananas, were also observed; but to see this most generous of all fruit-trees in perfection, one must go north toward the Equator, into Queensland.

Now and again a few thousand sheep were seen, and some small herds of horned cattle feeding on the hillsides or browsing among the forest glades; but the true pastoral districts are much farther inland. At Albury the Murray River was crossed, which here makes the boundary between New South Wales and Victoria, though which side of the watercourse belongs to the former and which to the latter is a constant source of dispute between them. An examination of baggage took place at Albury, as though the traveller were passing from one European nationality to another. The two colonies, however, have tariffs materially differing from each other, and duty is demanded upon all merchandise passing either way between them. The custom-house officers are quite discriminating, and unless they have reason to suspect a person of designs against the customs they do not put him to unnecessary trouble in the examination of his effects.

Not until one comes to within fifty or sixty miles of Melbourne upon this route does the country become attractive; but here it begins to open into broad green fields and rich meadows, forming a choice succession of agricultural districts, affording the best of pasturage and showing upon a large scale the careful cultivation of root-crops, corn, oats, wheat, and barley. Government owns and operates the railroad with a fair degree of liberality, though the prices charged for transportation are much higher than with us in America. The cars are often of the English style, formed into coaches which are cheaply upholstered, though they are reasonably comfortable.

It is but little more than half a century since an Englishman named John Batman ascended the Yarra-Yarra and bargained with the chiefs of the native tribe located here, to sell "to him and his heirs forever" so many thousand acres of land as now embrace the area occupied by the city of Melbourne and its immediate environs, covering six or eight miles square. For this grant of land Batman paid the chiefs in goods, which are said to have consisted of one dozen cotton shirts, a dozen colored woollen blankets, a handful of glass-bead ornaments, twelve bags of flour, and two casks of pork. These were all otherwise unattainable articles to the savages, who, however, had land enough and to spare. It is said that the aborigines pleaded hard for one or more guns to be added to the payment, but Batman was too wary to supply them with weapons which they could in an emergency turn against himself or other white men. The Englishman came and settled upon his purchase, built a stock-house, and proposed to surround himself with friends in order to form a sort of small independent State. But only a brief period transpired before an authorized agent of the English Government appeared upon the spot and declared the bargain between Batman and the savages to be null and void; in justice, however, to the purchaser, Government paid him some thousands of pounds sterling, and he turned over all his right and title to the authorities accordingly. Neither party could possibly have anticipated that in so few years this land would be valued at many millions of pounds sterling. Five years ago a monument was erected to Batman's memory, he having died in 1839; this monument stands in the old cemetery of Melbourne. To-day the site once so cheaply purchased, with the population now upon it, is classed by English writers as forming, in point of wealth, numbers of inhabitants, and general importance, the tenth city in the world!

The first sight of Melbourne was quite a surprise to us, though we thought we were fairly informed about this capital of Victoria. No stranger could anticipate beholding so grand a city in this far-away South-land of the Pacific. Where there was only a swamp and uncleared woods a few years ago, there has risen a city containing to-day a population of fully four hundred and twenty thousand, embracing the immediate suburbs. This capital is certainly unsurpassed by any of the British colonies in the elegancies and luxuries of modern civilization, such as broad avenues, palatial dwellings, churches, colossal warehouses, banks, theatres, and public buildings and pleasure-grounds. It is pleasant to record the fact that one fifth of the revenue raised by taxation is expended for educational purposes. Of what other city in the New or the Old World can this be said? Universities, libraries, public art-galleries, and museums lack not for the liberal and fostering care of the Government. No city except San Francisco ever attained to such size and importance in so short a period as has Melbourne.

The public buildings of the city are mainly constructed of a sort of freestone brought from Tasmania, as the local quarries, being mostly of a volcanic nature, are too hard for favorable working, though some use is made of their material. The new and elaborate Roman Catholic Cathedral, now nearly completed, is entirely constructed of this stone. Melbourne covers a very large area for its population; indeed, we were told by those who should be well informed in such matters that its extent of territory is nearly the same as that of Paris. In the environs are many delightful residences, embowered with creeping vines and surrounded with flower-gardens. These dwellings could hardly be made to look more attractive externally, though simple architecturally. They are mostly vine-clad; Flora has touched them with her magic finger, and they have become beautiful. Many of these suburbs are named after familiar European localities, such as Brighton, Kew, Emerald Hill, Collingwood, St. Kilda, Fitzroy, and so forth. The streets of St. Kilda must have been named about the period of the late Crimean war, as the following names were observed among them: Raglan, Sebastopol, Redan, Cardigan, Balaklava, and Malakoff.

Lake Yan-Yan supplies Melbourne with drinking-water by means of a system embracing a double set of pipes. This water-supply for domestic and general use is beyond all comparison the best we have ever chanced to see. The valley of the river Plenty, which is a tributary of the Yarra-Yarra, is dammed across at Yan-Yan, nearly twenty miles from the capital, by an embankment half a mile long, — thereby forming a lake nearly ten miles in circumference, with an area of over thirteen hundred acres, and an average depth of twenty-five feet. It holds sufficient water, as we were informed by an official, to furnish an ample supply for the use of the city during a period of two years, allowing fifteen gallons per head per day for the present population. This grand piece of engineering was expensive, but is fully worth all it has cost; namely, between six and seven million dollars.

The river Yarra-Yarra runs through the city, and is navigable for large vessels to the main wharves, where it is crossed by a broad and substantial bridge. Both the harbor and the river are being dredged by the most powerful boats designed for the purpose which we have ever seen. Above the bridge the river is handsomely lined with trees; and here, notwithstanding a somewhat winding course, the great boat-races take place which form one of the most attractive of all the local athletic amusements,—and Melbourne is famous for out-door sports of every form and nature, but principally for boating and ball-playing.

A whole chapter might be written describing the public gardens of the city and our inspiring visit to them. The variety of trees here collected is marvellous in its comprehensiveness. Oaks and elms of great size were observed among other exotics; one would hardly have thought they could have found time to acquire such proportions, but all trees grow with marked rapidity in this climate. Some very beautiful fern-trees were noticed, twenty feet in height, their fronds measuring fourteen feet in length, drooping plume-like about the graceful bending stems. Here were seen fine specimens of the magnolia-tree, bending to the ground under the weight of great yellow blossoms. The collection of tropical fruit-trees was remarkably complete. Wherever there are gardens in front of the dwellings in the environs of the city one is sure to see an abundance of the little pink and white daphne, fragrant and lovely as the violet, flourishing in great luxuriance. The abundance of maiden's-hair fern, in various sizes down to little leaves of pin-head dimensions, gives occasion for its very free use in bouquets. The variety of color found in this species of fern is quite noticeable here, the shades running from a deep dark green, by easy gradations, to almost an orange hue. The charming little daphne is the favorite button-hole flower of the Collins Street beaux, backed by a tiny spray of light-green fern. We saw some bouquets of cut-flowers in floral establishments on Swanston Street, exhibiting a degree of artistic taste in the arrangement which could not be excelled. The most delicate branches of maiden's-hair fern were so intertwined among the various colored flowers as to form a gauze-like veil, so that one seemed to behold them through a transparent cloud of misty green. Such combinations of tangible beauty cannot be equalled by the finest paintings.

This capital of Victoria, as we have intimated, is a city of public gardens. It is astonishing what an air of elegance, space, and wholesomeness is imparted by them. Besides the Botanical Gardens there are the Fitzroy Gardens, situated in the eastern suburb of the town, which contain some seventy-five acres of ground beautifully laid out and ornamented with a grand collection of trees, shrubs, and flowers, especially in the department of ferns. Fountains, rocky basins, and artificial waterfalls add picturesqueness to the place. The Zoölogical Gardens are in the Royal Park, containing a really fine collection of animals as well as a well-furnished aviary. We had as "fellow-passengers" on board the "Zealandia" a pair of young California lions designed for this collection, which arrived safely at their destination. These baby lions were quite sea-sick on the long voyage, but were in fine condition when we saw them in their new and spacious quarters at the Zoo-zoo.

Carlton Gardens are in the northern suburb, near the Parliament House; here also stands near by, the Exhibition Building, erected at a cost of over half a million dollars. It is now improved as a place for public amusements of various sorts, and contains a well-stocked and particularly well-arranged aquarium, somewhat after the style of that at Brighton, England. There are five or six other parks or public gardens more or less extensive, all charmingly laid out and beautified with trees of native and foreign species, with miniature lakes, aquatic plants and birds, and possessing picturesquely arranged fountains. Albert Park, in the eastern suburb, contains a lake so large as to render it available for sailing-boats and pleasant rowing-parties, for which purpose it is daily improved by both sexes and entire families.

The streets of Melbourne present a busy aspect, and there is ample space afforded for all legitimate business and pleasure purposes, these thoroughfares being each one hundred feet in width, — a gauge which is maintained throughout the city. They are all laid out at right angles, with mathematical precision. This liberal allotment of space for public use is carried out even in the suburbs, calculation having been made in advance for the growth of the city which is sure to come. The streets are for the most part paved either in blocks of granite or of wood, being in a few instances macadamized; but all are kept in admirable condition, both as to use and cleanliness. The stream of humanity pouring through them at all hours of the day is indeed vast and varied, though the population, while it consists of a mingling of nationalities, is yet distinctively English. It seemed to the writer that more Americans were to be found in this capital of Victoria than elsewhere in the colonies, quite a number being prominently engaged in speculative enterprises, and maintaining agencies for firms whose headquarters are in the United States. Several of our popular Life Insurance Companies are thus represented.

The busy activity in the streets was remarkable. Hansom cabs rattled about or stood in long rows awaiting patrons; four-wheeled vehicles of an inexcusably awkward style, also for hire, abounded;

messenger-boys, with yellow leather pouches strapped over their shoulders, hurried hither and thither; high-hung omnibuses with three horses abreast, like those of Paris and Naples, dashed rapidly along, well filled with passengers; men galloped through the crowd upon small horses, carrying big baskets of provisions on their arms; dog-carts driven by smart young fellows, with a flunky behind in gaudy livery, cut in and out among the vehicles; powerful draught-horses stamped along the way, drawing heavily loaded drays; milk-carts with big letters on their canvas sides made themselves conspicuous, rivalled as to the size of the lettering by the bakers' carts of similar shape; light and neat American wagonettes glided along among less attractive vehicles. Now and then a Chinaman passed by with his peculiar shambling gait, a pole across his shoulders balancing his baskets of truck; women with oranges and bananas for a penny apiece met one at every turn, — and still the sidewalks are so broad and the streets so wide that no one seemed to be in the least incommoded. The fruiterers' stands here and there, as well as the windows of the dealers in the same products, presented an array remarkable for its tempting variety. Among these fruits are the mandarin and navel oranges, apricots, figs, grapes, passion-fruit, pineapples, bananas, peaches, plums, and several other sorts, all in fine condition. With the exception of San Francisco, nowhere else can fruit of such choice character be found in so great variety and at such cheap rates as in Melbourne.

While driving in the environs of the city many plots of ground were observed cultivated by Chinamen, and kept in the neatest possible manner. As we have already said, John is a natural gardener. In the first place his knowledge of fertilizing materials suitable for the soil enables him to produce vegetables not only in abundance, but of the best quality. He is independent of markets, going personally to his customers, — thus making his body serve for both cart and horse, and accustoming himself to carry heavy burdens daily. By such means he realizes all the profit there is to be made on his products, not having to divide with the wholesale dealer or the middle-man. He thus shows business keenness as well as a capacity to endure great drudgery. So absorbed is the general attention, in other directions that only John attends to the raising of vegetables, — thus providing a necessary diet for those who would otherwise be liable to lose health and strength for the want of it.

One meets plenty of Jews upon the boulevards of Melbourne, with their strongly-marked features. There was an abundance of them also in Sydney; and indeed where are they not to be found, if there is money to be borrowed or trade to be vigorously pushed?

On the corners of the streets in Melbourne are to be seen a peculiar class of idlers. The eight-hour system of labor prevails here, and men hasten from work to the bar-rooms, there being one of these poison-dispensing resorts at every corner of the business thoroughfares. We calculated that there were four thousand "gin mills" in this city, and probably that is an under estimate. The common laboring classes of this city are not only universal drinkers, but they are also "hard drinkers." They are as a rule too ignorant or besotted to see, putting all other things out of the question, that the cup of any sensual indulgence if drained to the bottom has always poison in its dregs. They indulge grossly, and suffer accordingly.

The showy liveries worn by the retainers of some of the more wealthy (not the better) classes of the citizens of Sydney and Melbourne seemed to us strangely out of place. As nearly as we could get at the facts by casual inquiry, most of these buttoned and uniformed flunkies were in the service of persons concerning whose genealogy the less said the better, especially when we remember that the earlier residents of Australia were mostly composed of those who left their native country for their country's good. "You may safely calculate that the father of the latest Australian baronet was a nobody, or something worse," says a writer in one of the local magazines. Melbourne, however, seemed to us less open to any aspersions growing out of former penal associations than either Brisbane, Sydney, or Hobart in Tasmania, all which colonies were originally settled as penal stations. Victoria is one of the youngest of all these colonies, and was, up to the discovery of the gold-fields within her present borders, — that is, in 1851, — a portion of New South Wales; but to-day it is the metropolis *par excellence* of Australia. It has not the many natural beauties of Sydney, but it has numerous compensating advantages, and is undoubtedly the real centre of colonial enterprise upon the continent.

The admirable system of tramways in Melbourne is worthy of all praise, use being made of the subterranean cable and stationary engines as a motor. This mode of propulsion is safe, cheap, and cleanly. While we were in the capital tracks were being laid for several new and extended routes, one of which runs through Burke Street parallel with Collins. The public amusements of a large city often aid one in forming a just idea of its development in other directions. Those of this capital of the southern hemisphere are numerous, well conducted, and well attended, — a sure evidence of prosperity and general thrift. People from inland who have money to spend are attracted to such places as will afford them the greatest variety of reasonable amusements; and hence Melbourne, rather than Sydney, has become the resort of these pleasure-seekers.

It has been said that gold made Melbourne and wool made Sydney, — a remark which is based on fact. The experiences of both these cities in the early part of their career was peculiar. Money easily gained is seldom wisely spent; sums that fall as it were into the open palm will burn in the unaccustomed pocket; the excited recipient resorts to high revels and all sorts of excesses, be he never so quiet and reasonable under ordinary circumstances. At one time skilled labor in Melbourne commanded the extraordinary wages of ten dollars per day, and mechanics thought the millennium had come; they had not the wit to see that such extremes produce in the end a sure and severe reaction, but experience taught them that lesson by and by. "The greatest flood has the soonest ebb." The lavish earnings of the masses, whether at the gold-fields or at the bench, were soon engulfed in the beer-barrel and the wine-cask; the bar-rooms were the only places where uninterrupted industry was exhibited, and where unremitting application to a given object was conspicuous. "Our streets," said a citizen of Melbourne to us, "in the early days of the gold-rush swarmed with drunken revellers; nor could we see any ready way out of the trouble which afflicted the community. Finally, however, the diggings ceased to yield so lavishly; the surface ore was exhausted, and to get gold out of the earth a man was compelled to work hard for it. The great novelty also began to wear away, and those who were making money less easily, very naturally were disposed to spend it less foolishly." The exaggerated rates of wages were consequently reduced, inflated prices for all articles of consumption fell gradually to a reasonable figure, and affairs generally returned to their normal condition. Precisely the same experience was realized in the early days of the gold discovery in California.

Personal beauty is not the prevailing characteristic of the female portion of the community of Melbourne any more than it is at Sydney; and shall we be forgiven for saying that in our opinion the ladies do not dress in very good taste? Young and middle-aged women generally cut their hair short; but why such a fashion should prevail among them we could not conjecture, the boyish aspect thus produced being anything but becoming. The bar-rooms are very generally tended here, as they are also in England, by women; and the bar-maids universally cut their hair short, in boy-fashion. One would think that this fact alone would be sufficient to induce ladies of respectability to avoid such an extreme and questionable custom.

The wide sidewalks are here covered with stationary verandas, as noticed in most of the colonial cities and towns. These coverings are sometimes made of glass or of matched boards, but most commonly of corrugated sheet-iron, supported at the edge-stones by small iron pillars. They form a shelter from both rain and sun, — recalling the Rue Rivoli of Paris, or the streets of Turin in Italy, or of Bologna in Spain. The ladies and gentlemen strolling under these covered ways, before the fine display in the shop windows, present a gay and attractive picture at the fashionable hours of the day. But in broad contrast to these bright and cheerful centres, there are in the northeastern section of the town filthy alleys and by-ways that one would think must be, owing to their filth and squalor, hot-beds of disease and pestilence, well calculated to supplement the inevitable effects of the defective drainage of this rich capital on the banks of the Yarra-Yarra.

One cannot but notice the peculiar pronunciation and mode of speech common among the people here. It is what we call cockney in America, with some added local effects. The misplacing of the letter h is almost universal. This is a habit which appears to be infectious; one individual who practises it is liable to corrupt scores of others. The drawling hesitancy of the Londoners of a certain class is also easily transmitted, being as catching as stuttering or the measles.

One who passes through foreign cities and is able to spend rarely more than a couple of weeks in each capital, is not competent to speak authoritatively of its social life, or in detail of its best society. But it is safe to say that ladies and gentlemen are the same everywhere. They form perhaps the higher element of a social centre, but they do comparatively little toward determining its outward aspect or its political status. It is the people *en masse* who form the general character of a large population, — such individuals as one meets in omnibuses, railroad cars, hotels, places of public amusement, and upon the fashionable promenades at the favorite hours.

The General Post-Office of Melbourne is situated at the junction of Elizabeth and Burke streets, presenting a striking architectural aspect, with its tall tower, bold reliefs, illumined clock, and chime of bells. It is admirably designed for the purposes of this department of the Government, and covers an entire block by itself, with a pillared colonnade about it similar to that already described as forming the outer portion of the Post-Office at Sydney. It affords room not only for the several divisions of the Post-Office proper, but also for the savings bank, the money-order department, and that of the telegraph, all which are under the control of the Government. Spacious as the original design of the structure was, the business transacted in it has already outgrown its capacity, so that more room is now imperatively demanded. Additions are consequently making by extending the rear of the building, while at the same time the tower is being raised and a story added to the whole edifice.

The author does not pretend to describe the many public buildings of Melbourne, but briefly to mention such as most impressed him. Among these were the Town Hall, on the corner of Elizabeth and Collins streets, — a very large and solid building in the Renaissance style, erected in 1867, containing among numerous other rooms designed for municipal use the Executive Chamber, and one remarkable apartment capable of seating over five thousand persons. In this hall is a grand organ which is acknowledged to be the fifth largest in the world, — a noble and costly instrument of exquisite harmony and great power, a full description of which was given to us with much patient courtesy. The Town Hall is four stories high, and has office room for all the various branches of the city business, with ample accommodations for civic ceremonies.

Collins Street is the fashionable boulevard of the city, though Burke Street nearly rivals it in gay promenaders and elegant shops. To make a familiar comparison, the latter is the Broadway, the former the Fifth Avenue, of Melbourne. On the upper part of Burke Street there is a covered market consisting of two spacious floors occupying an acre and more of ground, which we visited in the early morning. The confused variety of articles and lines of goods here offered for sale was really ludicrous, recalling a similar display witnessed at Warsaw, in Poland, near the Saxony Gardens, though it lacked entirely the element of picturesqueness there so prominent. Here were displayed side by side dry-goods and green fruit, crockery ware and millinery, flowers and meats, clothing and jewelry, boots, shoes, and poultry, singing-birds and underwear. Indeed, what was there not to be had here for a price? A mile and more away from this, up Elizabeth Street, the regular vegetable and meat market was found. Here several acres were covered by sheds open at the sides, where country produce was offered at wholesale and retail. It is more than probable that "nice" people do not go to market in Melbourne, judging from the character of the noisy, jostling, and rather rudely-behaved masses who were encountered in these two markets, especially the last named. Here neatness and cleanliness in the surroundings were completely ignored. The garbage over which one was compelled to pass in order to get about the market was not only extremely difficult to encounter, but also disgusting. In European and American cities one meets representatives of all classes in such resorts at early morning, but it does not seem to be so in Melbourne. In Philadelphia and Havana the household mistress, followed by a servant with a basket, goes regularly to early market, — or if not daily, certainly on Saturday mornings. 'T is not so here.

There are four large arcades in the city all opening from Burke Street, and forming pleasant popular resorts for strollers, who are here sheltered from the weather and the noise of the public thoroughfares. They are respectively the Royal Arcade, nearly opposite the Post-Office, containing elegantly furnished shops; the Victoria Arcade, opposite the Theatre Royal; the Eastern Arcade, next to the market; and the Book Arcade, in the eastern part of Burke Street, — this last, as its name indicates, being devoted mostly to the sale of books. Free evening concerts are given also in these retreats, which always attract fair audiences. The Book Arcade is a very popular resort for students and the better class of evening idlers. The proprietor told us that he had two hundred thousand volumes upon his shelves, — a number which we judged from appearances not to be over stated. These books were so systematically arranged by subjects, that the inquirer for any special work could have it in hand in a moment; or if it was not in stock, the proprietor could ascertain that fact almost as quickly. The character of the books in this establishment was of a singular mixture, running from the higher classics down to a dime novel, and from the Encyclopædia Britannica to Mother Goose's Melodies.

The Public Library of Melbourne is a large and impressive building, standing by itself back from the street on rising ground, and would be creditable to any European or American city. It already contains a hundred and twenty-six thousand volumes, and is being constantly added to by public and private bequests. The collection of manuscripts and unbound pamphlets is large and comprehensive, especially in the latter department. The interior arrangements of the Library struck us as being particularly excellent, affording ample and accessible room for the books, besides all needed table accommodations for the use of the public. In this respect the Library was far in advance of our Boston institution, and is hardly surpassed by the Astor Library in New York. As to the Melbourne building, inside and out, it is superior to both of the libraries we have named in architectural effect. Under the same roof is a Technological Museum containing an extensive collection, especially of geological specimens, mainly comprised of those found in Australia. For entomologists and mineralogists the collection here exhibited will present also special interest. An entire wing upon the lower floor of the building — the library proper being up one flight of stairs — is devoted to statuary and to a public school of art. A third department is appropriated to a permanent exhibition of paintings. Here may be seen many choice modern pictures and some admirable copies from the old masters. All these departments come under the direction of the managers of the Library, and all are free to the public. Over one hundred persons were counted at the reading-tables of the Library during our brief visit. There were representatives among them of all classes of citizens, from the professional student in search of special information, to the laboring man seeking to improve himself by acquiring general knowledge. Many of these readers were clearly from a station in life that would furnish them no access to such books except for this public provision. What an admirable arrangement it is that here affords to the humblest well-behaved person books, shelter, warmth, and light, from ten in the morning until ten at night, free of all charge or onerous conditions! It is the multiplication of such facilities for culture and self-improvement which so emphasizes the real meaning of the words *civilization* and *progress*. This is a grand missionary work in the right direction. Now let the managers of the Melbourne Public Library open the doors of their institution on Sundays, and thus add to the usefulness of this noble benefaction.

Melbourne has its Chinese Quarter, like Sydney and San Francisco; it is situated in Little Burke Street, just back of the Theatre Royal, and forms a veritable

China-Town with its joss-house, opium-dens, lottery cellars, "fantan" cafés, low hovels, and other kindred establishments. Here one requires a guide to make his way understandingly and safely. The unintelligible notices posted upon the buildings in Chinese characters are a curious puzzle to the uninitiated. The signs over the shops are especially peculiar; they do not denote the name of the owner, or particularize the business which is done within, but are assumed titles of flowery character. Thus, — Kong, Meng & Co. means "Bright Light Firm;" Sun Kum Lee & Co. is in English "New Golden Firm;" Kwong Hop signifies "New Agreement Company;" Hi Cheong, "Peace and Prosperity Firm;" Kwong Tu Tye, "Flourishing and Peaceful Company," — and so on. John is an inveterate smuggler, and manages to get a large amount of his precious opium landed without paying any portion of the high rate of duty imposed by the Government. The Chinese are very impulsive, and will follow one another sometimes, like a flock of sheep after a leader. Not long since there burst out in their Melbourne quarter an epidemic of suicide, and many of them resorted to it. The mode they adopted was that of strangulation, which they effectually accomplished by knotting their pigtails about their throats.

There is a Chinese Doctor of Medicine in this Asiatic section of Melbourne who was educated in Pekin, and who is said to have been once attached to the family of the Emperor of China, but for some irregularity was banished from that country. We were told that he had performed some remarkable cures among the better class of citizens, in cases which had been given up by European physicians. It was said that he might command a large professional practice if he would remove from the locality where his countrymen lived and which is held in such bad odor.

John is nowhere a favorite, as we have already clearly demonstrated, however advantageous may be his frugal and industrious habits in the formation of new States. That he possesses at least this recommendation has been fully proved in the instances of California and Australia. In the official report of the completion of the first Atlantic and Pacific railroad, the following paragraph appears: "Labor was difficult to get, and when obtained, more difficult to control, until the Chinese arrived; and to them is due the real credit of the construction of the road." This paragraph of course refers to the Pacific end of the route. It is as a rule the worst type of the Chinese who leave their native land to make a new home elsewhere, and it is not to be expected that they will be much improved by intercourse with the Australian "larrikins," who are composed of the lowest and most criminal orders. These refuse of humanity are largely composed of the rabble of London and Liverpool, many of whom have had their passage paid by their relatives at home solely to get rid of them, while others have worked their passage hither to avoid punishment for crimes committed in England. Murders are by no means infrequent in the Chinese Quarter of Melbourne, or as some call it the "Hell of Little Burke Street." These crimes, however, are oftenest committed by the larrikins, sometimes undoubtedly by the Chinese. It is altogether a sheltering refuge for criminals of various nationalities, being a source of constant anxiety to the authorities and a puzzle to the police officials.

Poor, abandoned white women are mingled with the other habitués of this Mongolian district, and they too learn the subtle fascination of the opium pipe. An intelligent man, long engaged in missionary work in Melbourne, and particularly in this special region of the town, told us that the girls and women who had become fixed inhabitants of the Little Burke Street quarter were irredeemable. To break the once contracted habit of opium indulgence was next to impossible. He declared that in all his experience he had known but two veritable reformations among these women, and one of them finally ended her wretched career in a mad-house.

CHAPTER IX.

A Melbourne Half-Holiday. — Inconsistency of Laborers. — Vice-Royal Residence. — Special Gold-Fields of Victoria. — Ballarat. — Great Depths in Mines. — Agricultural Interests. — Sandhurst. — The Giant Trees of Australia. — The Kangaroo. — In Victorian Forests. — Peculiar Salt Lakes. — The Bower-bird's Retreat. — The Wild Dog. — Desirable and Undesirable Emigrants. — No Place for the Intemperate.

SATURDAY afternoon is made a weekly carnival in Melbourne, though it does not by any means assume so picturesque an aspect as in Honolulu. Here the shops are all closed soon after mid-day, work of every sort ceases, and amusements promptly begin, being kept up vigorously until after midnight. The parks and pleasure-grounds are crowded with foot-ball, base-ball, and cricket players, as well as by groups devoted to other games. In the evening the theatres and public exhibitions are all insufficient to accommodate the throngs that attend them, though there are five regular places in the city where dramatic entertainments are given. The bar-rooms reap a golden harvest, and are especially patronized, while a general spirit of license prevails among all classes. The streets are crowded by a careless, not to say reckless, throng of men, women, and boys, very many of whom were observed to be decidedly the worse for liquor. Burke Street, Elizabeth Street, and even Collins Street, which represent the best portion of the town, are tinctured for the time being with a spirit of rowdyism. Indeed, a general latitude of behavior appears to be condoned on this Saturday half-holiday, as it is with us to a certain extent on the Fourth of July. The workmen of Melbourne who have received ten hours' pay for eight hours' work also claim this gratuity of time on the sixth day, and by their use of it not only cheapen their labor, but impair both their health and their fortune. We could not but conclude on the whole that the Saturday half-holiday as employed by the masses of Melbourne was a weekly error, and that the class which most imperiously demand this release from occupation is unfortunately composed of those who most grossly abuse the privilege.

On Sunday few people were to be seen in the streets and fewer still in the churches, leading one to divine that the day was generally devoted to necessary recuperation after the gross excesses of Saturday. It was noticed that the bar-rooms were ostensibly closed on the Sabbath. This the local law requires, but there are always ways and means whereby the thirsty tippler gets his fill.

The laborers who place themselves under the control of some organized Union are in fact its slaves, the victims of designing theorists and cunning managers, who are themselves drones in the human hive. The ordinary workman does not think for himself; he does not realize that the less he gives for his day's wages the dearer must become those articles that are dependent upon labor. If the abbreviated time of eight hours per day for five days of the week, and four hours on Saturday, constitute a week's work, the laborer has more to pay for all of the necessities of life than he would have were full hours and a fair equivalent given for the wages he receives. It costs more to build houses in the former instance; therefore his rent must be increased. He must pay more for his food and clothing. An honest day's work is the true criterion of value; and so far as that is curtailed just so much more must it cost for family support, and just so much poorer shall we all be, both capitalist and laborer.

One sees no special signs of poverty in the streets of Melbourne, as we have already intimated; but there may be, and to a certain extent we know that there is, squalor existing, though it does not make itself visible in the public thoroughfares. There are "back slums" that do not by their appearance invite one to penetrate them, and which would best be avoided at night; but these are the concomitants of all large and promiscuous gatherings of humanity. Though the city is well situated for drainage, there seems to be at present only a very defective mode adopted, mostly dependent upon surface flow to clear the daily accumulation of débris. We were told, however, that this objection was fast being remedied, and that there already exists a partial system of drainage which has been applied to the most important sections of the town.

The heavy clouds of fuliginous coal-smoke which envelop Melbourne are caused by the steam-launches, ferry-boats, coasting and ocean-going steamers, and manufactories, all which create their motive-power with Sydney bituminous coal, — a good steam-producing article, but which covers everything in its neighborhood with a fine black dust, the formidable enemy of clean faces and white linen. The smoke and dust nevertheless are significant of life and energy. They indicate that business is active, that the channels of trade are not blocked; and therefore they are cheerfully submitted to. "Dirt," said a certain shrewd philosopher, "is not dirt; it is something in the wrong place."

The finest site near the city has been selected for the residence of Vice-royalty; so that quite a prominent feature of the suburbs is the Government House, which is situated about a mile from the city proper, and is an imposing but ugly-looking building. It has a central tower twenty-five feet square more or less, and of considerable height. It is pleasanter to say a good word concerning any object than a harsh one; but the Government House in Melbourne is irredeemable ugly, though it must have cost a mint of money. This immense edifice is only half improved on the inside, being large enough for a European royal residence requiring accommodations for a large number of retainers; the Governor of Victoria, however, finds it necessary to count the cost as regards his manner of living, since his official salary is by no means sufficient to keep up a royal court. The ball-room of this residence is somewhat famous for its size and general appointments, being of such proportions as would easily accommodate a marching regiment under arms. It is however on certain occasions thrown open and lighted throughout for its original purpose. The public park which joins the grounds of the Government House is beautiful indeed, being a botanical garden in itself, and the one redeeming feature of the establishment.

Victoria is the special gold-field of Australia, and has produced two thirds of all the precious metal which statistics credit to the country at large. One of the localities which has proved to be most prolific in gold is Ballarat, now a charming and populous city, and next to Melbourne in importance. It lies nearly a hundred miles north of the capital, at an elevation of some fifteen hundred feet above sea-level, and is accessible by rail. This is thought to be the centre of one of the richest gold-producing districts in the world. Beechworth, one hundred and seventy miles northeast of Melbourne, at a higher elevation than Ballarat, is nearly as populous and well-nigh as prolific in the precious metal. The diggings of Maryborough district, situated a hundred and fifty miles northwest of Melbourne, are also of great extent and quite famous. There are over eight thousand miners at work here. Castlemain, some seventy-five miles north of the capital, has proved to be very profitable in its yield of gold. Nearly forty square miles of auriferous lands are being worked by Europeans and Chinese in the district of Ararat, about a hundred and fifty miles from Melbourne, northward. From these several sources of mineral wealth there flows constantly toward the capital a stream of riches, making it the greatest gold-producing locality on the globe. There are about fifty thousand people in all engaged at gold-mining in the several parts of Victoria, at least ten thousand of whom are Chinese. The latter operate almost entirely in the alluvial workings, while the Europeans are occupied almost wholly in quartz-crushing. Some of the shafts sunk for procuring paying quartz are over two thousand feet in depth. The Stawell mine is, to be exact, two thousand four hundred and twelve feet below the surface of the ground, from which depth is brought up stone yielding over four ounces of gold to the ton. We have by no means exhausted the list of noted diggings in this region, but have only mentioned a few of them, such as came most readily to mind; moreover, new deposits of recognized value are being discovered every few months. Still, we repeat here that reliable figures show that in the aggregate the corn and wool of Victoria alone are of more monetary value than is the result from all the alluvial and quartz-yielding mines within her entire borders.

Three days from Melbourne will suffice for visiting the interesting and handsome city of Ballarat. It is now a place containing over fifty thousand inhabitants, owing its existence entirely to the finding of gold on the spot which it occupies; indeed, it has not inappropriately been called the city of Midas. Where thirty years ago the land was covered with miners' tents and log-huts, an arid and treeless expanse lying between two low hills, there is now a fine modern city. It is a metropolis with broad boulevards, substantial stone buildings, massive warehouses, sumptuous residences, elegant official structures, and good schools, supplemented by many philanthropic and religious institutions. The environs of Ballarat are also beautified, having many choice trees planted all about them, especially California pines, which are great favorites here and multiplying continually. Trees grow in this climate with such rapidity as to encourage their planting. They are particularly desirable here, where the surroundings were redeemed from such original crudeness, as they impart a certain grace and home-like appearance to otherwise desolate places.

A glimpse only may be had of Ballarat in the time we have named, but let no one who comes hither neglect the Public Garden, which the reader of these notes has by this time learned is one of the prime necessities of each of these colonial capitals. The wealthy citizens of Ballarat have expended freely of their gold upon this delightful park, which, if it does not rival in some particulars those of Sydney and Melbourne, certainly comes quite up to them in general excellence and beauty. There is plenty of water to be had in the city for irrigating and all other purposes, an artificial lake having been created in the hills not far away, whence pipes bring the water to every one's door. This reservoir is of admirable workmanship, and of inestimable value to the town. The pleasant streets are rendered shady and attractive by long lines of bordering trees. The mining here is carried on in the environs, not in "every man's back yard," as is said to be the case at Sandhurst, another famous mining point of which we shall speak further on. All the ground upon which Ballarat is built, however, has been faithfully and profitably dug over and passed through the sieve or over the amalgamating tables. Surface mining is no longer prosecuted here to any extent. These deposits are naturally the first to fail in productiveness, but the neighboring hills are formed of a gold-bearing quartz which is being crushed, night and day, by hundreds of powerful machines; and the works still pay ten thousand miners fair day-wages, besides giving the organized companies who employ them satisfactory dividends. Thus mining has been largely robbed of its adventurous character in this neighborhood, and perhaps also of most of its alluring charm, having become a sort of regular industry, like coal-mining, or even brick-making.

Ballarat being situated on elevated ground, the air here is particularly bracing and healthful, so that Melbourne physicians sometimes send invalids hither. It is plainly the centre of a former volcanic region, and in many places near at hand extinct volcanoes can be counted by the score, — some filled up to their summits with the débris of ages, some forming deep depressions, and some filled with small lakes of bitter water. There is plain evidence of these volcanic cones and craters having discharged basalt, lava, scoria, cinders, and the like within a comparatively modern period. The natives who were found in this region had legends of eruptions having taken place hereabout, but as to how long ago they could give no idea, having no means of measuring periods of time.

Although gold-mining, as we have said, is a prominent feature of the general industry of Ballarat, the prevailing business of this immediate district is farming. It is now a great agricultural centre as well as a gold-producing one, and this legitimate pursuit is becoming daily of more and more importance, — thus once more demonstrating that even in Eldorado gold-mining is a means to an end, not the grand object itself. We were told that the great wheat-fields in this district have been ploughed, planted, and reaped for fifteen consecutive years, without the least thought on the part of the occupants of using any fertilizer. To-day these fields yield as uniformly as at first, and seem inexhaustible in their fertility.

Five million pounds sterling in gold is annually produced in Victoria; yet it is perfectly well known that the cost of its production, in labor and money, amounts to about the same sum. The original cost of the mines, the expense incurred for machinery, the daily wages of the thousands of miners, and the interest upon the capital invested, are each factors in the calculation, not forgetting that there are frequent expensive exigencies sure to occur. For instance, we were told of an accident which happened in a Victoria mine just previous to our visit, resulting in the loss of the lives of eight miners. Owing to a defective metallic rope, a "lift" containing eight men suddenly fell while ascending a shaft, killing instantly every one of its occupants. The court held that the company was responsible for the lives of these men, because it permitted its agent to use a defective rope. The agent promptly settled with the representatives of the unfortunate men at a thousand pounds for each life, making an aggregate sum of forty-five thousand dollars; and it cost another thousand pounds to repair the injured machinery of the mine.

The author looked somewhat carefully into the subject of gold-mining with the desire to arrive at a correct conclusion concerning it, and was fortunate in meeting intelligent men who were ready to impart their experience in this field of enterprise, — among them being some who had been personally interested in all departments of mining for many years. At the risk of some repetition, we would here say that gold-mining has profited most those who have never engaged in it; that the cool-headed traders, brokers, bankers, and agriculturalists have reaped the real benefit growing out of the gold discoveries in Australia, not the eager, hard-working, excited digger himself. In short, we believe that the same amount of patient labor and steady application bestowed upon almost any other industry would yield a better return to the toiler.

We have spoken incidentally of Sandhurst, one of the famous gold-fields of Victoria, which was originally known by the name of Bendigo. This place, situated a hundred miles from Ballarat, more directly inland, has matured into an attractive and important city, well laid out into broad streets lined with ornamental trees, and containing many fine public and private edifices. Sandhurst possesses all the elements that go to form a progressive and intelligent community, having ample school facilities, churches, hotels, and charitable organizations. The population is an increasing one, and already numbers some thirty-five thousand. Its array of well-furnished shops affords a bright and attractive feature. The environs, unlike those of Ballarat, are rough and uncared-for, presenting many acres of deserted diggings, with deep holes, broken windlasses, ruined quartz-tubs, rusted and useless pieces of machinery, and a profusion of other mining débris. Alluvial or surface mining is entirely worked out in the vicinity of Sandhurst, but quartz raising and crushing still gives employment to thousands of laborers; and as there seems to be a comparatively unlimited supply of the gold-bearing rock, we can see no reason why the place should not go on prosperously for any length of time to come. There are here some of the most extensive works for reducing the quartz-rock that have ever been erected. The principal mine of the neighborhood has reached a depth of twenty-six hundred feet, fresh reefs of rich quartz having lately been struck and developed, concerning the existence of which there were no signs whatever at the surface of the land. We were told that a true reef had never been exhausted, or worked out in Australia, though alluvial deposits often cease to yield in a few months. The deep mine of which we have just spoken is the property of a wealthy Englishman named George Lansell, a noted gold-miner of Victoria.

About five miles from Sandhurst is the town of Eaglehawk, perched upon an eminence, having its own municipal government, and even aspiring to be a rival of Sandhurst; but it is really at present scarcely more than a suburb of that city. At Eaglehawk there are some exceptionally rich gold mines, where quartz is raised which we were told yields from four to five ounces of pure metal to the ton of rock handled. There are shafts here varying from five hundred to one thousand feet in depth, with the usual drifts and galleries. The depth of the shafts is being steadily increased, and new lateral workings started. The depth to which these mines in Victoria and elsewhere in Australia may be profitably worked is not yet demonstrated, though geologists until within a brief period have confidently asserted that beyond one hundred feet the quartz rock would not be found sufficiently rich to pay for the labor of raising it to the surface and crushing it. Theory and fact, however, have come into collision upon this point, as demonstrated both in California and Australia. The laws which govern these deposits are not understood, and the best-informed often find themselves at fault in their calculations. The mines do not invariably grow richer as they descend, but vary near the surface. "Twenty-five years of mining experience," said a Victorian to us, " have taught me that no one knows at what depth quartz lodes or reefs will be found to pay, and there is nothing to show that the quality or quantity of the yield of metal depends upon the depth from which it is taken." Statistics show all sorts of yield of gold at all depths; it is indeed as the working miners say regarding the gold, "Where it is, there it is, and no rule applies." We were told of the appointment of a Government commission in Melbourne not long ago, whose members travelled over the colony to inspect personally the mining operations, and make a proper report thereon. After due consideration these gentlemen prepared and published their report, with much official flourish, each member doubtless tincturing it with some favorite theory of his own. The result was simply ridiculous, as within a twelvemonth, and by practical results at the various mines which they had inspected, every deduction of their report was proved to be entirely wrong.

It is in this colony of Australia that the traveller finds the giant trees, considered to be one of the great wonders of our times, and which exceed in dimensions those grand conifers of California in which

Americans feel such pride. These big trees of Victoria are called the mountain ash, though why so named we do not understand, as they are not of that family. But they are certainly the tallest trees in the known world, often measuring four hundred feet and more in height, and from fifty to sixty feet in girth a couple of yards from the ground. When we say that these trees exceed in dimensions those of California, we refer especially to their height, inasmuch as the American trees equal them, if they do not in some instances surpass them, in circumference. The Australian trees rise a hundred feet more or less from the roots without putting forth a lateral branch. On beholding them one is not at first impressed by their exceptional size or monarch-like appearance; but they grow upon one by further observation. A trip of a hundred miles from Melbourne due east to Sale — a remarkably pleasant town of between three and four thousand inhabitants, situated on the Gippsland railroad — takes one to the region where these immense forest giants are to be seen, and at the same time introduces the traveller to some of the finest scenery in the mountain range of this district.

It is in this neighborhood that one finds the kangaroo in his wild state; but a good local guide is necessary to insure success in the search for these animals. Though the kangaroo, like everything else aboriginal, is gradually disappearing in Australia, the onslaught and ceaseless war which is waged against the wild dog, the only enemy except man which the kangaroo has to fear, leaves the latter a chance even for increase in some districts, as we found to be the case in Queensland. It is calculated that one kangaroo eats as much grass and consumes as much food generally as do five sheep, and consequently he is looked upon as an enemy, to be hunted with the one idea of exterminating him altogether. In roaming the woods one is almost sure to fall in with more or less of these animals. They are usually found sitting upright in circles of a dozen or more, as grave as though engaged in holding a formal council. Their short fore-paws hang limp before them, while their restless heads and delicate ears turn hither and thither in watchful care against surprise. Notwithstanding their huge paunch, big hind-quarters, and immense tail, there is something graceful and attractive about these creatures, even with all their proverbial awkwardness. When they are young they are as playful as kittens. Even when running away from pursuit, — a process performed by enormous leaps, often covering a rod at each flying jump, — there is a certain airy grace and harmony of movement attending their motions. Dogs and horses have more power of endurance than the kangaroo, and are thus enabled to run them down; but neither horse nor dog can achieve the same degree of speed for moderate distances. If the chase occurs in a wood where there are numerous obstacles, like heavy logs, the kangaroo is safe, since he can surmount all such impediments without diminution of speed.

In the forest glades of Victoria one becomes acquainted with some of the most interesting of the birds of Australia. It is said that very many of those which are now abundant are not indigenous, but have been introduced from time to time by the new-comers from Europe and elsewhere. At all events, the birds of this region are abundant enough now and of great variety, adding much to the charm of inland districts. The shrill whistle of the blue-jay saluted us constantly; and equally frequent were the monotonous notes of the green thrush. Now and then the confused utterances of the leather-head were heard, a peculiar bird resembling a small vulture. As to the screams of the cockatoos and parrots, they are at times quite deafening. There was observed one diminutive feathered creature called the diamond-bird, arrayed in gorgeous plumage, and having a rich dark crimson tail, while the body was mottled like the iris colors upon a blue pigeon's throat, or the surface of an opal. Now and again the small pheasant wren flitted by, lighting upon some delicate branch of tree or bush, with its long tail trailing behind it. One specimen of the lyre-bird was seen, though it is so shy and wild as to be seldom captured.

It is mainly to behold the big gum-trees, however, that one visits the Fernshaw Mountain district; and they alone richly repay the trouble of going thither. We were told of one fallen monarch which was measured by a government surveyor, which had a length upon the ground of four hundred and seventy-four feet. The Pyramid of Cheops is not so high as was this tree when it stood erect. The average height of these marvels is from three hundred and fifty to four hundred feet. They are situated in a valley protected from winds, and are favorably located to promote their growth, and also to preserve them from destruction by gales or sudden tornadoes, such as have prostrated some of the largest trees in our own valley of the Yosemite.

There are some picturesque lakes in Gippsland which deserve mention, separated from the sea only by narrow necks of land, though in some instances there are passages between navigable by small steamboats. The largest of these lakes is that known as Lake Corangamite, which is salt, though it has no visible connection with the sea. The great amount of evaporation which takes place here in the summer months leaves on its shores large quantities of salt crystals, the gathering of which forms an important local industry.

In these inland excursions large districts were seen devoted to the raising of grapes and the production of wine therefrom. We were told that the wine made from these Victoria vineyards was admitted to be the best produced in the country. Much land is also given up to the raising of hops, which recalled the thrifty fields of Kent, in England. There were seen here immense expanses of oats, which are mostly cut green,— that is, just before ripening,— for fodder. Together with these several interests, there were also plenty of copper and tin mines being worked; and we were informed by good authority that one third of the total area of the colony is believed to be occupied by gold-bearing quartz. Extraordinary as this assertion appears, it is fully credited by the author.

A most curious and remarkable example of bird-life and bird-instinct was pointed out to us, in the instance of what is known as the bower-bird. This peculiar little creature builds a cunning play-place, a tiny shady bower, which it ornaments with vines and high-colored feathers of other birds, besides the yellow blossoms of the wattle-tree and dainty ferns. In this ingeniously devised sylvan retreat the feathered architect runs about and holds a sort of carnival, to which he apparently invites others of his tribe. At all events a select company come hither and join the builders for an hour or so, chirping vigorously and strutting about together in a most ludicrously demonstrative manner.

Scarcely any of the animals found in other countries were native to this land. There were no apes, no ruminants, no lions, tigers, or wolves. We were told about the wild dog, already spoken of, familiarly known as the "dingo," which is such a serious pest to the sheep-raisers, and which closely resembles the Scotch collie. This creature is the wildest and fiercest animal found in the Australian bush, evincing a destructive propensity merely for the sake of spilling blood. Its habit is to kill a dozen sheep when it attacks a flock, though one would more than suffice to satisfy its hunger. It seizes the unresisting victim by the throat, and its fatal work is quickly accomplished. A price is placed upon the head of the dingo by Government, and there is a class of men who are particularly fond of hunting it, and who obtain a living by waging a constant war upon the species. Undoubtedly this animal was introduced here by Captain Cook when he landed a second time in the country, and a century of wild life has given to it a new nature. The hunters of the dingo also make rabbits a special object of onslaught, for which Government pays a liberal premium of so much per brace, the heads being required as evidence of their destruction. But all efforts to destroy these prolific creatures have so far proved inadequate.

A packet ship arrived from London with emigrants while we were at Melbourne. its passengers being of a very mixed character. Some few of them were doubtless real workers honestly desirous of benefiting their circumstances in a legitimate manner; but the majority seemed to be idlers, of little use to themselves and hardly desirable additions to the colony. These new arrivals appeared entirely unlike the emigrants who come in such vast numbers to our own shores from all parts of Europe. While a majority of these Australian immigrants were obviously from the lower classes of the big English cities, the arrivals in America consist mostly of those coming from the rural districts of Northern Europe.

As already intimated, characters which cannot be

whitewashed in England are often encouraged to emigrate to Australia. Originally such persons were sent hither by the courts; now they come by the persuasion of their friends. We believe there is enough of sterling worth and responsibility established in Australia to overrule the unfortunate elements thrown upon her shores by the inflow of questionable humanity. At all events such a class of immigration is the inevitable outgrowth of circumstances beyond the control of the colonists. They have so successfully lived down the early penal associations attached to their country, that the best result may be hoped for as regards this matter. Australia is certainly a good place to bring people to their true level. The shiftless and helpless quickly sink to the bottom, while energy and tact, whether in the low born or those from the higher walks of life, cause their possessors to rise to the surface and become a power in the land.

The author saw some examples of a sad and painful character in the cases of individuals who had been reared in luxury at home, in England, but who were nearly starving in Melbourne. They would willingly have worked their passage back to the old country, but as they could not be rated as able-bodied seamen, they could find no such chance. There is room and opportunity enough in Australia for any number of sober, hardy, frugal men and women who have a special business or regular calling. An industrious and worthy person is sure to make a good living there, and perhaps to realize a fortune; but he cannot *pick* it up, — he must *work* it up. That which comes by laborious effort and self-abnegation remains with us, and constitutes a lasting capital. The gold nuggets which are occasionally found here never amount to much as regards the benefit of the finder. It is upon the whole a fortunate day for the respectable immigrant who has any degree of ability, when he concludes to turn his back upon gold-digging and adopt some more legitimate business. The great elements of success are the same in Australia as in California, Africa, or Massachusetts; namely, steadiness of purpose, application, and temperance. One thing we would impress upon every one: let those who cannot resist the fascination of the bottle, avoid Australia; for it is the very hot-bed of dissipation, and no place for the weak and irresolute.

The laboring classes of Melbourne and Sydney especially make great efforts to prevent emigration from Europe, on the ground that it will have a tendency to reduce wages, — a view palpably narrow and contracted beyond all reason. There cannot be too many good immigrants; and any policy tending to limit their numbers is as short-sighted as most of the ignorant schemes of organized Labor Unions. Even a larger number of the despised Chinese would be desirable in the present state of things in Australia; but the landing fee of fifty dollars acts almost as prohibitory in regard to the Asiatic race, besides which all sorts of lawless impediments are instituted to operate against their well-being.

CHAPTER X.

From Melbourne to Adelaide. — Capital of South Australia. — New Gold-Fields. — Agricultural Interests. — City Institutions. — Inducements to Immigrants. — Public Buildings. — A City of Churches. — Australian Ladies. — Interior of the Country. — Irrigation. — German Settlers. — The Botanical Gardens. — West Australia. — Perth the Capital. — The Pearl Fisheries. — Commercial Advantages Considered.

WE shall now leave Victoria and take the reader into another colony, by no means less interesting than those already visited. The distance from Melbourne to Adelaide, the capital of South Australia, is about the same as that from Sydney to Melbourne, — say, six hundred miles. Australia is an immense territory, and its capital cities are a long way apart. The cars upon this route are constructed upon both the American and English plan, and one is not annoyed by having to change cars to accommodate a difference in the gauge, as upon the Sydney route, where for this purpose he is aroused at midnight on the borders of Victoria. On passing the limit of South Australia the traveller finds his watch to be twenty-five minutes too fast, and makes the necessary alteration to accommodate the local time in accordance with western longitude. It is a tiresome journey, — or at least we found it so. There were few first-class passengers, none of whom particularly interested a stranger beyond general observation; moreover the road passes through what is called the Ninety-mile Desert, which is desolate and barren indeed. The miles seemed interminable; and it was a great relief at last when a wooded country was reached, and there came into view open, well-fenced fields, with here and there small groups of choice breeds of cattle and sheep, and an occasional neat homestead.

In the course of this journey the Murray Bridge was crossed. This iron structure spans the breadth of that great Australian water-way here known as the Murray River, but which finds its source thousands of miles to the north, in Queensland, where it is known as the Darling River. After leaving Murray Bridge two large engines were necessary to draw our train up the steep incline among the hills and mountains which separate Adelaide from her eastern territory. These mechanical giants puffed and panted with an almost human expression, in their vigorous struggle to drag the train forward, — now and again hovering upon the very verge of inability, and then, as it seemed to us, by putting forth renewed energy and extraordinary effort, pressing forward and finally surmounting the steep way. The aspect of the scenery rapidly changed for the better as we advanced, and our spirits rose accordingly. Everything looked bright and thrifty. Gardens, orchards, well-cultivated fields, and pleasant roadside stations, with the summer residences of the citizens of Adelaide, were rapidly passed, until Mount Lofty station was reached and the descent toward the plains began. The traveller was soon gratified by a bird's-eye view of the capital of South Australia, lying spread out upon the plain, with the broad sea beyond glittering with mottled sunshine.

Adelaide is surrounded by an amphitheatre of wooded hills rearing their heads not far away from the city, and forms a very fine picture when thus approached. The capital is so perfectly level that to be seen to advantage it must be looked upon as a whole from some favorable elevation. Though this colony is called South Australia, it should be known as Central Australia in respect to its actual geographical position. It is destined in the near future to merit the name of the granary of the country, being already largely and successfully devoted to agriculture. This pursuit is followed in no circumscribed manner, but in a large and liberal style, like that of our best Western farmers. Immense tracts of land are also devoted to stock-raising, for the purpose of furnishing "dead beef" for shipment to England in fresh condition. South Australia contains nearly a million square miles, and is therefore ten times larger than Victoria, and fifteen times the size of England. It extends northward from the temperate zone, so that nearly one half of its area lies within the tropics, while it has a coast-line of five hundred miles along the great Southern Ocean. A vast portion of its interior is uninhabited and indeed unexplored. The total population of the whole colony is about four hundred thousand. Wheat, wool, wine, copper, and meat are at present the chief exports.

Though gold has been found in this province to a very large extent, it is not so abundant here as in other parts of Australia, — and yet since these notes were begun new gold-fields have been discovered in this section which are reported to be exceedingly rich. Statistics show that somewhat over seventeen million pounds sterling in gold have been exported from South Australia since its first discovery here. One mine alone, known as the Moonta, has paid its shareholders in dividends the large sum of twelve hundred thousand pounds sterling. Gold-digging as a business, however, grows less and less attractive in the colony, though the precious metal must continue to be produced here for many years to come, by well-organized companies who possess ample machinery for raising and crushing the quartz rock. But good wages, equalling the average earned by miners, are now paid here by a dozen easier and more legitimate occupations, — among the rest the large vineyards which produced last year over three million gallons of pure native wine. The great trouble is to procure laborers at all, notwithstanding the liberal scale of wages paid. No community or section of country has ever yet reached a permanent success, according to the usually accepted idea of success, upon what may in this connection be denominated a gold basis.

"Let us cherish no delusions," said a San Francisco preacher on a certain occasion; "no society has ever been able to organize itself in a satisfactory manner on gold-bearing soil. Even Nature herself is deceitful: she corrupts, seduces, and betrays man; she laughs at his labors, she turns his toil into gambling and his word into a lie!" The preacher's deductions have proved true in California, South Africa, New Zealand, and Australia. And yet we have freely admitted in these pages that the finding of gold mines has stimulated labor, immigration, and manly activity in many directions, and has thus indirectly been the agent of good in other than its own field.

As we find gold king in Victoria, so in Adelaide we have pastoral millionnaires. Some of the men who have become enriched by this means possess fortunes of over two million pounds sterling, and have gone back to England to enjoy their wealth in their native land; others, and these are the larger portion of the successful settlers, still remain here, promoting the local interests of the colony.

Adelaide, thus named for the queen of William IV., we found to be the depot of a large and growing trade in wool and grain especially derived from the fertile agricultural district of which it is the capital, and is furnished with numerous arterial railways to bring these products to market. We were told by reliable parties here that there are at present about four million acres of land under the plough. Preference is universally given to the grain produced in this colony, because of its uniform excellence. New South Wales and Victoria hamper their people in the use of this grain by the imposition of most unreasonable and aggravating tariff laws. "Protection," said an earnest citizen of Melbourne to us, "does anything but protect; it makes much of our food cost us twenty per cent more than it would naturally if the ordinary laws of trade were permitted to adjust themselves." The mass of the people favor free-trade, but the leaders and the officials favor high tariff, for they realize a living through the collecting of dues that arise under its provisions. It was admitted to the author by local political economists that it costs fifty per cent of the aggregate sum collected to keep "the machine" moving, — a fact which alone forms a strong argument against the entire system.

Adelaide, with a population of a hundred and fifty thousand, has a noble University, quite equal in standing to that of any city in the country. When we remember how youthful she is, it becomes a matter of no small surprise that Adelaide has achieved such a condition of progress in all the appointments and possessions which go to make up a great city of modern times. This remark will apply indeed to all the Australian capitals, none of which are deficient in hospitals, libraries, schools, asylums, art galleries, and charitable institutions generally. Few of the European cities of twice the size of these in Australia can boast a more complete outfit in all that goes to promote a true civilization. We must not forget, however, that a city established in the nineteenth century has a lamp to guide its feet in the experience of all who have gone before, — thus enabling it to start upon a wise and proper basis from the very outset.

Though South Australia presents little of the glamour of auriferous fields to attract new settlers, those who come here are as a rule of the best class. This colony offers officially the most liberal inducements to new-comers, while the natural advantages of its agricultural and stock-raising districts are unsurpassed in either of the other colonies. A land-order is given gratuitously to every qualified person upon his arrival at Adelaide, which is good for one hundred dollars for each adult, and fifty dollars for each child, at the Government Land Office; besides which other liberal inducements are offered that are calculated to interest representatives especially of the agricultural class of Great Britain.

King William Street is a broad and elegant thoroughfare, the principal one of the city. It is lined on either side with grand palatial buildings, — banks, insurance offices, warehouses, shops, and hotels. On this street also are the Post-Office and the Town Hall. One looks about at the solid and pleasing architectural effect of all these buildings with no small degree of surprise. Everywhere within the limits of the city, especially extending eastward and westward of the Post-Office, spacious edifices are to be found, either completed and occupied or in course of construction. The material used for building purposes consists very largely of a handsome white stone, which produces a remarkably cheerful general effect. By ascending North Adelaide Hill one gets an admirable view of all the space between Mount Lofty and the city proper, which space is dotted with villas, gardens, and pleasant domestic surroundings, and profusely ornamented with trees. There is an aspect of thrift and business prosperity in the very atmosphere; civic and suburban improvement is the order of the day. The churches of all denominations are numerous and handsome. Comparisons may be odious, and especially so as regards different portions of these colonies, between which there is rampant a spirit of exaggerated and endless jealousy; but we cannot refrain from saying that to the casual observer Adelaide manifests greater evidences of enterprise and rapid growth than either Sydney, Melbourne, or Brisbane. The citizens are especially alive to all educational interests. There is here a Minister of Education, a Training and Model School, three Colleges, and an ample number of common and primary schools. The South Australian Institute and Museum is designed for the promotion of art studies, science, and philosophy.

King William Street is nearly two miles long, certainly rivalling in many respects Collins Street in Melbourne, and is more elegant and effective as a whole than George Street in Sydney. Some enterprising parties should introduce a few hundred Hansom cabs into the city, to take the place of the hideous four-wheeled vehicles which are drawn about town by two horses. Victoria Square, situated in the very heart of Adelaide, is a busy quarter, where at a single glance one has a view of the principal public buildings, including the Town Hall, a noble structure, the colonnade of which is built over the surrounding foot-way. Opposite this building is the General Post-Office, the main features of which are like the Post-Office of Sydney, — a tall square tower rising from the centre, which seemed in both instances quite out of place. The city is remarkable for the compactness of its business centre. Queen Street runs from bank to bank of the river, so that the masts of the shipping are visible from either end of the thoroughfare.

The city proper is separated from its suburbs by a wide belt of park lands, and all the approaches are lined with thrifty ornamental trees. Great liberality and good judgment presided over the laying out of Adelaide. All the streets are broad and regular, running north and south, east and west. There are no mysterious labyrinths, dark lanes, or blind alleys in the city; all the avenues cross each other at right angles and are uniform in width. Somehow we missed the irregular ways of old European cities and those of the far East, where one can get delightfully lost and bewildered now and then.

Adelaide has been called the city of churches, and as already intimated it certainly is well supplied in that respect; but it is still better entitled to be called the city of public parks.

There was a grand Industrial Exhibition open at Adelaide during our visit, to which all the sister colonies had contributed; and hosts of strangers were consequently attracted to the town, imparting a business aspect to everything and a general life to its streets which doubtless was not its normal condition. Still, be this as it may, the capital of South Australia is growing steadily in population and material wealth. The present Exhibition Building stands in the Adelaide Park lands, fronting North Terrace, adjacent to the Botanical Gardens. A direct line of railway, seven miles long, connects the Exhibition with the wharves at Port Adelaide, where ships of the largest tonnage can lie at the pier and discharge their cargoes. The completeness, thorough organization, and amazing variety of this Exhibition of Industries here in the South Seas was a subject of great surprise and admiration to us. It is not, however, our intention to go into a description of the Exhibition, but it was certainly worthy of all commendation.

The Australian ladies of this section are essentially unlike their sisterhood of the colonies in general. They are characterized by a bright, buoyant, piquant manner which charms and captivates the stranger who is so fortunate as to enjoy their proverbial hospitality. Without being in the least flippant, they are debonair and winsome in the display of their many accomplishments, which always embrace music, drawing, and dancing. They are more like the women of America in height and general figure than their English progenitors. They have none of the English stoutness which indicates a plethora of blood and vigor; indeed, there was a marked delicacy generally apparent in the matter of health, which is to be attributed doubtless to climatic influences,— and yet statistics show a low scale of mortality in Adelaide, as in most parts of Australia. Regarding amusements, dancing is a favorite one, quite as much so here as among the ladies of Spain. Among gentlemen belonging to what is termed the best society in Adelaide, it is a fact worth remarking that one finds no idlers; all have some legitimate calling, and would evidently feel ill at ease without it. Idling is not popular; each citizen is expected to contribute in some form to the general condition of thrift and progress, as well as to do his share toward developing the natural resources of the State. This is imperative in a youthful colony, and not out of place in any community.

It is believed that the interior of the continent, which is largely embraced within the territory of South Australia, was at a comparatively recent period covered by a great inland ocean. Here are found the mammoth bones of animals of the marsupial species, now extinct, which have afforded much interest to scientists. On some portions of these plains it is said that the heat absorbed from the sun in the daytime is radiated from the soil at night to such a degree as to be insufferable to human beings. The soil is represented to be at such times like burning coal; and when the air moves over it, an effect is produced as from a furnace, or from a sirocco blowing off the coast of Africa. The effect of these winds is occasionally felt in Sydney and Melbourne; and while it lasts, humanity becomes inert, and exertion impossible. It rarely continues, however, more than three days, and in the vicinity of Adelaide is seldom experienced more than twice in a season.

Several lakes are represented to exist in the interior, as shown by maps of Australia, — among them Lake Torrens, Lake Eyre, Lake Gardiner, and Lake Amadeus, apparently covering large areas; but these localities are little more than muddy swamps or salt marshes, which are completely dried up in summer. Their level is believed to be considerably below that of the sea; and it has been proposed to cut a canal from Torrens to Spencer Gulf: if that proved advantageous, then Lake Eyre could be connected with comparatively little labor. Spencer Gulf is the deepest indentation upon the south coast, and would flood these swamps with permanent water, rendering them not only navigable, but producing a favorable change in the climate. At present, during the summer season the thermometer rises in the lake region to 110° and even to 115° Fahrenheit.

This district is regarded as a desert waste because of its want of a permanent supply of water, being "eaten up," to use a local phrase, with drought. And yet this want of water at certain seasons while there is an abundance at others is a matter so obviously within the ability of the people to remedy, that one cannot sympathize much with them in their present deprivation. Why the intelligent means of irrigation so well known and so thoroughly tested elsewhere are not adopted here, it is difficult to understand. We heartily agree with the position assumed in regard to this matter by a certain English Bishop, of whom we were told. He came to Australia to make it his home; and being applied to in a dry season to issue a circular-prayer for rain, he answered that a fair average quantity of water fell upon the land already, and that he declined to petition the Almighty to work a miracle until the colonists had themselves done what they could to preserve the rains by constructing proper reservoirs and sinking artesian wells. These people must not expect that Hercules will help them, unless they first put their own shoulders to the wheel.

The river Darling shows well upon paper, and judged by its aspect on the map it is a river which might rank with the Volga and the Amazon. But the truth is that it forms a watercourse dependent at present upon floods, admitting of navigation for hundreds of miles at certain seasons, and at others being as dry as the Arno at Florence or the Manzanares at Madrid. By a series of dams and canals this river might be navigable all the year round. The same remark applies to several of its tributaries, and to rivers generally running toward the inland centres and flowing into the Murray. The governments of the several colonies have long realized the importance and the necessity of a grand and comprehensive system of irrigation. They seem to be never tired of talking about the matter; but the time has now come for action. Some of the most enterprising of the pioneers as they have advanced inland have built dams on the small tributaries of the two rivers named, and have found it to pay them tenfold. Some have sunk artesian wells, and have in their turn reaped commensurate advantages. We were shown great reaches of country where ten years ago cattle would have starved had they been turned out to find a living there, but which now support large herds of domestic animals.

Africa's interior is scarcely less mapped out and explored than Central Australia. There are thousands of square miles upon which the foot of a white man has never trod. Tartary has its steppes, America its prairies, Egypt its deserts, and Australia its "scrub." The plains so called are covered by a low-growing bush, compact and almost impenetrable in places, composed of a dwarf eucalyptus. The appearance of a large reach of this scrub is desolate indeed, the underlying soil being a sort of yellow sand which one would think could surely produce nothing else. We were told of one large section of South Australia ten thousand miles square, which is solely covered with this scrub. "Yet," said our informant, himself an agriculturist of experience and a large landholder, "experiment has shown that if a watercourse were turned upon this ground and the scrub cleared away, it would give us a soil nearly as fertile as the valley of the Nile." And he added: "After a year or two more of useless talk, irrigation will be applied in all directions."

The climate of Adelaide and the surrounding country is of much greater warmth than that of the region about Brisbane, Sydney, or Melbourne. It is not uncommon for the thermometer to register 100° in the shade during the summer months. The vegetable products are almost identical with those of South Africa, and the soil is equally productive, yielding crop after crop with no signs of exhaustion. The food of the common people is cheap, abundant, and good. Mutton and beef do not cost one tenth as much as is charged for them in England or America, while bread is but four cents per pound. The flour produced here we were told won prizes wherever it was exhibited, and was considered as ranking with the very best manufactured anywhere. All kinds of vegetables are also cheap, and thanks to the Chinamen they are also in good supply: no one but John pretends to raise them. Everybody eats meat three times a day, rich and poor; but of the cooking,— well, as we cannot say anything complimentary about it, we will not dilate upon this theme.

The large number of German residents in and about Adelaide is particularly observable, and whole villages were found to exist in South Australia where

German was the one language spoken. This people form the best class of settlers, for they come hither with a well-considered purpose, almost always in the direction of agricultural enterprise; and this they pursue undeviatingly. Many of them are from the Rhine districts of Germany, and interest themselves in the planting and culture of the grape and in wine-making, having brought with them a special and valuable experience obtained in their native land.

The large, well-kept parks which surround this capital of South Australia form a magnificent drive, eight or ten miles long, outside of which are the villas and pleasant flower-gardens of the citizens, where one sees tropical fruits growing in great abundance, — including the orange, lemon, citron, pineapple, and the like. Some of the floral displays were truly gorgeous, embracing the flaring warratah and the glowing banksias, decked with curious and lovely foliage. Here and there were to be seen the Norfolk Island Pine, of which one never tires, and which is a great favorite all over this country. It branches straight out from the trunk with a succession of hard prickly leaves inclining upward at the ends. Its color is always of the deepest green.

The Botanical Gardens of Adelaide cover a hundred and thirty acres, the hedges of which are formed of a picturesque variety of yellow cactus, acacias, magnolias, and myrtles. Here we first saw the Australian bottle-tree, which is native only to these colonies. It receives its name from its resemblance in shape to a junk-bottle. This tree has the property of storing up water in its hollow trunk, — a well-known fact, which has often proved a providential supply for thirsty travellers in a country so subject to drought. Here also was seen the correa, with its stiff stem and prickly leaves, bearing a curious string of little delicate pendulous flowers, red, orange, and white, not unlike the fuchsia in form. The South Sea myrtle was especially attractive, appearing in flower with round clustering bunches, spangled with white stars. The styphelia, a heath-like plant, was a surprise to us, with its green flower, the first of its species the author had seen. We were shown a specimen of the sandrach-tree from Africa, which is almost imperishable, and from which the ceilings of mosques are exclusively made; it is supposed to be the shittim-wood of Scripture. The Indian cotton-tree loomed up beside the South American aloe, this last with its bayonet-like leaves, ornamented in wavy lines like the surface of a Toledo blade. The groupings of these exotics, natives of regions so far apart upon the earth's surface, yet quite domesticated and acclimated here, formed an incongruous picture and an interesting theme for contemplation.

West Australia, of which Perth is the capital, is eight hundred miles in width and thirteen hundred long from north to south, actually covering about one third of the continent. It embraces all that portion lying to the westward of the one hundred and twenty-ninth meridian of east longitude, having an area of about one million square miles, — or, to make a familiar comparison, it is eight times as large as the United Kingdom of Great Britain and Ireland. It has but few towns, ports, or settled districts, and Perth itself has less than eleven thousand inhabitants. The city is represented to be an attractive place, possessing a fine climate. Its oranges and tropical fruits generally are said to be excellent. It is situated on the Swan River, better known locally as Perth Waters. This river runs from Fremantle to Perth, and is a noble water-way, commercially spoiled however by a dangerous ledge of rocks about six feet under water, which shuts off the entrance from the sea. Of course, in due time dynamite will settle the business for that ledge.

The population of the entire colony known as West Australia is at the present writing hardly forty thousand, scattered along the sea-board or within a hundred miles of it. The results accomplished by this small number of inhabitants show very clearly of what the country is capable, and indicate what it would doubtless yield under more generous cultivation. The colony exported last year over a million dollars' worth of wool, besides copper, sandal-wood, timber, cattle, and so on. Late statistics show that there are over two millions of sheep in this section of the country, and we were told that it could support as many more as are found in Queensland and New South Wales united.

Pearl-oysters abound on the coast of West Australia, and pearl-shells are a ready source of income to the people, being exported in large quantities. These are most freely procured at the north. There are merchants in Sydney who annually fit out boats of from six to ten tons each, and send them to this locality for the pearl-oyster fishing. This is best prosecuted nearest to Torres Strait, which separates Australia from New Guinea. Next to the great island-continent itself, New Guinea is the largest island in the world, being three hundred and sixty miles wide by thirteen hundred miles in length; but while Australia as a whole is so remarkably healthy, not even the African Gold Coast is so dangerous to health as New Guinea. Its flat, densely-wooded, swampy coast is simply deadly to white men, and even the natives suffer constantly from low fever. These natives are probably the most barbaric of any savages living in this nineteenth century; they have no notion of even the rudest agricultural operations, living altogether on fish, berries, and roots.

The pearl-fisheries of which we were speaking give employment to a singular class of laborers, consisting of Malays, Lascars, South Sea Islanders, Australian aborigines, runaway sailors, and West Indian negroes. Formerly the oysters were raised from four or five fathoms' depth solely by divers, but dredging has lately been adopted with good success. The pearl-oyster is a large mollusk, the shell weighing sometimes as much as eight pounds. The divers are paid fair wages, and whatever pearls they find become their perquisites, it being the shells alone that the employer seeks to secure. These, when properly dried and cleansed, he ships to Europe, where they bring an average of five hundred dollars per ton. When diving is depended upon for raising the oysters, a boat is very fully equipped, and the captain, who is the diver, descends in a full set of armor. Air-pumps supply the necessary atmosphere to enable him to remain for half an hour and more under water, during which time he fills the canvas bags which are sent down to him empty and drawn up by those remaining in the boat. Considerable capital is embarked in this business. One enemy the divers have to look out for is the shark. These dreadful creatures do not swarm on the coast of West Australia, but are nevertheless sometimes seen there; and when that is the case the diver signals his crew to draw him to the surface, for though he is armed with a long knife, he could hardly cope with these ravenous monsters in their own element.

The coast-line of the colony is set down as being three thousand miles in length on the Indian Ocean, and some hundreds upon the Southern Ocean. The country is known to be auriferous, but to what extent it is impossible to say. There are two or three hundred miles of railroad here belonging to the Government, and more is under contract to be built in this year of 1888, covering short routes between comparatively populous points. Immigration is encouraged by liberal appropriations, and the population is increasing steadily if not rapidly. The late discovery of gold-fields at the Kimberly district on the Fitzroy River has already turned public attention thither, and settlers and adventurers are sure to follow fast. Government survey has shown that on the territory traversed by the Mary, Margaret, Elvira, and Ord rivers an immense number of gold-bearing quartz-reefs exist, besides surface diggings along the river courses and valley from which "good color," as miners express it, can be got from the sand almost anywhere. Already diggers have gone to work successfully in this region, where it seems the country is well-watered most of the year, and where the Government surveyors say there is no trouble in storing water against possible drought. All these facts simply signify that Perth, the western capital of the colonies, is in the near future to go through the same experience as have Melbourne, Adelaide, Ballarat, and Brisbane, and that she is sure by and by to become like them a great and prosperous city. What is called a "rush" in the colonies has not yet taken place in the Kimberly district, but there is a steady trend of gold-miners thither, and one or two extraordinary "finds" would draw to this part of the country as eager a throng as ever swarmed in New South Wales or Victoria bent upon the same errand.

Were we to write more in detail of West Australia it would be simply from what we learned through intelligent persons at Melbourne, Sydney, and Adelaide. We did not visit Perth. A glance at the map will show the reader how great are the distances between the capitals of Australia, over which we traversed hither and thither three thousand miles and more. From Adelaide to Perth, overland, would be a distance of fifteen hundred miles, which would require to be accomplished mostly on horseback. By water across the Australian Bight and Indian Ocean, it would be a voyage of about the same length.

The climate of West Australia was represented to us as being extremely fine; and one great pride of the people there is the variety and abundance of the wild-flowers which cover hill and dale near the coast-line of the entire colony. The pearl-fisheries to which we have alluded produce some of the most valuable gems that find their way to the markets of the world; for though by general consent the choicest pearls come from Ceylon and the Persian Gulf, those found on the west coast of Australia are deemed by many equal to the best. Beautiful specimens were shown to us in Melbourne which we could not recognize as in any way inferior to the Oriental gems that bring such fabulous prices in Paris and London. In a jeweller's shop on Collins Street we saw several which had come from the region near Torres Strait, and which were valued at a hundred pounds sterling each, and one which on account of its size was prized at two hundred pounds, it having already been sold for that sum.

On preparing to leave Australia proper, some facts were noted as deduced from careful observation and diligent inquiry. It seems that this country can command the markets of the world in three articles at least, — wool, meat, and wine. For producing these she has the advantages of breadth of territory, of climate, and of general adaptation beyond those of any other land. At the present writing it would be safe to add gold to the other three staples, since Australia, in combination with Tasmania and New Zealand, is producing more of it annually than any other country in the world. In competition with the United States in the home market, — that is, in England, — Australia is handicapped by some eight thousand miles of distance, and must therefore count just so much relative additional cost of transportation. But Australia can produce two of the special articles named, — meat and wool, — at least ten per cent cheaper than our own country. As regards cereals, Australia is capable of raising at present double the amount of grain which she can consume. In that staple, however, the United States and some other countries can compete with her for reasons which favor them, independent of the additional distance she must overcome to reach a market.

CHAPTER XI.

From Australia to Tasmania. — The River Tamar.— Bird Life. — City of Launceston. — Aborigines of the Island. — Tattooing. — Van Diemen's Land. — A Beautiful Country. — Rich Mines. — Mount Bischoff. — Down in a Gold Mine. — From Launceston to Hobart. — Rural Aspects. — Capital of Tasmania. — Street Scenes. — A Former Penal Depot. — Mount Wellington. — Personal Beauty. — An Unbecoming Fashion.

From Adelaide and Perth let us turn our steps toward another of this group of British colonies in the South Sea. To reach Tasmania one takes a coasting steamer at Melbourne, passing down the river Yarra-Yarra, the muddiest of water-ways, until Bass Strait is reached, across which the course is due south for a hundred and twenty miles. This is a reach of ocean-travel which for boisterousness and discomfort can be said to rival the English Channel. As the coast of Tasmania is approached, a tall light-house, one hundred and forty feet in height, first attracts the attention, — designating the mouth of the Tamar River. The land formed a lee for the steamer as we approached it, giving us smooth water at last, whereupon the strained muscles of the body gradually relaxed, and it was delightful to be once more upon an even keel. At sea the human body is constantly struggling in the vain effort to preserve its equilibrium.

During our short but tumultuous voyage across Bass Strait our steamer was often surrounded by a great variety of sea-birds, — among which were the Cape-pigeon, the stormy petrel, and the gannet, which last is the largest of ocean birds next to the albatross. On drawing still nearer to the shore flocks of pelicans were observed upon the rocks, and that most awkward of birds, the penguin, was seen in idle groups. The penguin is a good swimmer, but his apologetic wings are not intended for flying. As these birds stand upright, they always suggest the unpleasant idea of men with arms amputated above the elbows.

The winding Tamar with its tree-covered islands, green headlands, and bold background of undulating hills affords a varied and beautiful picture. Beyond the nearest range of hills was seen a second and much higher series, whose tops were covered with snow. Our passage of the Strait had been partly made in the night, and as we entered the mouth of the river the sun rose, turning these frosty peaks into sparkling crowns. The rise and fall of the tide in the Tamar is quite remarkable, being characterized by a difference of some fourteen feet.

It is singular that no enthusiastic traveller has written of the great beauty of this river of Tasmania, which deserves the highest appreciation for its natural loveliness and interesting variety of scenery. True, it has the disadvantage of extreme tides, which at one hour of the day expand it into broad, lake-like proportions, and at another reduce it to a narrow, intricate channel, disfigured by unsightly mud-banks and half-submerged ledges; but nevertheless, for a large portion of the twenty-four hours it is a scene of diversified beauty. Even when the receding tide has left so much of rock and soil uncovered, one is rendered picturesque by varied bird-life, and the other by large reaches of bright-green sea-vegetation. Here and there isolated houses dot the shore, surrounded by well-cultivated fields, — not temporary cabins, such as prevail through the inland districts of Australia, but neat and permanent structures, consisting of comfortable dwellings and large barns, with other appropriate buildings. These barns signify the necessity in Tasmania of affording a shelter in winter for domestic animals, while at the north we had not seen such a structure in the entire country from Brisbane to Adelaide.

We pass up the Tamar River through its winding channel for a distance of forty miles before coming in sight of the harbor and town of Launceston. The many tall, smoking chimney-shafts which meet the eye indicate that the town is busy smelting ores dug from the contiguous mineral hills and valleys. Approaching it in the same manner in which we first came to Parametta, at the head of river navigation, it was natural to compare the aspect of that drowsy though picturesque place with this vigorous, wide-awake community. Launceston is no Sleepy Hollow, but is a pleasant and thrifty little city, slightly addicted to earthquakes and their attendant inconveniencies. The place is named for a town in Cornwall, England, and the Tamar from a river of the same name also in that country. At our hotel numerous cracks in the walls and ceilings were silent but significant tokens of what might be expected to occur at almost any moment; but it was observed that the residents do not give this subject a second thought.

We have left Australia proper far behind, but the Bass Strait which separates that country from **Tasmania** is evidently of comparatively modern formation. The similarity of the vegetation, minerals, fauna, and flora of the two countries shows that this island must at some time in the long-past ages have been connected with the mainland. And yet the aborigines of Tasmania were a race quite distinct from those of Australia, — so different, indeed, as only to resemble them in color. They were a well-formed, athletic people, with brilliant eyes, curly hair, flat noses, and elaborately tattooed bodies. This ingenious and barbaric ornamentation of the body, practised by isolated savage races, seems to have been universal among the inhabitants of the Pacific Islands, though the great distances which separate them, as well as the lack of all ordinary means of intercommunication, would lead to the belief that they could not have borrowed the idea from one another. We are also reminded that singularly enough the rite of circumcision has been found to exist among some of the most completely isolated tribes of the Pacific, which causes the ethnologist to exclaim in wonder whence these savages could have got the idea. The isolation of the Samoans is so complete that one is half inclined to believe their own tradition that they originally sprang from the sea; and yet this people are even more elaborately tattooed than the natives of the Feejee Islands.

The Tasmanian aborigines " wore no clothing whatever when first discovered, leaving even those parts of the person exposed which an innate sense of decency causes most savages to conceal. They hunted the kangaroo with spears, and brought down birds with a heavy whirling stick," says an old chronicler; but whether he means by "a heavy whirling stick" to indicate the boomerang, we cannot say. If these savages possessed that ingenious instrument, it would show that they must have been more or less intimate with the Australian aborigines, who doubtless invented it. They are said to have been low in the scale of barbarism; but they were not stupid, lighting fires by the friction of two pieces of dry wood, and roasting their fowls, fish, and prisoners of war before eating them. They were openly addicted to cannibalism to the very last, until association with the whites gradually ended this barbarism. They however secretly practised infanticide until formally interfered with by the laws of the white invaders.

So late as sixty years ago there were three or four thousand of these people still in existence in Tasmania, but to-day not one soul is living to represent the race; civilization to them has indeed proved to be an active agent of destruction. They were bold and independent, prompt to resent an injury, but very poorly provided with the means of avenging themselves. Their weapons were mere toys when compared with the fire-arms of the whites. The war constantly waged between the two races was most unequal, and ended only in the extermination of the natives. These savages had to deal largely with escaped prisoners and ex-convicts, who were hardly less savage, thinking no more of shooting a black man than they would of shooting a kangaroo; and it is affirmed that this class of whites banded together and hunted the aborigines as they would wild beasts. No wonder that the natives retaliated in kind, and that when they found an unprotected family of whites they savagely destroyed women and children, and burned down their homes. Thus mutual destruction went on, the whites being annually reinforced by numbers from across the sea, and the barbaric natives dwindling rapidly away.

When the country cast off the disgrace of being a penal colony, the name it bore was very judiciously changed from Van Diemen's Land to that of Tasmania, in honor of its first discoverer, Abel Janssen Tasman, the famous Dutch navigator of the seventeenth century. We should perhaps qualify the words "first discoverer." Tasman was the first accredited discoverer, but he was less entitled to impart his name to this beautiful island than were others. Captain Cook, with characteristic zeal and sagacity, explored, surveyed, and described it, whereas Tasman scarcely more than sighted it. However, any name was preferable to that of Van Diemen's Land, which had become the synonym for a penal station, and with which is associated the memory of some of the most outrageous and murderous acts of cruelty for which a civilized government was ever responsible.

The whole island has now a population of about one hundred and thirty thousand, and a total area of over twenty-four thousand square miles, being really as much a part of Australia as Ceylon is of India, and sustaining the same relative geographical position. As Ceylon is called the pearl of the continent it so nearly adjoins, so Tasmania may justly be called the jewel of Australia. The climate is so equable and healthy that it bears the name among the Australians of the Eden of the Colonies. Its size is not quite that of Ireland, one hundred and seventy miles long by a hundred and sixty in width. There are no extremes of heat and cold, the winter mean being 47° Fahrenheit, and that of summer 65°. Lying so much nearer the Antarctic Circle it is of course cooler than the continent, but the influence of its sea surroundings renders its climate more equable. For many years it has formed a popular summer resort for the citizens of Sydney and Melbourne, as well as of other portions of the mainland. It may be the result of a local prejudice, but it is universally admitted that its native-born women are remarkable for personal beauty: we mean those born here of European parents.

The general aspect of the country is that of being occupied by thrifty farmers of advanced ideas, such as carry on their calling understandingly, much more like well-populated America than like Australia. Our native fruits — apples, peaches, pears, and the like — thrive here in such abundance as to form a prominent item in the exports, besides promoting a large and profitable industry in the packing of preserved fruits, which are in universal use in Australia and New Zealand. These canned fruits have an excellent and well-deserved reputation, there being an extensive demand for them on shipboard. Here also we saw enormous trees, with a circumference of eighty feet near the ground and a height of three hundred and fifty feet. Fern-trees, with their graceful palm-like formation, are frequently seen thirty feet in height. The country is well wooded, and traversed by pleasant watercourses; is singularly fertile, and rich in good harbors, especially upon the eastern coast. In short its hills, forests, and plains afford a pleasing variety of scenery, while its rich pastures invite the stock-breeder to reap a goodly harvest in the easiest and most profitable manner. The familiar description which occurs in Deuteronomy seems to apply exactly to this favored island: "For the Lord thy God bringeth thee into a good land; a land of brooks of water, of fountains and depths that spring out of valleys and hills; a land of wheat and barley, and vines and fig-trees, and pomegranates; a land of oil-olive and honey; a land wherein thou shalt eat bread without scarceness, — thou shalt not lack anything in it ; a land whose stones are iron, and out of whose hills thou mayest dig brass."

Tasmania is already largely occupied for the purpose of sheep-runs and wool-raising, and is studded with lovely homesteads carefully fenced in, the grounds being covered with fruit and ornamental trees. There seemed to us scarcely an acre of waste land to be seen in passing through the country upon travelled routes. The roads in many districts are lined with thrifty hedges symmetrically trimmed, consisting sometimes of the brilliant yellow gorse, and often of the double, stocky species of geranium in scarlet bloom. This species, which is not particularly fragrant, grows almost like a wild scrub here, requiring little or no cultivation; the more it is trimmed down the more stocky it becomes, until a hedge of it is quite impenetrable.

The interior of Tasmania develops into a mountain range of from two to five thousand feet in height, while its valleys and plains give support and ample pasturage to two million five hundred thousand sheep, not to enumerate the large herds of horned cattle which also abound. The wool produced upon the island has long been a favorite in the market on account of its uniformity and general excellence, always commanding the best prices. In and about the mountain ranges, gold, tin, silver, copper, and coal abound, so that the land teems with undeveloped mineral wealth, besides being full of beautiful lakes and fertile valleys.

Tasmania indeed might well be the Elysium depicted by Hesiod and Pindar, the Island of the Blest in the far Western Ocean. As a whole it pleased us greatly. The women were handsome, the children bright-eyed and rosy-cheeked, the men dignified and intelligent. The dwellings were neat and substantial, the grounds and gardens trim and picturesque. The walls were ivy-grown, and the fields divided by hedges. Prosperity and good taste were observable everywhere, presenting a succession of landscapes like those of populous New England. The roads are equal to the best European highways, having been built at great expense by convict labor, winding through fields that recall, as we have said, the finest of American rural scenery, presenting at the same time scarcely a shade of newness. The people who have built such complete cottage homes here have surely done so with the intention of staying. The very sunshine seemed more golden, the trees more green and graceful, and the skies clearer and bluer than on the continent left behind. Indeed, Tasmania might be a big slice detached from England and drifted into the South Sea. The rural scenery of Kent or Surrey is not more charming, while the thrifty hop-fields here heighten the general resemblance. Gold-mining, though followed to a certain extent in Tasmania, has not seemed to demoralize the people, and is really a secondary occupation to others that pay better both in a moral and a pecuniary sense.

As we have shown, Launceston is situated at the head of navigation on the Tamar River, where the town nestles in the lap of a valley surrounded by hills. The population numbers about twelve thousand. It is regularly laid out in broad streets lighted by gas, and has a good water-supply brought from St. Patrick's River fifteen miles east of the city. There are numerous substantial public buildings of brick and stone, and everything bears a thorough business aspect indicating great prosperity. There is a Public Library containing over ten thousand volumes, and there are also five or six well-appointed schools of the several grades. The Town Hall is a very fine and substantial building of dressed stone, and several large brick buildings for business purposes were observed to be in course of erection. The city is not without its Botanical Garden, embracing twelve or fifteen acres of land near the centre of the town. The walks and drives in and about the neighborhood are quite attractive. The North and South Elk rivers rise on different sides of Ben Lomond, and after flowing through some romantic plains and gorges, they join each other at Launceston. This sky-reaching mountain is worthy of its Scotch counterpart; between it and Launceston is some of the finest river and mountain scenery in all Tasmania. Ben Lomond is the chief object in the landscape wherever one drives or walks in this part of the island.

One of the first places of interest in this vicinity

to which the attention of the visitor is invited, is a locality reached by a drive of four or five miles from Launceston called Cora Linn, which is notable for its romantic scenery. It consists of a deep gorge, through which the North Elk River rushes noisily, forming seething cascades and dashing waterfalls of a grand character. To reach this spot one passes through the pretty village of St. Leonard, where there is a neat little Wesleyan chapel and plenty of handsome villas most home-like in aspect.

The winter is here like that of Nice and Mentone, while the summer is much like that of New England, though not subject to such extremes. One sees many bronze-winged pigeons here, a very fine domestic bird, blazing with color under the sun's rays.

Of all the vast mineral wealth of Tasmania, the most thoroughly developed enterprise is that of the Mount Bischoff tin mine, which is situated about one hundred and fifty miles from Launceston. It is accessible from the city either by land or water. The land-route passes through a highly interesting district, diversified by river and mountain scenery, pleasant homesteads, cultivated fields, and some of the largest sheep-runs on the island. The quartz or tin-bearing rock of this mine may be said to form the entire hill to the height of three hundred feet, — Mount Bischoff itself being three thousand feet above sea-level. Several shafts have been sunk to a depth of a hundred feet each, showing that the metallic deposit reaches to that depth with a " breast " (as

miners term it) as broad as the hill itself. The
deposit is therefore practically inexhaustible, and of
such value that it has already greatly enriched its
stockholders. The tin is shipped direct to England
in the form of "pigs," and the demand from that
country seems to absorb the entire product of this
mine. The price for tin ore is said to be as uniform as that for gold. The company's pay-roll at
the mine averages twenty thousand dollars a month,
the men receiving from two dollars a day upwards,
none, however, exceeding two dollars and a half as
day-laborers.

This mountain of tin, for that is really what it is,
has been tunnelled through its greatest dimension,
showing it to be equally rich in all parts. It is a
busy place, but so well organized in every department
that there is no confusion, each man working intelli-
gently and to the best advantage. We were told by
the superintendent that the shares of this mine originally cost five dollars each; to-day they are selling
for three hundred dollars per share, and not always
to be had at that price. They are almost wholly
owned in this neighborhood, and on them the owners
receive monthly dividends. We were told of other
tin mines in this island, but Mount Bischoff is *the* tin
mine of Tasmania.

A view from the summit of Mount Bischoff across
the wild forest and densely-covered hills is a picture
to be long remembered. The query suggested itself,
Is it possible that this immense wild tract of country,

these miles upon miles of seemingly impenetrable forest, will ever be cleared and dotted with the homes of settlers? Being in the heart of a rich mineral district, where not tin alone but gold also is found, doubtless it is destined, in the near future, to have a similar experience to that which transformed Ballarat and Sandhurst from deserts into cities.

A trip to the Beaconsfield gold mine, which is situated some thirty miles from Launceston, will well repay the traveller from other lands. The town of Beaconsfield ranks next to those of Hobart and Launceston in importance, and has a rapidly increasing population. It is of quite recent establishment, and owes its rise solely to the discovery of the attractive metal within that district.

The Tasmanian mine, so called, is considered one of the most valuable and prolific on the island, possessing also a very perfect "plant" in machinery and the usual appliances for quartz mining. Before descending the main shaft of the mine one must assume suitable clothing, as mud and water are to be encountered in extraordinary quantities. The great difficulty to be overcome in working nearly all of these subterranean mines is the profuse influx of water, often involving the necessity for a steam-pumping apparatus of immense power, which must be worked night and day in order to keep the various sections of the mine sufficiently dry for working. Armed with candles, we descended two hundred feet by the "lift" to the first level, or drift, forming a passage just high enough and wide enough for a man to swing a pick in, but as wet as a river, one being often over shoes in water and mud. From the far end of this passage we got now and then a breath of fresh air, which seemed to come down a ventilating shaft. A few dismal-looking laborers were seen chipping off the rock amid the misty shadows caused by the fitful light. What a place to work in day after day, — and all for gold, "saint-seducing gold"! After a short exploration on this level, we descended still another two hundred feet, penetrating a second drift almost identical with the first in size and general character. Here some Chinamen were engaged with picks, drills, and shovels, — dark, mysterious figures, who seemed to glare at us from out the uncertain rays of light as though they were brooding over some fancied wrong, for which they would gladly avenge themselves then and there. The quartz rock which they break away from the walls of the drift is all the time being hoisted to the surface of the mine to be crushed and passed through various processes to extract the precious metal. The next gallery was still two hundred feet lower down the shaft, — that is, six hundred feet from the surface. Here, after passing through the same experiences as above, we mildly but firmly declined to go any farther into the bowels of the earth simply for the sake of saying that we had done so, since there was really nothing to be seen essentially different from what had already been examined. It was no slight relief to get once more to the surface, and to see the light of day. On looking about us and reflecting on the network of galleries we had threaded far below this upper earth, there was seen a quarter of a mile away, on the other side of the lagoon, the ventilating shaft which gave air to the mine.

The name of another successful mine in this immediate vicinity is the Florence Nightingale mine, very similar to the Tasmanian, and therefore requiring no description. The gold-workings are mostly of the quartz, though there are some paying alluvial diggings along the banks of running streams, where it would seem as though some Midas had bathed, and filled the sand with scales of gold, — places the sight of which at once recalled that far-away river Pactolus of the Lydian country.

Many fortunes are staked and lost in the sinking of these deep shafts, where the indications have been so promising at the surface, but which not being thoroughly understood have led to operations ending in great disappointment. As a rule, however, the miners have become sufficiently experienced to work unerringly; and when a quartz-bearing vein has once been discovered, they can follow its course, or strike it at various levels, almost with certainty.

The trip from Launceston to Hobart, a distance of one hundred and twenty miles more or less, takes us into the centre of the island, — the direction being from north to south through lovely glades, over broad plains, across rushing streams, and around the base of abrupt mountains. The narrow-gauge railroad which connects the two cities is owned and operated by a private company, whose charge for carrying a passenger over the short distance named is six dollars. The cars are so poorly constructed, so narrow, and so meanly upholstered, as to appear like worn-out omnibuses built forty years ago. To add to the traveller's discomfort, the road-bed is as bad as it can be and not derail the cars constantly. One fellow-traveller suggested that there should be printed upon each passenger's ticket the condition that the holder would be expected to walk round all the sharp curves, and to help push the train up the steep grades. The engine seemed to be of that minimum capacity which always left a doubt upon the mind whether it would not give out altogether at the next up grade. In short, this railroad is a disgrace to Tasmania. Travellers, however, must learn not only to carry ample change of clothing with them, but also an ever ready stock of patience and forbearance, — better currency with which to insure comfort than even silver and gold.

It was mid-winter in Tasmania, and yet ploughing, sowing, and harrowing were going on at the same time along the route, — an agricultural anomaly rather puzzling to a stranger. The road passes through many pleasant though small villages. Ben Lomond, with its white crest, overlooks the scene for many miles after leaving Launceston. This grand mountain is in the north of the island what Mount Wellington is in the south, — the pride of the residents who live beneath its shadow. It is prolific in mineral deposits, including gold and coal; but at the present time mining operations are only prosecuted for the purpose of producing a domestic supply of the latter article.

About thirty miles from Launceston the traveller arrives at Campbelltown, which is the centre of a pastoral district. The place lies embosomed in hills, the highest point being Mount Campbell, — an elevation rising twenty-three hundred feet above sea-level. Next the town of Ross is passed, — a pretty little village, beautified by ornamental trees, and having a long arched stone bridge and lovely rural surroundings. Tunbridge, which follows, is half-way between the two cities, and seemed to be a very thrifty settlement. This, as we were told, was the nearest point to what is known as the Lake District of Tasmania, where a series of large and permanent deposits of water, lying three thousand feet above the average inhabited portions of the island, form a centre of considerable interest. It is proposed to tap these lakes in the best engineering style, for the purpose of irrigating hundreds of square miles of soil, — the country here, as upon the mainland, being subject to occasional droughts.

As we proceeded southward the picturesqueness of the scenery increased, now winding through valleys or creeping over mountain passes. Wherever the valleys widen into plains there are seen numberless rural homes, substantial and attractive, surrounded by fertile fields, cultivated gardens, and large fruit-orchards, — the latter leafless at this season, though the general foliage of the country is evergreen. Thrifty gorse hedges are prominent everywhere, blazing with yellow blossoms which lighted up and warmed the landscape like sunshine. Oatlands, Jericho, and Melton Mowbry follow one another, — each a thriving town graced with substantial buildings, often constructed of white freestone wrought from neighboring quarries. All the way the tall mountain ranges are in full sight, with patches of snow here and there high up on their sides. At the town of Brighton the river Derwent is first seen not far away, shining under the sun's rays like silver; after which Hobart is soon reached, and we are relieved from the imprisonment of the uncomfortable cars.

Hobart was so named by Colonel Collins, its founder, in 1804, in honor of Lord Hobart, who was then Secretary of State for the Colonies. It is surrounded by hills and mountains on all sides except where the Derwent opens into lake form, making a deep and well-sheltered harbor, whence it leads the way into the Southern Ocean. Among the lofty hills in this vicinity Mount Wellington towers grandly forty-two hundred feet above the others, so close to the city on the northwest side as to seem almost within rifle-range. The shape of the town is square, built upon a succession of low hills, being very much in this respect like Sydney. It has broad streets intersecting one another at right angles, lined with handsome well-stocked stores serving an active and enterprising population of thirty thousand or more. Of these shops, two or three spacious and elegant bookstores deserve special mention, being such as would do credit to any American or European city. Their shelves and counters were found to contain a remarkably full assortment of both modern and classic literature. There must be many cultured and intelligent people here to afford sufficient support to such admirable establishments.

Many fine public buildings were observed, with elaborate façades, nearly all built of light freestone; while quite a number of handsome edifices, both for public and private use, were noticed as in course of construction of the same material. Churches, banks, insurance offices, and the like, all in this bright cheerful stone, give not only an imposing aspect to the thoroughfares of the city, but one always pleasing whether viewed under cloud-shadows or in the rays of the sun. And yet Hobart has hardly outlived the curse of the penal associations which clustered about its birth. Thirty or forty years ago the British Government expended here five thousand dollars per day in support of jails and military barracks. The last convict ship from England discharged her cargo at Hobart in 1851, since which year the system has gradually disappeared. The loss of a large, profitable, and regular business incidental to a penal depot, however objectionable in some of its associations, gave the place a check from which it has taken a series of years to recover; but its far more legitimate and agreeable growth is now one in which the citizens may and do take a commendable and natural pride. The past history of the place, so characterized by official cruelties, brutalities, and crimes, will not bear recall or exposure to the light of day. What Cayenne was to France, Hobart was to England; namely, the convict's purgatory, where order was maintained only by the lash, the halter, and the bullet; where official murder formed a part of the daily routine. What a broad contrast exists between that picture of the past and the surroundings of the present; between the penal life that reigned here in 1840, and the healthy, contented existence characterizing the Hobart in which the author is writing these notes!

The view from Mount Wellington is justly famed for its varied and comprehensive character. The city with its gracefully undulating conformation, lying at the visitor's feet, is framed by a three-quarter circle of tree-covered hills, relieved by the river Derwent, which conducts the eye seaward by its bright, sparkling, and winding stream. Turning to the view inland, there lies beneath a beautiful blue sky, just touched here and there by fleecy clouds, a fair and lovely land diversified by rivers, lakes, forests, villages, and towns, — some of the latter in the valleys, some on the open plains, some perched on the mountain-sides, and all together forming a most fascinating, far-reaching picture of the fairest section of Australasia.

Hobart also has its Botanical Garden, covering an area of over twenty acres near the centre of the town. It is filled with ornamental trees, flowers, and fruit-trees from every part of the world, the sweet-scented shrubs rendering the dewy morning atmosphere fragrant even in mid-winter. Geraniums, cacti, tiger-lilies, and many creeping plants were flowering as though in a tropical climate, not at all abashed by the snow-caps upon some of the mountain ranges in sight. This garden slopes down in beautiful form to the waters of the harbor, and is washed by the blue Derwent. The city is supplied with good drinking-water from a copious, never-failing crystal spring, situated half-way up Mount Wellington. The street scenes have the usual local color; like those of Launceston, they embrace the typical miner, with his rude kit upon his shoulder, consisting of a huge canvas-bag, a shovel and pick. The professional chimney-sweep, with blackened face and hands begrimed, whom we lost sight of years ago in Boston and London, is seen here pursuing his vocation. Market-men have the same singular mode of delivering purchases to their customers as we noted elsewhere, and are seen constantly galloping upon little wiry horses, bearing upon their arms large well-filled baskets. Women with scores of slaughtered rabbits cry them for sale at sixpence a pair, besides which they realize a bounty for killing the pests. Let us not forget to mention the lovely, rosy-cheeked children and handsome maidens met at every few steps going to or coming from school, with their glowing promise of health and beauty.

It is remarkable how certain communities are characterized by handsome girls and boys, together with lovely children, while another locality, either far away or near at hand, is notable for the almost painful plainness of its rising generation. Such experiences are sure to force themselves upon the notice of the traveller in foreign lands, personal beauty being oftenest encountered where least expected, and usually under such circumstances as to be the more impressive. The same inclination to cut the hair short like that of boys, which we had noticed among women single and married still farther north, prevails here to even a greater extent. Though it was so common, it nevertheless repeatedly suggested their late possible recovery from some serious and depleting fever.

CHAPTER XII.

Lake District of Tasmania. — Mount Wellington. — Kangaroos. — The Big Trees. — A Serenade. — The Albatross. — Marksmanship at Sea. — Dust of the Ocean. — A Storm. — Franklin's Proposition. — A Feathered Captive. — Bluff Oysters. — Most Southerly Hotel in the World. — Invercargill. — Historical Matters. — Geographical. — The Climate of New Zealand. — Colonial Hospitality.

THE river Derwent, which rises far inland where the beautiful lakes St. Clair and Sorell are embosomed, itself broadens into an inland lake six miles wide, where it forms the harbor of Hobart, famous for the summer regattas that are rowed upon its surface. Here the largest maritime craft that navigates these seas can lie close to the wharf and the warehouses to discharge cargo, while the fine large stone Custom House is within pistol-shot of the shore. Let us emphasize the importance of a visit to the Lake District of Tasmania, where the lakes just referred to lie in their lonely beauty, — now overhung by towering cliffs, like those bordering a Norwegian fjord, and now edged by pebbly beaches, where choice specimens of agate and carnelian abound. They are dotted here and there by verdant isles with sedge-lined shores, and present sheets of a glassy surface unbroken for miles in extent. The neighborhood is one of primeval loneliness, invaded only by an occasional traveller; but a brief visit to Lake St. Clair and Lake Sorell leaves a delightful picture upon the memory not soon to be obliterated.

The charming cloud-effects which hang over and about the lofty hills that environ the capital of Tasmania recall vividly those of the Lake of Geneva, near Chillon, and the Dent du Midi; while the Derwent itself, reflecting the hills upon its blue and placid surface, forms another pleasing resemblance to Lake Leman. We should not forget to mention that in ascending Mount Wellington, the lion of Tasmanian scenery, where the visitor reaches a height of about two thousand feet, the Old World ocean floor is reached and clearly defined, as we have seen it exhibited among the heights of Norwegian mountains. Here there are plenty of lithoidal remains of the former denizens of the ocean, — fossils telling the strange and interesting story of terrestrial changes that have taken place in the thousands upon thousands of years that are past. Hobart is one of the very few cities with which we are familiar whence Alpine elevations can be so easily reached. Its broad streets run to the base of snow-covered mountains at one end, and at the other terminate on the busy shore of the harbor.

A walk up the precipitous sides of Mount Wellington affords special delight to the lover of botanical science. The ferns to be found in the gullies and elsewhere are singularly attractive in their great variety and natural beauty of combinations. One spot is so marked and monopolized by them as to be called Fern-Tree Bower. The difference between this species of plant as found in Tasmania and those indigenous to the mainland is that the former maintain their entire freshness and summer colors all through the year, — though this is a characteristic in a general way of all Australian vegetation, as seen in the perpetual and vigorous freshness of the forests. On this mountain-side mosses, lichens, and blue-striped gentians are mingled in close companionship, with here and there dainty specimens of the white wood-sorrel, — lowly, but lovely examples of Nature's gardening. Here was also seen the cabbage-palm twenty feet high, imparting a marked tropical aspect to this cool region. Some delicate specimens of ferns were seen depending from the trunks of trees in damp and low-lying places, where they also lined the shallow water-ways.

On returning from an excursion from Mount Wellington we saw some domesticated kangaroos. This animal can easily be tamed, and will then follow a person about like a dog, evincing remarkable attachment and intelligence. One of those which we saw followed its mistress, the lady of the house, wherever she went, but would follow no one else. When she sat down, it came and nestled by her side with all the confidence imparted by a sense of perfect protection. The kangaroo has a wonderfully expressive face, more than half human, with a head and large plaintive eyes quite like those of a fawn of the red-deer species. The ears are long, nervously active and extremely delicate, seeming to be almost transparent when seen against a strong light. Tasmania once swarmed with kangaroos, but the hunters here, as upon the mainland, have nearly obliterated the species. Full-grown males sometimes measure six feet when standing upright, and weigh about one hundred and fifty pounds. The sharp claws of the short fore-feet are powerful weapons, and if brought to bay by the dogs when hunted, the male kangaroo will sometimes turn upon his pursuers and with his claws disembowel the largest dog. When unmolested, however, they use these fore-paws like a squirrel, holding their food and carrying it to their mouths with them as we do with our hands.

The fish-market of Hobart was to us quite interesting. The local denizens of the sea here seem to have a physiognomy, so to speak, all their own, differing in shape, colors, and general aspect from those with which we were elsewhere familiar. Long, slim, pointed fish are here a favorite; and others, so like young sharks as to make one shudder at the thought of eating them, found ready purchasers. The lobsters were quite unlike our New England species; indeed, they are here known as cray-fish, or crawfish. They have, in place of a smooth, soft shell, a corrugated one, pimply like the red face of an inveterate toper, and so hard are they as to require a hammer to break out the meat that forms the body, while they are entirely lacking in the claws which form so prominent a portion of our common lobster. The oysters here seem to be equally uninviting, as the shells are so crumpled that it becomes a mystery where the knife should be inserted to obtain the very small quantity of edible matter forming the body of the oyster. How Wareham, Blue Point, or Shrewsbury Bay oysters would astonish people who are satisfied with these apologies for first-class bivalves!

About twenty miles from Hobart one finds a forest of the remarkable gum-trees of which we have all read, — trees which exceed in height and circumference the mammoth growths of our own Yosemite Valley, and fully equal those of Victoria. The immediate locality which contains them is known as the Huon District. A walk among these forest giants fills one with mingled emotions of wonder and delight. Surrounded by beautiful fern-trees nearly forty feet high, whose plumed caps tremble and vibrate in the breeze, one's eyes seek the lofty tops of these grand forest monarchs which are nearly lost in the sky to which they aspire; no church steeples, no cathedral pinnacle reared by the hand of man, but only mountain peaks reach so far heavenward. These forests are so abundant in their yield that local steam sawmills are constantly engaged in cutting and preparing the lumber in various dimensions for the market. All the trees are by no means of the great size of which we have spoken, and yet all are extraordinary in this respect. The people of Hobart claim that they can show trees in the Huon forests taller and larger than any to be found in Victoria. We measured only one in the former District, which had lately fallen, the dimensions of which we can vouch for; namely, three hundred and thirty feet in length or height, and seventy-one feet in circumference. The average reader will not be able to realize the remarkable figures here given as applying to the trunk of a tree, except by comparison with some familiar object.

A century ago, before Tasmania was settled by the English, the whole country was covered with dense forests, remarkable for the size of individual trees. Even now the western half of the island remains mostly unchanged and unexplored, traversed by wild mountain ranges, full of deep, gloomy, and nearly inaccessible ravines shut in by giant precipices. Many of these districts were untrodden even in the days of the aborigines. The abundance of land already available to accommodate the present sparse population, together with the impenetrable nature of the forest growth of the west coast, have caused that region to remain unexplored.

Our hotel in Hobart was the Orient, which is situated upon high ground; and by ascending to its roof at night a grand, awe-inspiring view of the heavens was obtained, — the blue vault being thickly strewn with stars. As we stood gazing at them our thoughts wandered back to the period of the Nativity and the journey of the Wise Men. The surrounding hills terraced by dwellings which were brilliantly lighted, and which crept up to the sky line, made it difficult to decide just where the artificial lights ended and heaven's lamps began. It is marvellous how clear and bright the constellations and single stars shine forth in these latitudes presided over by the Southern Cross, — which was in the zenith, emphasized by the great stars in Centaurus pointing toward it, and accompanied by the mysterious belt of the Via Lactea and the illumined Magellan Clouds.

> "This brave o'er-hanging firmament;
> This majestical roof fretted with golden fire."

The tardy moon was somewhere behind the dark shadowy range of hills, but the stars filled the valley and plain with a soft, dreamy, exquisite light. Just at that moment a band of local musicians broke forth with the air of "Home, Sweet Home," as a serenade of welcome to the "Tasmanian Nightingale," Miss Amy Sherwin, who had returned that day to her native land from a foreign professional tour. A lonely, unheeded stranger was also there, under the deep sea-blue canopy studded with stars, whom those familiar strains moved to quickened tears. Presently, over the height of Mount Wellington a broad light was gradually developed, covering the mantle of snow with silver spangles, and the moon burst forth upon the scene with a calm, mellow radiance, sweeping grandly on its upward course. Then the vocalist came out upon a balcony, and in her clear contralto voice gave the words of the touching song, to the delight of the welcoming group below. But one may not delay for sentiment. "This world is a bog," said Queen Elizabeth, "over which we must trip lightly. If we pause we sink!"

This was our last night in Hobart. The next day we sailed for New Zealand. A state-room was secured on board the steamship "Mararoa," which had just arrived from Sydney, and which was bound for the east coast of the country just named. The ship sailed at mid-day, and as we steamed down the Derwent seaward we were followed by a myriad of Cape-pigeons, a small graceful bird of the gull family, with which we have not before chanced to meet.

The twelve miles of river between Hobart and the open sea virtually forms the harbor of this city, just as Sydney harbor begins when the "Heads" are passed seven miles below the capital. The undulating shore of the river on either side was beautified by rural residences and cultivated fields near the water's edge. But a little way inshore we could see a continuous range of elevations, backed by those still higher; and finally in the distance we descried a series of cloud-embraced mountains. As soon as the mouth of the river was reached the ship's course was laid a little south of east, the dull green of the water on soundings changing to the navy-blue of the broad ocean. We were then fairly launched on our twelve-hundred-mile voyage. The prevailing winds of the season blow from the west, which with the Australian current and the Antarctic drift were all in our favor, and so the good ship sped bravely on her way. The

"Mararoa" is a fine vessel of twenty-five hundred tons' measurement, possessing most admirable passenger accommodations; so fine, indeed, were her appointments as to make her seem to us rather out of place upon a track of ocean so little frequented by travellers. It appeared on inquiry, however, that she was originally built for the route between San Francisco and Australia, but proved insufficient in freight capacity.

The tedium of the voyage was beguiled by watching critically the graceful movements of the wandering albatross, the fateful bird of nautical romance, which is seen in large numbers below the thirtieth parallel of south latitude. The peculiarities of this sea-bird's flight are a constant marvel, for it scarcely ever plies its wings, but literally sails upon the wind in any desired direction. What secret power, we wondered, could so propel him for hundreds of rods, with an upward trend at the close? If for a single moment he partially lights upon the water to seize some object of prey, there is a trifling exertion evinced in rising again until he is a few feet above the waves, when once more he sails, with or against the wind, upon outspread, immovable wings. With no apparent inclination or occasion for pugnacity, the albatross is yet armed with a tremendous beak, certainly the most terrible of its kind attached to any of the feathered tribe. It is from six to eight inches long, and ends in a sharp-pointed hook of extreme strength and hardness.

A preserved specimen of the albatross was mounted in the saloon of the "Mararoa," as an ornament appropriate for a vessel sailing in the latitudes where this bird-monarch roams. This was easily measured, and though not of the largest size reached by them, its dimensions seemed to us extraordinary. The body measured three feet in length, from the beak to the end of the short tail; the spread of wing from tip to tip was ten feet eight inches. The web-feet were seven inches across, and armed with three sharp claws an inch and a quarter long; these were very strong, and capable of sustaining twenty or thirty pounds. The prevailing color of the albatross is a slate-white over the upper part of the body and wings; but the breast and under surface generally are of pure white. Of course the birds vary in color, but this is the most common description. Ermine itself is not whiter than the breast of the albatross; living in the air and bathing constantly in the sea, there is no encounter liable to soil its purity. The feathers are pearl-like in their lustre. It has been said that if he pleased, the albatross might breakfast at the Cape of Good Hope and dine in New York, so swift is it in flight and so powerful on the wing.

While we were watching from the ship's deck the tireless movements of these birds, an officer of the "Mararoa" told us that on the previous voyage some English passengers who had rifles with them shot at the graceful creatures, but found it almost impossible to hit them. The deck of a vessel in motion was under any circumstances an uncertain base from which to take aim; moreover, the birds were always on the wing; and again, the missiles were bullets, not shot. It is particularly difficult to calculate distances under such circumstances, and so these marksmen found it. An albatross was sometimes barely touched by the leaden messenger, so that the tip of its wing perhaps shed a few feathers, or a similar effect was produced upon some part of its body; but this did not serve to frighten them, as the detonation of fire-arms was so unusual a circumstance at sea. They had not learned the trick of the rifle, and would require to see the fall of more than one of their number following its report, before they would connect cause and effect in such a way as to be a warning to them. These birds are hardy, and must be touched in some vital point in order to disable them; a slight wound would not affect them any more than the partial hooking of a fish affects it, — failing, as is often the case, to prevent it from again biting at the fatal barb. At last one of the birds at which the Englishmen of the "Mararoa" were firing was struck in the body, and fell headlong into the sea. Then it was demonstrated that albatross nature is as cannibalistic as that of the Russian wolf. The wounded, bleeding, and helpless bird was almost instantly fallen upon by its late companions and torn quickly to pieces to fill their greedy crops. "That," said a lady passenger who had overheard the officer's story, "was not only cruel, but terribly unnatural." The officer's respectful answer was very significant. "Nay, madam," said he, "it was only too natural!"

While dreamily watching the throbbing surface of this mystery of waters through which our good ship steadily ploughed her way, the thought occurred to us of how many uses the various seas and oceans were to man besides forming the great pathway of commerce reaching to the uttermost parts of the globe. The animals it produces are among the mightiest and the smallest, from monstrous whales and walruses down to the tiny animalcules. What an inexhaustible supply of food it yields for the support of man! Its contributions to various industries are almost limitless, while the treasuries of art are enriched by the abundance of tortoise-shell, mother-of-pearl, and the lovely pearl gem itself, with delicate shells, coral, amber, and other choice articles of decoration. A very interesting chapter might be written upon the prolific yield of the sea in the various departments of food, industry, and art. While we were musing thus, a school of dolphins, as they are often called, appeared on the surface near the ship's side. The proper name of this fish is the porpoise. The dolphin belongs to the whale family, breathing atmospheric air; while the porpoise has no blow-holes, but receives the water into its mouth to be thrown out at the gills. Porpoises seem to be the most sportive fish that swim in the sea, and while they remained in their playful mood near our ship, it was amusing to watch their gambols.

At night the phosphorescence of these lonely waters lying just north of the Antarctic Circle, between southern Tasmania and New Zealand, was indeed marvellous. Liquid fire is the only term which will properly express its flame-like appearance. A bucketful was drawn and deposited upon deck; while it remained still it appeared dark and like any other water, but when agitated it emitted scintillations of light like the stars. A drop of this water placed under the microscope was found to be teeming with living and active organisms. A muslin bag was suspended for a few moments over the ship's side and then drawn up, and after being permitted to drip for a few seconds the contents left in the bag were placed in a glass tumbler, when the quantity of living forms was found to be so great and abundant as to be visible to the naked eye. No two of these minute creatures seemed to be of similar form; the variety was infinite, and their activity incessant. Most of these animalcules are so small that if it were not for the microscope we should never even know of their existence.

One day at table a lady passenger complained of the dust of the sea, which she said got into her eyes and caused them to smart severely, and also soiled her clothing. Others laughed at her, and declared that there could be no dust at sea; but they were mistaken. There is a salt dust which rises from the spray and impregnates everything, even filling one's mouth with a saline taste. While the sun shines, this deposit, like the dew on land, is less active and perceptible; but to walk the deck at night is to become covered with a thin coating of salt dust, so fine indeed as to be hardly noticeable, but which in time becomes sufficiently crystallized to be obvious to the eye. The dust of the sea is no fable. The officer who stands his night-watch on the bridge will testify to this fact; and his cabin steward will tell you that he has often to resort to something more potent than a whisk-broom to cleanse clothing which has been exposed to sea-dust.

Winter upon the sea and winter upon the land in this extreme southern region are two very different things. On shore (save on the mountain-tops) there is scarcely any snow, the climate being mild and equable; but upon the ocean the fickle element does not forget boldly to assert itself. Three uneventful days carried us nearly a thousand miles upon our way toward New Zealand; but as night came on at the close of the third day, the barometer — which had been falling ominously for some time, after reaching a most significant figure — suddenly jumped several points, foretelling the heavy weather into which we were now rapidly driven. Everything had been made as snug on board the "Mararoa" as was possible, which was only the part of prudence, for the ship began to waltz in the wildest fashion to the hoarse music of the on-coming storm. It was a dismal and trying night, the raging sea breaking over and about the ship, drenching everything fore and aft, and causing the stout iron hull to tremble all over like a delicate fern in the wind. It was so cold that it seemed strange that the water did not freeze where it struck the deck and the rigging. There were no means provided for heating the cabins or the saloon, and the result was that a shivering discomfort was realized everywhere. On, on we drove into the dense darkness, with extra lookouts stationed forward, although it was impossible to see half a ship's length ahead. Timid passengers blanched with fear, and most of those who had thus far escaped sea-sickness now succumbed to that dismal disorder. "He that will learn to pray, let him go to sea," says George Herbert. To undress before taking to one's berth was quite impossible, since both hands were required to keep the body from being thrown thither and hither like a ball; but once fairly in the berth, the friendly brace of the lee-board and the firm gripe of the metallic bars united, served to keep one in position. Sleep was out of the question, and so one was forced to exercise as much patience and philosophy as possible under the circumstances.

Sailing-vessels making this voyage, as we were told, carry casks of cheap oil, which in some cases they use to still the boisterous sea about them when "God maketh the deep to boil like a pot." Is it generally known that our own Benjamin Franklin first suggested, about a century ago, the carrying of oil to sea by vessels for this purpose? Our shrewd

American philosopher was also the first to propose, about the same period, that ship-builders should construct the hulls of vessels in water-tight compartments, thus affording them sufficient sustaining power to float when by accident portions of the hull became leaky or broken in. After the lapse of a century both precautions have been generally adopted. If oil can be used to good effect anywhere upon troubled waters, we should judge that it might be on the track of vessels between Tasmania and South New Zealand.

The longest night must have an end. The half-hour strokes of the sonorous ship's-bell rang upon the ear through the fierce howling of the gale, until the morning light finally broke, which seemed to be a signal for the abating of the storm, as by and by the sun rose bright and clear from behind the yet mountainous waves. No observation had been obtained on the previous day owing to the cloudy condition of the sky, so that it was impossible exactly to define our position; but dead reckoning showed we must be nearing the land, and as the sea began rapidly to subside, it was evident that we were under the lee of the shore. As the day advanced, the sun burned away the mist and revealed to us the mountains of the southern coast of New Zealand, with their tops clad in virgin white. Midway between summit and base cloud-wreaths decked the range of hills, which in the sun's rays seemed struggling with one another for precedence. We skirted the mainland for hours, encountering numerous islands, now and again opening dark mountain gorges which came down to the very shore, enabling one to look deep into the mysterious heart of the hills and discover new peaks extending far inland. Clouds of sea-martins wheeled about the ship, saluting us with strange cries, some alighting upon our very topmasts, where they paused for a moment and then launched into the air again. This sea-bird, in size between the common gull and the Cape-pigeon, is peculiar to this coast; we had never seen a live specimen before. As they settle upon the water or rise from it, their red legs become conspicuous, and are in singular contrast to their soft white bodies and light slate-colored wings. They are a tame and fearless bird, flying about the ship almost within arm's reach. One was secured by a foremast hand and brought aft, seeming to care no more for his temporary captivity than a domestic fowl would have done. Their feathery covering is exquisitely soft and glossy, the under part of the wings and the body having a covering as delicate as the downy plumage of young goslings. Our feathery captive when released joined his companions, and was saluted by loud cries of welcome.

The west and southwest coasts of New Zealand, which we were skirting, are indented with deep fjords almost precisely like the coast of Norway from Bergen to Hammerfest; and singular to say, these arms of the sea, like those of the far north, are much deeper than the contiguous ocean, — a practical evidence of their being of similar original formation. While we were remarking upon these peculiarities, the captain of the "Mararoa" recalled the fact that it is always the west coast of any land which is indented in this remarkable manner, let the cause be what it may.

Just as the sun set like a blazing fire-ball in the sea upon the western horizon, the ship rounded the bold promontory known as "the Bluff," and winding up the narrow channel into the harbor was soon moored to the one pier of the place. This was none too promptly done, for no sooner was the ship made fast than the darkness of night enshrouded both land and water.

A woman who had anticipated the arrival of the "Mararoa" had set up a temporary oyster-stand on the pier, by placing a couple of boards across two barrels, beside which she had raised a powerful blazing flambeau. Here she opened and dispensed fresh bivalves. And *such* oysters we have rarely seen; they were in their prime, large, full, and perfect in flavor. Blue Points could not excel them. It seems that oysters are a specialty here, whence they are shipped in large quantities to Tasmania and Australia. It was a weird and curious picture presented by the group on the pier, — the blazing, flickering flambeau casting flashes upon the many faces, and all surrounded by deep shadows and darkness. Among the spectators of the ship's arrival who had come to the pier were a score of half-breeds, — Maori girls and men, laughing and chattering like monkeys. A night's sleep, a quiet night in harbor and on board ship, was a needful process of recuperation after the experience of the previous one on a raging sea, and we rose wonderfully refreshed the next morning. At breakfast we were regaled with New Zealand oysters and fresh fish.

The Bluff — also known as Campbelltown — is located in the very track of storms, and is open to the entire sweep of the great Antarctic Ocean. Its shelving side, sloping toward the harbor, forms a sort of lee, — a sheltered position which is occupied by a pretty little fishing village of some sixty houses, with a population of less than a thousand. These people gain their living mostly from the neighboring sea, and from such labor as is consequent upon the occasional arrival of steamships on their way to the north. Here we took refreshment at the Golden Age Hotel, — a primitive little inn, quaint to the last degree, its reception-room ornamented with many species of stuffed birds, mostly sea-fowls, among which was a preserved specimen of the albatross even larger than the one whose dimensions we have already given. There was a well-preserved seal hanging from a hook in the wall; also a sword-fish, and a young shark of the man-eating species. On one side of this room was a glass case of curious shells, large and small; and on the opposite side was an open bar presided over by a ruby-nosed Bardolph.

The Golden Age is noticeable as being the most

southerly public house of entertainment in the world. Twelve months previous, being exactly one year to a day, we had partaken, at Hammerfest, in Norway, of the hospitality of the most *northerly* hotel on the globe. When this coincidence was casually mentioned to the host of the Golden Age, he would have immolated us on the altar of his hospitality had we not discreetly retreated to the ship.

A single day was passed at the Bluff, a place so small that one could "do" it in an hour; and yet there was much of interest here to be observed. One is paid for ascending the high point of the Bluff, some nine hundred feet, by the fine view afforded of land and sea. Many half-caste people were observed, born of intermarriage between Europeans and the aborigines. Some of the young women of this descent were remarkable for possessing fine eyes, rich brown complexions, white teeth, clear-cut features, and a great wealth of long black hair. These answer to our quadroons of the Southern States in appearance, having the same dainty touch of color on the cheeks and lips. In figure they were tall and well-formed; but we were told that, like our quadroons, they are a short-lived race. There are a few half-breed men to be seen about the town, mostly engaged in service to the whites as boatmen and fishermen. They are said to make excellent and intelligent seamen.

Taking the cars at the Bluff one can run up to Invercargill, a distance of seventeen miles, consuming, however, a full hour in the transit. This was found to be quite a pleasant and busy town of about eight thousand inhabitants, which has grown to its present condition very rapidly. We were told that twenty-five years ago it had less than a hundred inhabitants. It is now the chief town of what is known as the District of Southland, — a large and fertile district. The town is built upon a perfectly level plain; the streets are unusually wide, and the place is neat and thrifty. The principal thoroughfare is Dee Street, in which are the banks, insurance offices, the Post-Office, and the Athenæum. A liberal provision by those who laid out the town was made for its future growth, which is reasonably expected to be rapid on account of its commercial advantages. The buildings of Invercargill are substantial and handsome, including several fairly good hotels. Some building was observed to be in progress, and other evidences of growth and prosperity were manifest. The town is situated one hundred and fifty miles south of the city of Dunedin, with which it has considerable trade, and is the terminus of the Southern Trunk Line of New Zealand. The neighborhood is mostly taken up for pastoral and agricultural purposes, fruit-raising, and the like. There are valuable coal-fields here, and it is a considerable wool depot. Our visit was of the briefest, as we took the cars the same afternoon back to the Bluff, whence we were to sail northward.

It is a curious fact, probably remembered by few of our readers, that Franklin proposed in a printed article to colonize New Zealand from our own country, so highly did he regard the possible advantages to be thus derived. This plan, if it had been adopted, would have anticipated by nearly a hundred years the action of the English Government in that direction. As early as the year 1800 our whalers had learned to seek the sperm whale in these waters, and to enter the harbors of New Zealand for wood and water and to make necessary repairs. American sailors, as well as others, shipped on board these vessels, and while in port here took Maori mistresses; and the children who sprang from these unions became numerous, their descendants being at once recognized to-day. Such have generally sought European connections, and are occasionally found here and there in all parts of the country, frequently engaged in the walks of business life. It will be remembered that New Zealand did not become a recognized British colony until the year 1840. For three quarters of a century after Cook's first visit the native tribes remained in free possession of their country. It is true that England was constructively mistress of these islands by right of discovery, but she made no formal assumption of political domain until the period already named, when it was formed into a colony subordinate to the Government of New South Wales. Up to the year 1840 English and American trading-vessels and whalers bought and sold articles from the natives, mostly consisting of flax (the wild growth of the country), for which they paid in fire-arms and powder, — though the weapons thus disposed of to the Maoris were such generally as had been condemned as useless in American or European lands. The sale of fire-arms to the islanders was stopped as soon as the English took formal possession; but in the mean time the Maoris had possessed themselves of sufficient weapons to make them dangerous enemies in the warfare which so soon became a settled condition of affairs between them and the white invaders. As early as 1815 white men of a venturous disposition began to settle in small numbers among the natives; but often their fate was to be roasted and eaten by cannibals. Before 1820 missionaries, no doubt influenced by truly Christian motives, came hither and devoted their lives to this people, — in more senses than one, as it is well known that they not infrequently met with a fate similar to that of their secular brethren.

In 1839 an incorporated association in London, called the New Zealand Company, sent out a ship loaded with emigrants to settle in the country. These were the pioneers who established the city of Wellington, the present capital of the islands. The country was still under the jurisdiction of New South Wales; but in 1841 it was constructed into an independent colony, and the first Legislative Council was held at Auckland. Thenceforth special settlements were regularly made by shipments from England; and in 1852 the Imperial Parliament granted the people of New Zealand a charter of self-government. By this act the sovereign power was vested in a General Assembly, consisting of a

Governor appointed by the Crown, and two Houses, — a Legislative Council, or Upper House, the members of which are nominated by the Government, and a House of Representatives chosen by the people at large.

Before taking the reader to the several cities embraced in the route we followed through New Zealand, a few preliminary and general remarks, embracing information which is the outgrowth of subsequent experience, may add interest to these pages and render our progress more intelligible. First, as to position, New Zealand lies as far south of the Equator as Italy does north of it. It is divided into the North and South Islands by Cook's Strait. The South Island is also known as Middle Island, to distinguish it more fully from Stewart Island, which belongs to the group, and which lies to the south of it. This last-named island is separated from Middle Island by Foveaux Strait, some fifteen or twenty miles across from the Bluff. It is about fifty miles long by thirty broad, and has a mountain range running through it, the loftiest peak of which is a trifle over three thousand feet high. There are some fishing hamlets here, but very few inhabitants. All these islands are believed to have once been a part of a great continent, which is now sunk in the sea.

The Southern Alps of the South Island, which were thus named by Captain Cook, are wooded up to the snow-line, the greatest height reached by any portion of the range being thirteen thousand feet;

and let us add that in frosty grandeur they are unequalled outside the limits of Polar regions. Vast snow-fields and glaciers exist among them, whence flow icy streams to the lakes of the table-land. The southwest corner of the island, as already intimated, is peculiarly indented by glacial action. There are numerous large lakes in both the North and South islands, notably in the district called Southland, in the South Island, where there are twelve large bodies of fresh water. These lakes are usually called the Cold Lakes of New Zealand, in distinction from those in the North Island known as the Hot Lakes. Many of these bodies of water in both sections are of enormous depth and of great scenic beauty. One is often reminded of Scotland by the general scenery in New Zealand, both countries being characterized by dark, serrated mountains casting sombre shadows into still, deep bays. Lake Taupo in the central part of the North Island covers an area of two hundred and fifty square miles. There are numerous mountain ranges in the North especially, which are mostly covered with forests, and three giant snow-capped mountains, — Ruapchu, Tongariro, and Mount Egmont, — ranging from seven to ten thousand feet each in height. The several portions of these islands differ materially from one another; the strange volcanic developments of the North Island are not repeated in the South. Of local peculiarities we shall speak in detail as we progress.

It is not yet a hundred and twenty years since

Captain Cook first landed in New Zealand, and the numerous native population that then swarmed upon its shores have dwindled to a comparative shadow of a once formidable race. But it is the present, not the past, with which we have mostly to do, — the present aspect of mountains, valleys, rivers, and lakes; with the wonderful volcanic developments and present activity of submerged forces that are exhibited in this peculiar country. Though heroic deeds and historic associations have not hallowed these localities, they are sufficiently unique in their own inherent charms to be intensely attractive. One does not pause amid burning mountains, boiling springs, and rushing geysers, to dwell on the want of human or historic background; the marvellous sublimity of Nature is sufficient. The bleaching bones of men and of extinct enormous birds, found among the brown tussocks of these lonely plains and in these curious caves, tell of a period long past, — and yet a period unhistoric and unheroic. These pages will clearly show that there is no lack of grandeur and beauty in this isolated land, but there is an utter lack of pathos.

Unlike Australia, New Zealand is rarely visited by drought; the whole eastern coast, north and south, abounds in good natural harbors, while the rivers and streams are ever-flowing and innumerable. Though it is a mountainous country, it differs for instance from Switzerland, in that it has no lack of extensive plains, which seem to have been left by Nature ready to the hand of the farmer, requiring scarcely ordinary cultivation to insure large crops of cereals. The diversity of surface, as well as the fact that these islands extend over thirteen degrees of latitude, give New Zealand a varied climate; but it is a remarkably temperate one, its salubrity far surpassing that of England or any portion of the United States. While snow is never seen in the North Island except upon the highest mountain peaks, the plains of the South Island — as far south as Otago — are sometimes sprinkled with it, but only to disappear almost immediately. The rivers are generally destitute of fish, and the forests of game. It is no sportsman's country; but vegetation runs riot, the soil being remarkably fertile, clothing the wild lands with perpetual verdure and vigorous freshness. Persons competent to express an opinion, compare the climate in the north, say at Auckland, with that of Spain; the middle, represented by Wellington, with that of France; and the southern, say at Invercargill, with that of England. The area of the islands is about one hundred thousand square miles, being a few more than are contained in England, Wales, and Ireland combined. The entire coast line is four thousand miles in length. There are here nearly seventy million acres of land, forty millions of which are deemed worthy of cultivation. The soil being light and easily worked, favors the agriculturist, and New Zealand is free from all noxious animals and venomous reptiles.

There are other islands besides the two principal

ones named (adding Stewart Island), but they are too small to require mention. The wonderful collection of geysers, sulphurous springs, and natural baths of the North Island are famous all over the world, and we shall presently ask the reader to visit them with us. Slight shocks of earthquakes are not uncommon here, but only one serious volcanic eruption has occurred for many years. The remote situation of the country, surrounded by the greatest extent of ocean on the globe, has kept it in a measure unknown to the rest of the world, even in these days of rapid communication. Wellington, the capital, is about sixteen thousand miles, more or less, from the Colonial Office in London; in other words, New Zealand forms the nearest land to the actual antipodes of England. The precious metals are distributed over the land in gold-bearing quartz reefs, rich alluvial diggings, and in the sands of its many rivers; mines of tin and iron and other deposits are supplemented by an abundance of the most important of all minerals, coal. In 1861 the gold-fields were discovered in Otago, stimulating fresh immigration, until at the present writing the country contains in round numbers six hundred thousand souls.

In these general remarks let us not forget to express hearty appreciation of the pronounced hospitality of the people of these British Colonies, both in Australia and New Zealand. It was almost impossible to escape its generous importunity, or to steal from it a few hours daily for personal observation and reflection. Intelligent, kind-hearted persons sometimes forget that even the best meant hospitality may become oppressive by over-effusiveness. We might have passed free over every railroad in Australia and New Zealand, the coasting steamers had a cabin quite at our service without charge, and even our hotel bills would have been handed to us receipted without pay, had we permitted it; but no service of whatever sort was accepted without the current charge for the same being paid. We wish, however, to bear testimony to the whole-heartedness which was so liberally displayed to a stranger. A chance newspaper paragraph printed by a Sydney journal on our first arrival, whose editor recognized the author's name, went the rounds of the Colonial press, and we were thus promptly recognized on appearing at each new locality.

As regards the matter of federation, spoken of in connection with Australia, it seemed to us hardly to apply to New Zealand, since this country is already one in this respect. There is no such folly recognized in New Zealand as a tariff between the different sections. As to federation with Australia, twelve hundred miles and more away across the sea, the citizens of Dunedin, Wellington, and Auckland say they do not see any possible advantage to accrue to them from it. On the contrary, they would lose more than they could by any possibility gain. New Zealand looks askance upon all high-tariff methods, and would gladly have free-trade. "We do not want to see public enterprise thus handicapped in Dunedin," said a prominent merchant of that city to us,—a sentiment echoed a few weeks later by an English resident doing business in Auckland, who said to us frankly, "We hope your country will keep up its high tariff; it suits us exactly. If you were to adopt free-trade principles in the United States you would eventually ruin the trade of England in the markets of the world."

CHAPTER XIII.

The City of Dunedin. — Scotch Residents. — The Enchanter's Wand. — Chain-Cable Tramways. — Volcanic Effects. — The Salvation Army. — Local Gold-Fields. — Enormous Aggregate Product. — Trees and Flowers. — The Rabbit Pest. — Port Littleton. — Market Day in Christchurch. — An Interesting City. — Wonderful Extinct Bird. — Strange Record of an Unknown Race. — The New Zealand Forests.

WE sailed from the Bluff at sunset on our return from Invercargill, having a boisterous voyage of fourteen hours to Dunedin, the chief city of Otago District, and indeed the chief city of New Zealand, if we make the number of inhabitants and the wealth of the place a criterion of comparison. Port Chalmers, situated a few miles below Dunedin, forms an outer harbor, so to speak; but vessels drawing twenty feet of water moor at the city wharves at high tide. We were told that the channel from the sea to the town was to be deepened so as to admit of vessels reaching the wharves at all stages of the tide, and that dredging for this purpose would begin at once. The lower harbor is land-locked, being surrounded by hills which slope gracefully down to the water's edge, the general conformation here recalling the scenery about the Lakes of Killarney. All the way up the river from Port Chalmers, a distance of nine miles, the banks are dotted with pleasant rural residences, picturesque acclivities, and low wooded ranges. Here and there were seen broad fields of grain and rich pastures, with domestic cattle grazing, and a few score of choice sheep, — the whole forming an aspect of rural thrift and peaceful abundance. If, as was the case in our instance, the tide is too low to admit of the steamers going up to the town, one can land at the Port and proceed to Dunedin by rail, — an opportunity which was gladly availed of, as we had "enjoyed" quite enough of sea-travel for some weeks at least.

The cities of both Australia and New Zealand have a habit of locating themselves among and upon a collection of hills, up the sides of which the houses creep in a very picturesque manner. Dunedin is no exception to this rule, rising rather abruptly from the plateaux where are the wharves and business centre of the town, to the summit of the foot-hills about which it lies. The town is more undulating in its conformation than Hobart, so lately described. A portion of the level plain near the shore, upon which broad streets and fine substantial blocks of buildings now stand, consists of made land, redeemed at great expense and trouble from the shallow water front. This whole section is as level as a dining-table. Heavy shipping business cannot well be conducted on a hillside; therefore the construction of this plateau was a necessity, as the town grew in size and extended its commercial relations. A couple of mountains close at hand, each of which is considerably over two thousand feet in height, dominate the city.

The Scottish character of the early settlers of Dunedin, as well as that of the present population, is emphasized by the names of its twenty odd miles of well-lighted and well-paved streets, of which nearly all the names are borrowed from the familiar thoroughfares of Edinburgh. The only monumental statue in the town is that of Scotland's beloved poet, Robert Burns, which is situated before the Town Hall, in a small enclosure. The first settlement here was as late as 1848, by a colony nearly every member of which came from Scotland, from which source the city has continued to draw many of its citizens. The Scottish brogue salutes the ear everywhere; the Scottish physiognomy is always prominent to the eye; indeed, there are several prevailing indications which cause one half to believe himself in Aberdeen, Glasgow, or Dundee. This is by no means unpleasant. There is a solid, reliable appearance to everything; people are rosy-cheeked, hearty, and good to look at; there is a spirit of genuineness impregnating the very atmosphere, quite wanting in many places named in these pages.

The wand of the enchanter touched the place in 1861, from which date it took a fresh start upon the road of prosperity. It was caused by gold being discovered in large quantities near at hand, and from that date Dunedin has grown in population and wealth with almost unprecedented rapidity. Large substantial stone edifices have sprung up on all the main thoroughfares devoted to business purposes, — banks, public offices, churches, store-houses, and schools, — giving a substantial aspect quite unmistakable. Numerous large buildings of white freestone were in course of erection while we were in the city, the material being brought from a neighboring quarry. This stone very much resembles that which we found in such general use in Tasmania; it is very easily worked, but rapidly hardens upon exposure to the atmosphere.

The market gardening for the supply of vegetables to the citizens of Dunedin was found to be carried on in the immediate vicinity by the Chinese, just as it is in and about the cities of Australia. No one attempts to compete with them in this line of occupation. There was found to be here about the same relative number of Asiatics as elsewhere among these South Sea colonies, and a small section of the town is devoted to their headquarters.

There are numerous tramways in this capital, the cable principle being adopted in most of them. Dunedin, indeed, was the first town in Australasia to adopt this improved motor; and although horse-power is still employed upon some of the thoroughfares, the former mode has the preference both in point of cleanliness and economy, — besides which, horses could not draw heavily-laden cars up some of the steep streets of Dunedin. The sensation when riding on one of these cable roads up or down a steep grade in the city, was much the same as when ascending or descending the Rigi in Switzerland, by means of the same unseen motor. The car is promptly stopped anywhere to land or take in a passenger, by the simple movement of a lever, and is as easily started again. There is no painful struggle of horse-flesh to start forward again after each stop. The powerful stationary engine situated a mile away, by means of the chains beneath the road-bed, quietly winds the car up the declivity, however heavily it may be laden, without the least slacking of power, irregularity of motion, or any visible exertion of force. It seemed to us that no better motor could possibly be devised, especially when rising grounds are to be surmounted. The principle is well demonstrated in some of the steepest avenues in San Francisco, where cable tramways have long been successfully operated.

Dunedin has two capacious theatres; also a public library containing about thirty thousand volumes, attached to which is a cheerful reading-room supplied with all the best magazines and journals of the times, including several of the most popular of our American issues.

Not to contain a Botanical Garden within its limits would be for the place to take a retrograde step among its sister colonial cities; and so Dunedin has a very creditable one, with many exotic trees and plants, which have readily adapted themselves to the climate. Among these there were observed some beautiful larches, junipers, cypresses, Chinese gingko-trees, Irish yews, Indian cedars, American birches, and many magnificent tree-ferns. Mingled with these were flower-beds of heath, laurestinus, daphne, and yellow gorse, all in gorgeous bloom, though it was mid-winter. The daphnes had both blossom and red berries upon their stems at the same time. The palm-like cabbage-tree is indigenous, and imparts an aspect of Equatorial Africa to the whole. To us there is a pleasing revelation in these trees and plants, however simple they may be in themselves. There is a refinement, a delicacy of taste, a love of the beautiful in Nature evinced in all such gathering of the products of widespread countries and different hemispheres, and placing them in juxtaposition. Wonderful are the lovely contrasts and striking natural peculiarities presented to the eye in so comparatively a small compass. Time was when one must travel the wide world over to see these arboreal representatives of varied climes; now they may be enjoyed in an afternoon stroll through the flower-decked paths of some local botanical garden.

Real appreciation looks deeper than the surface; there are stories and legends always ready to be whispered into the ear of the inquiring traveller. These singularly formed hills about Dunedin are not mere barren rocks; they have their suggestiveness, speaking of volcanic eruptions, of wild prehistoric upheavals dating back for many thousands of years. Scientists tell us these islands are of the earliest earth formations. The ground upon which this city stands, like that of Auckland farther north, is composed of the fiery outflow of volcanic matter.

It goes without saying that Dunedin has all the usual educational and philanthropic institutions which a community of fifty thousand people demand in our day. Especially is it well supplied with educational advantages, which seem to be conscientiously improved by the rising generation. The sum expended upon the public schools by the Government is very large; the exact amount is not now remembered, but we recollect being impressed with the fact that it was remarkable for a community of no greater numbers. Throughout New Zealand there are over eight hundred registered public schools of the various grades. The public buildings, notably the University, High School, Provincial Council Hall, and the Presbyterian Church, — this last of a very white stone, nearly as white as marble, — are all imposing and elegant structures.

These cities have not escaped the nuisance of the "Salvation Army," whose principal arguments consist of instrumental noise and torchlight parades. Here in Dunedin, as in Sydney and Melbourne, Auckland and elsewhere in the colonies, they constitute a chronic bore. They are composed of about one third women, and two thirds men and boys; the women beat crazy tambourines, wear poke bonnets, and sing aloud in cracked voices, while the men form themselves into instrumental bands, and produce the most hideous discord. These designing, or deluded, creatures tramp through the streets, in rain or shine, howling and uttering meaningless shouts until they are hoarse. The authorities do not interfere with such demonstrations, though they are clearly a public nuisance; but the mob deride and jeer them. Doubtless the persistent and remarkable exhibitions indulged in by these noisy religionists attract the vulgar imagination, and make followers if not converts. The public house at which we were stopping — the Grand Hotel — faces upon Prince's Street, which is the principal thoroughfare of the city, and in which is a square, ornamented by a monument erected to the memory of Captain William Cargill, the leading pioneer of this region. About the base of this well-lighted monument, it being night, a band of Salvationists were alternately playing upon brass instruments and singing hymns while we were endeavoring to write. The impression was thus strongly forced upon us that this open-air piety, this noisy and gratuitous religious serenading is more disagreeable than efficacious for good.

Having spoken of the Grand Hotel of Dunedin, let us add that it is one of the best houses of public entertainment we have found in all Australasia. It is a large, elegantly-appointed freestone building, under admirable management, — a little in advance perhaps of the present requirements of the city, but the population is rapidly increasing, to which end a first-class hotel largely contributes by attracting strangers and making their visit agreeable in all that conduces to their domestic comfort.

Within about seventy-five miles of Dunedin are some of the most productive gold-fields in the country. Gabriel's Gulch, so called, has proved to be a mint of the precious metal so rich that all the tailings of the diggings which have been once worked at a handsome profit, are just being submitted to a second and more scientific process in order to obtain the gold which is known still to remain in them. The amount of these tailings in gross weight is doubtless hundreds of thousands of tons; what percentage of gold to the ton will be realized, remains to be seen. An interested party informed us that it was confidently expected that more profit would be obtained by this second treatment than had been realized by the first. Some average samples sent to England for scientific treatment yielded at the rate of two ounces and one half of gold to the ton of tailings. If even two ounces can be realized, these diggings of Gabriel's Gulch will prove a Bonanza indeed.

New Zealand in proportion is nearly as rich in gold deposits as is Australia, and the precious metal is found under very nearly the same conditions; that is, in quartz reefs and in alluvial deposits. Much gold has been found here in what are termed pockets, under bowlders and large stones that lie on the sandy beach of the west coast. This gold is popularly believed to have been washed up out of the sea in heavy weather; but undoubtedly it was first washed down from the mountains by the rivers, and deposited along the shore. Official returns show that New Zealand has produced over fifty million pounds sterling in gold, or two hundred and fifty million dollars, since its first discovery there. Besides Europeans there are several thousand Chinese engaged in mining for gold; and here as in Australia these Asiatics work upon such claims and such tailings as have been abandoned by others.

Fern-trees abound in and about Dunedin, often growing to a height of thirty feet, with noble coronals of leaves, — far more effective and graceful than the fan-palm which is seen in such abundance at Singapore, Penang, and in Equatorial regions. The fuchsias grow to mammoth proportions and to a giant height here. We have never seen this favorite so large elsewhere, with one exception, — in the Summer Gardens of St. Petersburg, where an exotic plant of this beautiful flowering shrub had grown to the size of a tree, twenty feet high. About the suburban residences of this colonial capital laburnums, roses, laurels, and lilies abound, blooming all the year round. Innumerable exotics have been brought hither, and as was remarked to us by a citizen who was exhibiting a fine display on his own grounds, "the plant that will not thrive in New Zealand in any month of the year with ordinary care, out of doors, is yet to be found." This gentleman showed us a tiny flower in bloom, so like the Swiss edelweiss that we asked whence it came, and learned that it is a native of the mountain regions of New Zealand. It was surely an edelweiss, the simple but beautiful betrothal flower of the European Alps. It has a different name here, which we cannot recall. As to trees, the elm, beech, willow, fir, ash, and oak have so long been introduced from England, have been so multiplied, and have grown to such proportions, that they seem native here. Botanists tell us that there are not quite fifty different species of trees in England; but we are assured by equally good authority that there are a hundred and fifty different species found in New Zealand,— an assertion we could easily believe after having been in the country a few weeks, and enjoyed the beauty of its abundant forests.

When Captain Cook first came hither, he fully understood the cannibal habits of the native race, and desired to take some practical steps toward discouraging and effacing such inhuman practices. Upon his second visit, therefore, he introduced swine and some other domestic animals, including goats, in the vain hope that they would ultimately supply sufficient animal food for the savages and divert them from such wholesale roasting and eating of one another. The goats and some other animals were soon slaughtered and eaten, but the swine to a certain extent answered the purpose which Captain Cook had in view. That is to say, they ran wild, multiplied remarkably, and were hunted and eaten by the natives; but cannibalism was by no means abolished or even appreciably checked. Wild hogs are still quite abundant throughout the Northern Island, springing from the original animals introduced years ago.

With equally good intent, though not for a similar purpose, in later years rabbits were introduced into the country, but have in the mean time so multiplied as to become a terrible pest, consuming every green thing which comes in their way. "Like locusts they devour everything that grows out of the ground," said a stock farmer to us, "and would if left to themselves soon eat the sheep out of the fields." The flesh is recognized as good and suitable to eat, but it is so abundant that it is held in small repute, the skins only as a rule being preserved, and the carcasses left on the ground where they are killed, to be consumed by hawks and other carrion-eating birds. When brought to market, as they are daily, the retail price of rabbits is two pairs for sixpence, the seller retaining the skins and receiving the bounty paid by Government for their destruction. We were told that London and Paris are the largest consumers of the rabbit-skins, being freely used by the glove-makers for the manufacture of a certain grade of gloves. We also saw large cases of the skins securely packed and addressed to merchants in Vienna and Berlin. Thousands of bales of rabbit-skins are annually exported; indeed, so extensive is this trade that there is a large commercial room established in Dunedin called the Rabbit-Skin Exchange, where the article is bought and sold in enormous quantities. Thirty-five miles inland from this city, the author has seen by moonlight a whole sloping hillside which seemed to be moving, so completely was it covered by these little furry quadrupeds. They are poisoned, shot, trapped, and killed with clubs, but still so rapidly do they breed that there is no visible diminution of their numbers.

From Dunedin to Christchurch by sea is about two hundred miles, or the trip may be made by sail *via* Oamaru and Timaree. The harbor of Littleton, which stands in the same relation to Christchurch as Port Chalmers does to Dunedin, is a thoroughly sheltered deep bay, surrounded by a range of hills on three sides, — hills of cliff-like character rising abruptly out of the sea. Beyond those are higher elevations, their tops covered with snow, which the sun tinged with silvery hues as we sailed up the channel on a bright July morning. The surroundings are delightfully picturesque, the entrance to the harbor being as narrow as the harbor of Havana. It is formed by two breakwaters extending from opposite sides toward each other, each of which is over a thousand feet in length. Two huge dredging-machines were seen busily at work deepening the channel, so that vessels drawing not over twenty-two feet of water can lie at the wharves and discharge cargo. The spirit of commercial enterprise was very manifest here.

It was as late as the year 1850 that the first settlement was made at Christchurch, when a considerable company of immigrants, since called the "Canterbury

Pilgrims," came from Liverpool intending to form a community devoted to the Church of England. This design however was only partially carried out, though Christchurch is the chief seat of the Church of England in New Zealand, and has a magnificent cathedral testifying to the design of the original founders. It is said that the first people who arrived freely expressed their disappointment when they climbed the hills of Littleton and looked off upon the Canterbury Plains, with scarce a tree or shrub upon them, and not even a hillock to break the dull monotony of the brown tussock and low clumps of wild flax. A little over thirty years have since passed, and how different is the view to-day! Those lonely, dreary plains are now covered with thrifty farms, divided by broad fields of grain and well-fenced orchards, dotted here and there with pleasant homesteads surrounded by ornamental trees and blooming gardens, while as the centre and motive of it all there lies in the foreground, close at hand, Christchurch, the cheerful and populous City of the Plains. The lonely aspect of thirty years ago has given place to one instinct with busy life and modern civilization.

Littleton with its four thousand inhabitants is a most active and intensely busy seaport. We were not prepared to find so much shipping lying at its wharves. The long piers which are built out from the shore are lined with foreign and coasting steamers, and are also laid with iron rails connecting with the railroad which runs into the interior. Thus freight is brought in the cars alongside of the shipping, and it requires only a hoisting apparatus to fill rapidly with freight the hold of the largest vessel. The export of New Zealand produce from Littleton in 1886 reached the aggregate of nearly two million pounds sterling, and the revenue collected during the same year was two hundred thousand pounds sterling. The harbor is overlooked by a castellated signal-tower, situated upon a lofty cliff; and the town itself is terraced over the hillsides after the usual style of the colonies. Nothing could be more striking to the eye upon entering the harbor from the sea than these cliff residences.

Littleton is connected with Christchurch by a railroad, the tunnel for which is cut directly through the surrounding range of hills, which are almost worthy of the name of mountains. The tunnel is considerably over a mile in length. When this means of surmounting the great impediment presented by the hills was first suggested, it met with serious opposition, as being far too expensive an enterprise for so young a colony to undertake. So it was for a while given up; but as the colony grew in numbers, and produce for shipment poured into Christchurch, the necessity of the railroad was more and more fully realized. Without it, all exports by the way of the port of Littleton must be hauled by animal power over the hills at great expense. Finally the road was authorized; and once being determined upon, it was quickly built, at a cost of over one million dollars.

Having penetrated the range of hills by means of this grand improvement, one emerges into a broad level country, and passes through an agricultural district which is under a high state of cultivation, beautified here and there by pleasant rural residences, gardens, and wooded reaches. The land is divided into convenient lots and separated by tall hedges of gorse, blooming in all its gaudy yellow splendor, and impregnating the atmosphere with a sweetness which belied the season, seeming rather to belong to the balmy days of early spring. Eight miles of rail brings us to the outlying portions of Christchurch.

This metropolis of the Canterbury Plains is located upon ground as level as a chessboard, its broad streets intersecting one another with almost painful regularity and precision, but lined with fine substantial stone buildings, and rendered attractive by many shops displaying a great variety of goods. These avenues are full of busy life; horse-railroads, freight-wagons, coaches, and cabs are constantly passing before the eyes. The day of our arrival chanced to be that of the monthly races, and all the world of Christchurch and its environs had turned out to enjoy a holiday. Some of the shops were closed at noon, that all might participate in this gala occasion. Four-horse teams, with long ranges of extra seats rigged for the purpose, started from the public square laden with male passengers, the vehicles bearing great placards reading, "To the Races for one shilling." One might have imagined oneself in New

York or London, so rushing was the tide of life through Cashel Street and Cathedral Square.

The Public Garden of Christchurch is situated in a bend of the river Avon, on the western side of the city, about five minutes' walk from the business centre of the town. It occupies some eight or ten acres of land laid out in tasteful style. That portion which adjoins the river is lined with a beautiful border of weeping willows. A system is adopted in arranging the plants whereby all of a hardy nature are placed by themselves, the tropical vegetation being arranged together in the same manner; the plants indigenous to Japan, China, India, Australia, and Great Britain form each a group by themselves. This is called the geographical order, and has some advantages; but in adhering to such an arbitrary rule of adjustment, picturesqueness of effect must often be sacrificed. This whole collection of plants is of considerable beauty and scientific interest, though the garden is yet in its infancy, being less than twenty years old; but it is yearly undergoing much improvement.

A city built upon a perfect level is very rarely seen either in Australia or New Zealand, though there are exceptions, as in the case of Adelaide. Such a site is by no means so pleasant to the eye, albeit there are many practical advantages gained thereby. One feels shut up as it were in these long level reaches; the abrupt hills of Sydney, Dunedin, or San Francisco are preferable, even if often inconvenient. Nevertheless Christchurch is a pleasing, prosperous, and rapidly growing city, with much architectural beauty in its thoroughfares. As the commercial outlet of a broad-spread, fertile, and easily accessible district, it must continue to prosper commercially. Saturday is an especially attractive day here, when the country people — both men and women — from considerable distances come to town to dispose of their produce in the open market. The variety and excellence of meats, vegetables, fruits, and flowers accumulated here on such occasions is worthy of any large capital city. There is a conglomerate of humanity drawn together on this busy day of the week, which turns the streets and squares into a sort of out-door fair. We observed none of that abandon and careless dissipation which characterizes Melbourne on Saturdays; and yet Christchurch does not lack for an ample class who make pleasure-seeking a regular occupation.

At the Museum in this city a most interesting and perfect skeleton of that great prehistoric bird the Moa was seen, — a bird which was indigenous in New Zealand, and which is believed to have been extinct for about two thousand years, probably disappearing before any human beings came to these islands. The Maori Indians can be traced back but six or seven hundred years, and only very imperfectly during that period. They are believed to have come from the islands lying in the more northerly Pacific, presumedly from the Sandwich or Hawaiian group. Even the traditions of these natives fail to give us any account of this gigantic bird while living; but its bones are found in various sections of the country, principally in caves, and from these we must "gather and surmise." What is left of the Moa to-day is quite sufficient to form the greatest ornithological wonder in the world. The head of this reconstructed skeleton in the Museum of Christchurch stands sixteen feet from the ground, and its various proportions are all of a character to harmonize with its remarkable height. This skeleton shows the marvellous bird to have been, when standing upright, six feet taller than the average full-grown camelopard. It belonged to the Titans who dwelt upon the earth perhaps twenty or thirty thousand years ago, in the period of the Mastodon and the Dodo. What Niagara is to ordinary waterfalls, the Moa was to all the bird-tribe. It was a long time before incredulous scientists could be induced to admit these interesting facts, but the tangible evidence now existing in the Museum of this New Zealand city is indisputable. This Museum owes its great excellence and admirable scientific arrangement to Dr. Von Haast, the famous geologist and early explorer of New Zealand, and forms a worthy monument to his great fame in the world of science.

Some writers who have made a study of the subject are inclined to believe that the Moa was still existing when the first of the Maoris arrived in New Zealand; but this is only a supposition. It is an open question, indeed, whether the Maoris were or were not the first human beings to tread the soil of these islands.

There is sufficient evidence relating to this subject to whet the appetite of conjecture, but not to satisfy it. In the Takiroa caves of the South Island in the Waitaki Valley, and in a sheltered rocky glen or half cave near Canterbury, there are certain crude rock-paintings which are a puzzle to savants. These consist of figures representing men, birds, beasts, fishes, snakes, altars, and weapons, crude indeed as to design, but recognizable. The Maoris know nothing of their origin, and in the present light of the history of that race there is nothing which leads to the belief of these rock-paintings being of Maori production; in fact there seems to be sufficient evidence to prove their greater antiquity. The present natives have never been rock-painters, not possessing for this the requisite skill, though they have always been carvers in wood after a rude fashion. There seems to be some consecutive meaning in these rock illustrations, though what is designed to be indicated cannot be made out by careful and experienced men who have come hither from Europe solely to examine them. They are indelibly painted in red and black on the face of the rock, which is composed of calcareous sandstone. Close examination of the various figures shows that they are underlaid by others, which have either worn away under atmospheric influences, or have been partially obliterated by hand to make place for those which now are prominently visible. Writing in hieroglyphics is not the accomplishment of savages, but argues at least a semi-civilized condition. So do the colossal statues of Easter Island (South Pacific), which were never created by any such race of people as the present savage inhabitants; and yet these tribes have no traditions even of any previous residents of their island. It is the world to them, or rather was until Europeans first visited the place.

The population of Christchurch is from thirty-five to forty thousand. The plain upon which the city stands extends upon the same level for a distance of fifty miles inland, forming one of the best agricultural divisions in New Zealand, which is called the Canterbury District. Statistics show this immediate region to have produced in 1886 nearly seven million bushels of wheat, over four million bushels of oats, besides barley and potatoes in very large quantities. There are over three hundred miles of railroad in the District upon which to bring this grain and produce to market, a large percentage of which is shipped to Europe. We were informed that the number of sheep in this District would considerably exceed four millions, and that the annual shipment of wool was very large. The immediate environs of the city are dotted with cornfields and dairy farms, whose products find a ready home demand. Christchurch is famous for its annual agricultural fairs and pastoral exhibitions, which attract annually twenty-five thousand strangers to the town.

A horseback ride of a few hours from this city into the "bush" reveals a wealth of wooded richness almost indescribable. The trees, mostly of the pine family, yet totally different from the trees to which we give that name, were gracefully draped with luxuriant creepers, mingled with which were glowing red blossoms. Tall fern-trees and flowering aloes shared our admiration with variegated orchids, blending color and form in lovely combinations. In the low grounds the deep-green leaves of the wild flax stood forth with their tall, honey-laden flowers nodding in the breeze and tempting the bees to their embrace. The glowing afternoon sunlight was mottled with busy-winged insect life. The lowly ferns spread in most inimitable patterns a verdant carpet beneath our feet, such as no cunning of the loom could equal. It is well worth a pilgrimage from far-away lands to make the acquaintance, solitary and alone, of the primeval New Zealand forests, where there are no reptiles to dread and no wild animals to encounter. Only Nature, old but unchanged, — Nature, still and grand, — is here to be seen, presenting features which teach us in eloquent language of our own littleness and her immeasurable grandeur.

The beauty of the New Zealand forest will not soon be forgotten. Reclining upon the verdure-spread earth, and watching the far-reaching shadows, one is lulled into a dreamy mood by the mysterious whispers of the foliage, the influence of the soft resinous atmosphere, and the low drone of insects. The leaves seem to tremble and vibrate like the strings of an Eolian harp. Is it because the brain is over-stimulated by acute sensitiveness that tears — absurd tears — dim the eyes while one is surrounded by this delicious solitude? All Nature seems to be in harmony with one's feelings in this paradise of paroquets and love-birds, this Eden of the Southern Seas, this climate of eternal spring. We have somewhere read of the paucity of song-birds in the regions of Australasia, but let us hasten to correct such an impression. The notes that are trilled over one's head in these umbrageous solitudes constitute a bird-opera worthy of the great southlands overhung by the Southern Cross.

CHAPTER XIV.

Capital of New Zealand. — About the Native Race. — A City of Shops. — Local Earthquakes. — Large Glaciers. — McNab's Gardens. — A Public Nuisance. — Napier. — Maori Peculiarities. — Native Language. — Mythology. — Christianizing Savages. — Gisborne. — Cruelty to Dumb Animals. — Shag Island. — Sir George Gray's Pleasant Home. — Oysters Growing on New Zealand Trees!

WELLINGTON is situated on the north side of Cook's Strait, and is the capital of New Zealand. It is less than two hundred miles from Christchurch. Auckland was originally the seat of government, but since 1864 this city has been the political capital, in consequence of which the jealousy existing between the two cities nearly equals that between Sydney and Melbourne. Wellington has a grand harbor for all commercial purposes, is very capacious and entirely land-locked. After a narrow entrance is passed, the harbor opens into a magnificent sheet of water, in which the largest ships may ride in safety and discharge their cargoes at wharves built upon the busiest streets of the town. Here, as in Dunedin, a plateau of land has been reclaimed from the sea for business purposes. The curved line of Lambton Quay, one of the main thoroughfares of the city, represents what was once the strand, but a number of broad streets with long lines of warehouses have grown up between it and the sea; so that Lambton Quay is now in the centre of the town. The reclaiming of still more level land from the water-front is going on, in order to accommodate business requirements. The province of Wellington stretches northward a hundred and fifty miles, containing seven million acres of land, diversified by two mountain ranges, and having as grand scenery as can be found in the islands.

Our stay at Wellington was brief, for there is nothing of special interest to detain one here, and two days seemed a long time to devote to it. Were it not that this city is the recognized capital of the country, we should have passed it by with the briefest mention. It has its asylums, a college, hospital, botanical gardens, Roman Catholic cathedral, and colonial museum, — the latter being of more than ordinary interest in the excellence and completeness of its several departments. What is called the Maori House, built by the natives, is particularly interesting, being full of aboriginal curiosities such as domestic utensils, weapons, and elaborate carvings. This house is of ordinary village size, and is elaborately ornamented on many of its panels and posts by the Indians of the Ngatikaipoho tribe, who reside on the Bay of Plenty, and who are famous for their carvings. The Theatre Royal is a fine structure capable of accommodating a thousand persons. The spacious Botanical Garden occupies one hundred acres of ground, just about double the size of that at Sydney, and contains besides the usual collection of exotics the most comprehensive assortment of native trees that we chanced to see anywhere.

The city is surrounded by hills, except on the seaward side. By ascending the hill back of the town, upon which is the Roman Catholic Cemetery, one obtains an excellent view of Wellington as a whole, the harbor especially forming a charming portion of the picture. Soame's Island, which is the quarantine station, lies in the front, four miles from the city; to the left lie Petone and the Hutt; at the right is Mount Victoria dominating the bay, while many pretty villas cluster about its foot. Distant ranges descend toward the harbor, shutting it in by an amphitheatre of hills. There is no lack of shipping about the wharves, and there were plenty of row-boats and small sailing cutters; and as we viewed the scene, an ocean steamship was steering across the bay seaward, leaving a long line of black curling smoke behind her, which was in strong contrast with her snow-white foaming wake.

We found it somewhat cold and rather blustering on Cemetery Hill, though it was July. But this is New Zealand winter; and yet flowers were blooming luxuriantly in the open air in unexposed places. These islands are in one sense as tropical as Africa or Southern India; but it must be remembered that they are the most southerly of the South Pacific groups, and that there is a Southern or Antarctic Pole as there is a Northern or Arctic one. The farther we proceed either north or south from the Equatorial line, or centre of the globe, the cooler we shall find the climate. Thus Southern New Zealand being nearer the Antarctic Circle is less tropical than the northern portion, which is twelve hundred miles nearer the Equator.

A considerable number of natives, mostly in European costume, were met in the streets of Wellington, loitering aimlessly about the corners and gazing curiously into shop windows. The girls and women had heavy shocks of unkempt hair shading their great black eyes, high cheek-bones, and disfigured mouths and chins, which last were tattooed in blue dye of some sort. The males tattoo the whole face elaborately, but the women only thus disfigure themselves about the mouth and chin. It was most amusing to see them meet one another and rub noses, which is the Maori mode of salutation. It would be an exaggeration to call these people a cleanly race, though the tribes that occupy the Hot Lake District (whither we shall take the reader in another chapter) spend two thirds of their time in the water. The half-breeds are generally of fine physical appearance, the men especially being tall and well-developed; indeed it would be difficult to find more admirable specimens of physical manhood than exist among these Anglo-Maoris. As we have elsewhere intimated, the daughters of some of the unions between whites and natives are very pretty and intelligent, having received partial education and acquired some pleasing accomplishments. But there are few of these to be found among the tribes, and fewer still among the whites.

Among these natives, as a rule, the laborious work is put upon the women, while the men fill the rôle of idlers. It seems strange that while they were thorough barbarians and cannibals they continued to thrive, — certainly they did not largely decrease in numbers; but with semi-civilization has come almost annual decimation. As we have seen was the case of the aborigines in Tasmania, it is believed by many that the same fate of final complete extinction is in store for the Maoris in the near future.

The entire coast north of Wellington is extremely bold, tumbled together in true volcanic confusion. In the neighborhood of the capital this conformation begins to extend inland; thus the city has no near background of available country for population, from which to draw a certain amount of business, — no suburbs, so to speak. The town impressed us as being a city of shops; and how so many persons can realize a fair living from the amount of local business in Wellington is certainly a mystery. Here the dwellings creep up the hills as we have so often described the case elsewhere; and as the houses are mostly built of wood, fires have proved especially destructive. We found the general Post-Office in ruins by a recent fire, though it was a brick structure; the lofty stuccoed walls were still standing. Some large new buildings nearly finished were also observed to be of brick. For a number of years at first the fear of serious earthquakes prevented the use of any other material in building than wood. Even now there is a frequent tremulousness of the earth, and rumblings as of distant thunder are heard in the hills that run inland from the city toward the high mountains, — all which is quite sufficient to keep the fact in mind that this is a volcanic region. Earthquake shocks are frequent all over the islands, from Cape Maria in the far north to South Cape in the southern part of Stewart Island. It is believed that New Zealand was rent midway, and that Cook's Strait was thus created between the North and South Islands by volcanic explosion. There is known to be an extinct volcano at the bottom of the Strait in front of the entrance to the harbor of Wellington, over which the water is never absolutely calm. Thus it would seem that the city is situated very near a volcanic centre. A fellow-traveller in discussing the matter suggested that it was not just the place to seek for a "permanent" investment; but on the other hand an intelligent elderly resident assured us that these demonstrations are gradually dying out. Fires have latterly been so sweeping and disastrous in Wellington, that this element is coming to be more dreaded than earthquakes; and partially to provide against destruction by flames, stone and brick as building materials in the centre of the town are being almost universally substituted for wood.

The Southern Alps, as the range which runs north and south through New Zealand is called, are believed to antedate the Alps of Europe, while nowhere else is marked evidence of glacial action more clearly defined. The glaciers of to-day, though they are insignificant in comparison to those of ancient periods, are of vast size and full of awe-inspiring effects. In one respect these glaciers particularly resemble those of Norway; that is, in descending so nearly to the sea. The author has seen enormous glaciers in Scandinavia whose lower portions were within a hundred feet of the surface of the ocean, while it is well known that in Switzerland there is no instance where a glacier descends lower than thirty-five hundred feet above the level of the sea.

Willis Street is the fashionable thoroughfare of Wellington, being considerably more than a mile in length and nearly straight; but it is quite irregular in width. This street is lined on either side with stores and public buildings, some of large and pretentious aspect. We counted nine good-sized bookstores upon this avenue, all well stocked with modern literature. One may safely put down this fact as being a significant sign of the general intelligence of the neighborhood. Wellington is certainly growing with the prevailing rapidity of the several localities which we visited; new streets were being laid out, of better width and having more regularity of form, while the roadways were being thoroughly macadamized, and rolled with a heavy steam-rolling machine. In the harbor a large steam-dredging boat was also busy deepening and straightening the course of the channel. Eleven steamships and half-a-dozen large sailing-vessels lay at the wharves, five of the latter from England. It is natural that the trade of the colonies should be very generally retained by the mother country, though there is a considerable commerce carried on with the west coast of America.

The stranger coming to the capital must not omit to visit the Hutt, a pleasant village situated where the Hutt River enters the bay. Here also is located the Wellington race-course; and most interesting of all the attractions hereabout is a famous resort known as McNab's Gardens. The pleasant lawns, flower-beds, and fruit-orchards of this place form a charming resort for pleasure parties out on a ride or drive from the city. Some of the ornamental trees contained in these gardens were the finest we saw in New Zealand. The labyrinth of walks leads through exquisitely kept flower-beds, which specially exhibit the remarkably favorable nature of the climate for floral displays at any season of the year. The many fine exotics which are exhibited here must have been accumulated at a heavy expense. ·A small admission fee is very properly charged by the proprietor, who is prepared also to supply any desired refreshments at a reasonable price. As we write these notes there steals over the senses a delicious memory of atmospheric sweetness, daintily impregnated with mignonette, lilies, lemon verbena, and roses, at that pleasant resort on Wellington Bay.

The last scene witnessed at the capital, as we were about to embark on a steamer for the north, was an attempt at a parade by some "Salvationists." The procession moved in single file, consisting of three poke-bonnets with an equal number of young women under them, two men in red coats, and two in dark clothes, very shiny and greasy. There were also four or five small boys, who so straggled from the line that it was by no means certain whether they belonged to it or not. One of the girls vigorously pounded a cracked tambourine, one of the red-coated men blew occasional blasts upon a tin fish-horn, and all sang psalms much out of tune. The sight would have been ludicrous, had it not been saddening. In the midst of the chorus, "Glory, Hallelujah," the foremost girl, at the most critical moment of her performance upon the tambourine, made a misstep and fell at full length in the middle of the muddy street, while her noisy instrument rolled away through the slush. "There is something in the misfortunes of our best friends which is not entirely displeasing to us," says a certain French philosopher; and so the Salvationists supplemented their companion's misfortune and their "Glory Hallelujah" with uproarious laughter. As the poke-bonnet became once more elevated, both it and the wearer presented a wofully dilapidated appearance. It seems incredible that fanaticism can make such ninnies of men and women, for some of these ill-conducting persons are probably sincere.

Napier is situated about two hundred miles north of Wellington, upon an open roadstead and a very dangerous coast, — a fact sadly impressed upon us by the wreck of a large ship, the "Northumberland," an English freighter which was destroyed here a few days before our arrival and portions of which were still visible. With two anchors down, this fine vessel was driven on shore and completely wrecked, involving the loss of several lives and much valuable property. Almost superhuman efforts were made in behalf of the sufferers by the local life-saving boat's crew, but only with partial success.

The business portion of Napier is quite level, and regularly laid out; but the residences of the population creep up, tier upon tier, on the surrounding hills, one of which forms an extraordinary promontory extending into the roadstead. The six thousand persons who constitute the population of the town seem to be taking life very easily; indeed, there did not appear to be much of any business going on in the place, and the quietude of it was not a little oppressive. There were small crowds of men and youth loafing before the bar-rooms upon the corners of the streets, and among them were observed quite a sprinkling of half-castes and full-blooded natives. There was also a number of native women strolling about listlessly, wrapped only in their high-colored blankets and wearing a single skirt. The tattooed faces rendered these women and girls needlessly hideous, — an aspect which was partially redeemed by their fine eyes, the beauty of which nothing can efface; they are large, black as night, and brilliant, full of feeling and tenderness. If the term "ox-eyed" ever applied to humanity, it is appropriate to the Maori women, who possess this one feature in perfection.

We obtained some noteworthy and interesting information relative to these aborigines. For instance, they never eat salt; they have no fixed industry, and no idea of time or its divisions into hours and months; they are, like our North American Indians, constitutionally lazy; they are intensely selfish, and care nothing for their dead; they have a quick sense of insult, but cannot as a rule be called pugnacious; they excite themselves to fight by indulging in a hideous war-dance and by singing songs full of braggadocio, and when thus wrought up to a certain pitch they are perfectly reckless as to personal safety. The Maori is not however a treacherous enemy; he gives honorable notice of his hostile intent, warring only in an open manner,— thus exhibiting a degree of chivalry unknown among our American Indians. Money with the Maori is considered only as representing so much rum and tobacco. Alcohol is their criterion of value; bread and meat are quite secondary. They live entirely from hand to mouth, to use an expressive term, and never take heed for the morrow. As a rule they seem entirely thoughtless and happy in the present, so long as their necessities are satisfied and their animal pleasures are not interfered with. After all, this semi-barbarous race are like children, who follow bad example sooner than good. "White man drink whiskey, why not I?" said one of them to us at Ohinemutu when we declined to give him "drink money." As a rule the Maoris are not beggars, except for strong drink. They will importune a stranger for rum, but not for bread. We were told by an official of the district at Napier that it is quite impossible to imbue these Maoris with a sense of the importance of chastity; the idea is ignored altogether. But it is with them as with the Japanese; after a woman is married she becomes sacred, and to treat her with unchaste violence then is to incur the penalty of death. It would be impossible to imagine a more immoral people, when judged by the conventionalities of our civilization, than these New Zealand natives.

Ancient traditions are fast fading away among this people, dying with the elders of the tribes in whose memory they are locked up. Though the missionaries half invented and half transcribed an oral Maori language, it is almost solely applied to a translation of the Bible, and there cannot be said now to exist any native literature. Yet, could their legends be properly recorded, they would form a sort of barbaric literature by no means without considerable poetic value. Sir George Gray has attempted something of the sort, but with indifferent success. He speaks the native tongue fluently, however, and has always sympathized heartily with the aboriginal race, who call him their English Father.

"Maori" (pronounced *Mowre*) is the name which the aborigines gave themselves. If there were any human beings on these islands when the Maoris first arrived they doubtless fell a prey to the cannibalistic habits of the new-comers, whose insatiable appetite for human food was, as we have seen, irrepressible. When discovered by Captain Cook, they were the crudest of savage races; they knew scarcely anything of the mechanic arts, their skill being limited to the scooping out of a boat from the trunk of a tree, and the fabrication of fishing-nets from the coarse fibre of the wild flax. They also made spears, shields, and clubs. They had no beasts of burden, and so their women were made to supply the place. Their agriculture was confined to the raising of sweet potatoes and the esculent taro, while their more substantial food consisted of fish, rats, wild fowl, and human flesh. Yet we are told by well-informed writers upon the subject that they were of all the South Sea tribes the most intelligent. They are physically the most vigorous of any savages inhabiting islands south of the Equator, that we have met. They seemed from the outset to be desirous of learning from and affiliating with the whites, — a disposition which has led them to a degree of improvement in domestic life, manner of living, building of proper shelter for a home, and the manufacture of certain articles of convenience. Wherever they are now found in the neighborhood of populous centres, they have more or less adopted European clothing, — though we were told some amusing anecdotes of their going back into the "bush," from time to time, solely to indulge in the old savage habit of nudity, and to enjoy a sense of entire freedom from the conventionalities of the whites.

There is not much intermarriage between the white people and the natives in these days, although when there were fewer white women this was not so uncommon; but the licentiousness prevalent among the native girls is sufficient to prevent this at the present time. The race evinces to-day many of the wild traits of their ancestors, which have been transmitted to them in their blood, and which break out in odd ways now and then when least expected. You cannot quite tame an Apache warrior, a Spanish gypsy, or a New Zealand Maori; there will still remain a lingering desire toward the old life, which will often be resumed upon the first opportunity by the seemingly reclaimed savage. These natives exhibit very little family affection, though we saw evidences of tenderness toward their very young children. The old men and women are not infrequently abandoned when ill or too feeble to take care of themselves, — a trait which is sometimes exhibited by our own Indian tribes. Polygamy and slavery still exist among them. Indeed, a married woman is virtually the slave of her husband, whom she is expected to supply with food by gathering roots, berries, fruits, and the like.

We are told by the early missionaries that the Maoris possessed an oral mythology rudely resembling that of the classics. They firmly believed in a future state of existence, and built rude temples to a Great Spirit, but could see no harm whatever in making war upon neighboring tribes for the purpose of replenishing their larder. So late as 1840 their greatest delight was the war-dance, the cannibal feast, and the boasting war-song. The braggadocio of their fighting songs would do credit to Falstaff; but the Maori affords us the anomaly of a braggart who is not by any means a coward. Now and then there is seen among them a face of so unmistakably a Jewish cast as to set the imagination at work to find some possible connection, far back among the by-gone ages, between this race and the Hebrews. When this peculiar cast of features is seen among the girls or young women, it forms a face strikingly attractive.

The Maoris when first discovered had many games and sports which were identical with our own, — such as flying kites, skipping rope, cat's-cradle, gymnastic pole-exercise, hide-and-seek, dancing, and walking upon stilts. They are represented to have been good orators, and have handed down proverbs from generation to generation, — terse sayings, which are still preserved among them, and which are in spirit similar to many of those of Confucius. Captain Cook estimated when he first visited them that the Maoris had passed the period of their best days. He thought that in the century previous to his coming hither they had eaten about one fourth of their number. The race now numbers only thirty-six or thirty-eight thousand, though it is certain it aggregated a hundred thousand and more one century ago. It seems that a half-caste man or woman rarely lives to the age of forty years, and of the pure-blooded we saw comparatively few old persons. Now and then one was met, hideous of feature, whose deeply indented wrinkles rivalled the lines of tattoo, and who was bent in figure, decrepit, and bereft of most of the human faculties. Such a one, perhaps, was not so extremely old in years, but was prematurely aged. They are all most inveterate smokers, men, women, and children; and you can give a Maori maiden of "sweet sixteen" nothing more acceptable to her taste than a pipe and a plug of smoking-tobacco.

We were told before going among these New Zealand aborigines that they had been Christianized; that is to say, they had discarded idolatry and the doctrines of their fathers, and accepted the gospel as propounded to them by the white missionaries. But this was not found to be exactly true. If large numbers of them have at times professed Christianity, many of the "converted" have also returned to their mumbo-jumbo faith. Half of them, we judge, have never even pretended to be Christians. Before you can *convert* savages, you must in a degree *humanize* them; and this humanizing process has yet to be accomplished among this race. The Maoris live nearly like the lower class of animals, preferring that sort of life even after half a century of intercourse with the whites. They may for policy's sake listen to, and pretend to accept Christianity, as many of the Chinese are known to do; but both races, it is well understood, return to their original faith at the first opportunity. The modern Maori accepts the creed of the missionaries because it is the easiest thing for him to do; but he still believes in witchcraft, the evil-eye, and sorcery as openly practised by his designing priests. The Roman Catholic faith, which addresses itself so palpably to the eye by form and ceremony, is most popular among them, and has by far the largest number of professed adherents of any denomination.

The Maoris isolate themselves mostly in what is called the King's Country of the North Island, which embraces the Hot Lake District; and here they live under their own rule and customs. Their king is absolute in the domain claimed by them, which is held inviolate by treaty with the English Crown. Their decrease in numbers is as rapid in the King's Country as it is where they are brought into more close connection with the whites. As a people they have manifestly fulfilled the purpose for which Providence placed them upon these islands of the South Sea; and now, like the Moa, they must pass off the same and give way to another race of beings. So it is with the Red man of America, and so was it with the now totally extinct natives of Tasmania. No philanthropic effort can stop the fulfilment of the inevitable. It is *Kismet*.

The town of Napier is made up in the business portion of one-story houses, though in the main street there are found some establishments rising to the dignity of two stories. A skeleton frame of wood, covered on roof and sides with corrugated iron only, forms the material of many of the stores and dwelling-houses. There is a long esplanade just back of the town, within three minutes' walk of the centre, which has a most superb sea view. It borders upon a shelving beach two miles long, and though not suitable for bathing purposes on account of having a dangerous undertow, it is very charming as a promenade. Iron seats are arranged here and there upon the crown of the roadway, where one can sit at leisure and enjoy the hoarse music of the waves, at the same time looking off upon an immense area of wave-tossed waters, the scene occasionally being varied by the sight of a passing steamship leaving her long trail of smoke upon the distant horizon. It was a cool and somewhat boisterous winter's day when we were there, and yet the seats upon the beach were occupied by some romantic couples who seemed rather inclined to force the season by imitating turtle-doves, except that the latter are not supposed to mate until the genial spring-time.

One day was quite sufficient time to pass in such a place as Napier. We had come hither by steamer, and were glad to get on board ship once more as night came on, which found us directly steaming away northward. Next morning soon after sunrise we cast anchor in an open roadstead off the town of Gisborne, where we took on board a couple of hundred of sheep transported to our ship from the shore by means of a lighter, and which were to be landed at Auckland. It was a cold, dreary, foggy Sabbath morning; the ship rolled heavily, and the appearance of the little steam-tug, which was lifted at one moment above our bulwarks and the next plunged almost beneath our keel, was not sufficiently inviting to induce us to land, so we know nothing personally about the town called Gisborne, except that no place can ever amount to much commercially which depends upon such an exposed roadstead for its shipping facilities. The disagreeable smell, the dirt, and the discomfort generally caused by those poor sheep on their way to be slaughtered, is remembered with a shudder. They were so closely packed together upon our open and uncovered deck, as to be unable to lie down at all; and when the hour of slaughter came it must have been to them — thirsty, hungry, and weary as they were, after two days and nights on board — a great relief from suffering. The outrageous inhumanity exercised toward these poor helpless creatures rendered us quite miserable through those forty-eight hours.

From Gisborne we were bound to Auckland, and when we arrived off that port we passed Sir George Gray's island, which has a Maori name signifying Shag Island. It is situated over twenty miles seaward from the city of Auckland, at the entrance of the Hauraki Gulf. Here Sir George has pitched his tent for life, being now well advanced in age. As a young man, when in the engineer corps of the

English army, his rare ability and conspicuous talents commanded general respect, and he was rapidly advanced through the several stages of promotion. He received public honors at an early age, being Governor of South Australia at thirty; afterward he was Governor of Cape Town, Africa, and later on was made Governor of New Zealand, though he is now only a member of its House of Assembly. His name is held in great reverence here by all classes, as that of one who has ever been a true promoter of the best interests of these colonies.

Sir George has a refined literary taste, and is a profound ethnological scholar. Probably no European has so thoroughly mastered the Maori tongue as he, or done so much toward producing a correct impression concerning the race. In any serious trouble between the aborigines and the colonists, both parties are always ready to abide by his settlement of the matter. The natives know he has their best good at heart, and follow his advice under all circumstances. He was Governor during the last and most serious war which occurred between the Maoris and the whites, and to his influence was chiefly due its successful and amicable end. While he was firm and energetic during the war, at its close he saved the remnant of the race from beggary by securing to them the large tract of country which they now occupy. This left them still free and independent, though as victors Sir George's government might have confiscated all the native lands.

Sir George's home upon this spacious island, which he owns, is a most delightful retreat, where he has gathered his houschold gods about him, consisting of many books, works of art, and curiosities relating to these islands. Here, surrounded by a pleasant family circle devoted to his happiness, he has elected to live to the close of his life. He formerly possessed a library which he had been many years in collecting under peculiar advantages, and which numbered over ten thousand volumes, mostly historical works. This collection he has recently presented to the corporation of Auckland for the benefit of the public, and it has been added to the Public Library of the city.

Shag Island is now a tropical garden, producing the fruits of all lands and the flowers of all latitudes. Oranges, lemons, and bananas were seen growing down to its very shores, while its sloping sides were covered with palms, cocoanuts, and various tropical trees flourishing side by side with those of hardier climes. Sir George is an enthusiastic gardener, and has here met with phenomenal success in the acclimatization of plants, trees, fruits, and flowers of all regions. There is a peculiar tree which thrives on the seaward side of this island, named by the Maoris *pokutukawa*, which signifies, "wet in the ocean's spray." It bears a profusion of crimson flowers; but both its roots and its willow-like boughs seek the water with a very obvious natural inclination, and to them adhere the sweet little oysters native to the

Hauraki Gulf. Thus it has been said, half in fable and half in truth, that the trees in New Zealand bear oysters!

What a change has come over this island, which not long ago was covered with a tangled forest, making one of the special strongholds of the aborigines! It was the aggressive tribe of Momona that so long and so successfully held Shag Island, whence their chief made daring raids upon the mainland to keep his larder supplied with the flesh of his enemies. At last, however, the tribes of the mainland joined together and attacked the island in a body, putting its thousand defenders to the sword; and after feasting long upon their bodies, the successful invaders returned to celebrate their victory at the foot of Mount Eden, whose giant proportions overlook the present city of Auckland.

CHAPTER XV.

Historical Glance at Auckland. — A Remarkable Volcanic Region. — City Institutions. — Queen Street and Its Belongings. — Mount Eden. — Comprehensive View. — Labor Unions. — The Public Debt. — Kauri Forests. — Production of Kauri Gum. — Environs of Auckland. — The Native Flora. — An Admirable Climate. — A Rich Mineral District. — Agricultural Development.

AUCKLAND is the northern metropolis of New Zealand, and to us seemed to be its most representative city. As we have before mentioned, it was formerly the capital of the country until Wellington was selected for the headquarters of the Government, as being the more central and accessible from the various islands. So beautiful and picturesque are the bay and harbor of Auckland that we were not at all surprised to hear its citizens call it the Naples of New Zealand. Before the European settlers came hither, this was the locality where the most savage wars were carried on by the natives, and where the most warlike tribes lived in fortified villages. Though the country has virtually no history that is known to us, it has a recognized past extending back for some centuries. When the missionaries first came here, about the year 1814, the main subsistence of the natives who lived around what is now Auckland harbor, was human flesh. The first white immigrants, as well as the seamen of chance vessels driven upon the coast, were invariably killed, cooked, and eaten by the Maoris, until the white men became more wary, and by superior intelligence, backed by more effective weapons, proved themselves to be the masters. Thus the time soon came when the natives dared not attack the whites; but they still carried on their cannibalistic wars against one another, apparently determined upon mutual destruction. Not only did cannibalism prevail here at the time of the early discoveries, but also in Brazil, in the West Indies, in the Pacific Islands, along the coast of North America, and among the Indians of Chili, who ate the early navigators that landed upon their shores.

This province bears the same name as the city, and is a region of grand forests, fertile plains, and majestic rivers, — the very opposite of arid inland Australia. The variety and value of its trees suitable for timber are exceptionally noticeable; it was this fact which first drew to New Zealand the attention of European traders. Hence come the famous kauri spars, or ship-timber, the best for this special purpose which can be found in any land. The kauri-tree belongs to the pine family, yet is quite distinct from all other conifers, bearing a lance-shaped tapering leaf, and growing to great heights. It is only too well known, however, that the activity of this export trade is fast denuding these grand kauri-forests.

The isthmus upon which the city of Auckland is built is undoubtedly one of the most remarkable volcanic districts in the world, though the agency of subterranean fires is visible enough to the eye of the traveller all over New Zealand. Mount Tongariro, six thousand feet in height, is even now in constant activity, with occasional vigorous outbursts. The violent earthquakes which occur in both the North and South Islands cause alternate depressions and elevations. The severest modern earthquake took place so late as 1855, raising the coast-line four feet higher for many miles. As in the peninsula of Scandinavia, we here find a grand longitudinal mountain range extending from the extreme of the South Island through the Auckland district to the far north, forming a backbone, as it were, to the country. We were told that within a radius of ten miles from the centre of Auckland there are sixty-three volcanic cones, or points, in this range where eruptions have taken place. These hills vary in height from two to seven hundred feet; each of them was fortified and occupied by native tribes a century ago, the highest of all being Mount Eden, close to the present town. On this there are abundant evidences still left of the native fortification; but of the large Maori population that once covered the peninsula, and lived securely in these *pahs*, or fortified villages, not a soul remains.

Auckland is spread over a large territory; its villa-like houses, each with a pretty garden attached (except in the business section), cover the sloping hillside and valley from the foot of Mount Eden to the waters of the bay. Queen Street is the main thoroughfare of the town, — a broad avenue extending from the wharves to the suburbs, lined with a rather motley collection of buildings, some of which, however, are large and have fair architectural pretensions. There are upon this street a dozen or more fine stone buildings occupied by banks, insurance offices, warehouses, and some very handsome stores. Besides these there are several of brick, four stories high, with handsome façades. But the town is mainly constructed of wood, and — as we noted was the case in Wellington — has more than once been nearly swept away by conflagrations; so that a less inflammable material is now universally being adopted for building purposes. The principal public edifices are the Post-Office, Supreme Court House, Government House, Public Library, and the Hospital, while churches are to be seen in all sections of the town. There is also a University, a college for boys, and a high school for girls, with numerous primary schools.

The harbor is one of the largest and best in New Zealand, — indeed, we may say in Australasia. Though it is not so large or so varied in scenery, some unprejudiced persons compare it for beauty with that of Sydney. It has two dry docks, one of which is the largest in the South Pacific, being five hundred feet long and eighty wide. There is ample depth in the harbor for vessels of any size, and excellent wharf facilities. The shorter distance of Auckland from the ports of America gives it an advantage over any other seaport in Australasia. It is reached from London across the American continent in thirty-seven days, while to reach Sydney requires four days more of steam navigation.

This northern metropolis is situated, as already mentioned, in the centre of rich timber-lands, and also of abundant coal deposits. Should the Panama Canal be completed at some future day, Auckland would be the first port of call and the last of departure between Europe and the colonies of the South Pacific. Its present population, including that of the immediate suburbs, is something over sixty thousand; that of the whole province of Auckland is one hundred and thirty thousand.

The Ponsonby suburb and the village of Whou are composed of pleasant residences tastefully ornamented. Parnell, as it is called, forms another notable suburb, rendered attractive by hedge-rows, drooping willows, and prettily-arranged gardens. From this point one gets a fine view of the outspread bay lying below, exhibiting its various and busy craft. Steam ferry-boats are constantly gliding across the harbor, little white-winged cutters bend gracefully to the breeze, the tall masts of sailing-ships line the piers, and tiny row-boats glance hither and thither. The lofty marine-signal hill looms up across the harbor in its verdant garb, while volcanic cones, a little way inland on either shore, form an irregular line of background. Far away, and beyond all, the eye sees the swelling bosom of the restless Southern Ocean.

Both the level and steep streets of the town are "corded" with tramways, carried on at present by horse-power; but we were told that a cable-system with local engines was contemplated, and would doubtless soon be adopted, as the conformation of the town particularly favors this mode of transit. The pleasure-ground of Auckland is the Domain, with well-arranged walks shaded by an abundance of noble trees, both native and exotic; these grounds are bordered on one side by Parnell and on the other by the city. One pleasure-resort, the favorite of babyhood and nursery-maids, is called Albert Park, which is a small mountain rather than a park, as it is quite a climb to reach the summit, toward which zigzag paths are constructed, without which facility ladders would be required to reach the conical top. This reserve is but a few rods from Queen Street, and it rises therefore in the very centre of the town, which it overlooks in all directions; even Mount Eden, a mile away, loses one half of its commanding aspect when viewed from the top of Albert Park. On its highest point there is a tall flag-staff with signal halyards, which did not seem to be in regular use, except perhaps to raise the national flag on special occasions. Two or three large cannon were also found here, mounted upon awkward carriages; but it may be doubted if they could be made of much use under any circumstances.

As we have said, Queen Street contains many fine stores, and these are well stocked with a due mingling of a choice and a common class of goods. The necessities of life were found to be extraordinarily cheap. Meat, good beef and mutton, might be bought for four cents a pound; wearing apparel — all-wool goods — was offered at very low prices; the fish is good, in large variety, and cheap; oysters are abundant, and to be had all along shore simply for the gathering. These last are small, but of very sweet flavor.

The first excursion enjoyed after arriving at Auckland was a pleasant walk of a mile or more to Mount Eden, in the direction of the Khyber Pass. It is not a severe if a toilsome climb to reach the top, which is nearly eight hundred feet above sea-level. The terraced and pitted sides of the mountain show that it was formerly one of the Maori strongholds. At the top there is a hollow inverted cone of considerable depth, the sides of which are covered with creeping vines and ferns, the bottom being strewn here and there with rubble, slag, and hardened lava which looks as though it had not been cooled a very long time. Here we have clearly defined the mouth of an extinct volcano. If Vesuvius slept for centuries and then burst forth to overwhelm an entire city, why may not this mountain be expected in the course of time to do likewise?

The present view from Mount Eden, however, is indeed charming, and should not be missed by any one capable of appreciating such a pleasure. On the seaward side the whole of the volcanic isthmus lies at the visitor's feet; the portion sloping to the shore, known as the village of Remuera, is covered with handsome villas, cottages, luxurious groves and gardens, beyond which lies the city of Auckland, with its suburbs stretching away on either side. To the southward the volcanic hills called the Three Kings are conspicuous; and underlying them are many curious caves, where large numbers of human bones are still seen, testifying to the former orgies of the Maoris. Beyond the city lies the harbor, its clear waters sharply reflecting the sun's rays. A couple of miles away on the other side of the bay is Mount Victoria, once also an active volcano, but now only a signal station. The irregular north shore of the Hauraki Gulf, marked by promontories, inlets, green bays, and fertile meadows, spreads seaward on that side. Away to the right loom the triple peaks of Rangi-Toto, its well-wooded sides rising gracefully from the waters of the gulf toward Tiri-tiri and the open ocean. Looking inland, one sees a rolling country dotted here and there with smiling homesteads, wooded clumps, and volcanic knolls innumerable, — all together forming quite an incomparable picture. At the suggestion of a friend our second visit to Mount Eden was made by moonlight. The luminary in her last quarter was yet quite sufficient to lend a bewildering loveliness and light, which brought out the isle-dotted Hauraki Gulf and Manakoo Harbor clear in every outline, beautifying the dimpled waters with a silvery sheen. On the summit of Mount Eden there is to be seen an abundance of small shells embedded in the earth and mixed with the débris, showing clearly enough that the soil upon which one is standing, nearly a thousand feet above the level of the harbor of Auckland, must once have been the bottom of the neighboring sea.

Though we were told that the city was suffering from business depression, we saw some tangible evidences of growth and prosperity, — such as the erection of large and substantial buildings for business purposes, for offices and dwellings. A mammoth flour-mill, among other structures, was nearly completed; it was located very near to the wharves, between them and the railroad station. This mill was built upon the American plan, and all the machinery, as the proprietor informed us, was imported from the United States. This establishment is seven stories in height, substantially built of brick, and covers with its immediate outbuildings an acre of land. The business depression referred to had arisen almost entirely from the arbitrary acts of Labor Unions, scores of whose members were seen idling away their time about the bar-rooms of Queen Street, or being assisted to the police-station in a drunken condition. Many workmen who were doing well had lost their situations, and were now eking out a precarious living by resorting to the gum-fields, where with pick and shovel they could at least keep from starving. Even the noisy drones who had incited industrious men to bring about this state of affairs, were now themselves compelled to work or starve. Some few men have shown sufficient intelligence and independence to think for themselves and have cut loose from organizations which cost them so much to support, and which are only successful in involving in trouble all concerned.

We were a little startled when informed of the magnitude of the public debt of New Zealand, which aggregates nearly thirty-three million pounds sterling. This sum, large as it is, represents only the national debt, to which must be added an equally large sum representing the aggregate indebtedness of the several cities. The English creditors may be sure, however, that so long as they are prepared to lend money, New Zealand will be ready to borrow it. It has now become necessary to borrow large sums annually to pay the interest upon this growing debt. One is reminded of Falstaff's sentiments: "I can get no remedy against this consumption of the purse; borrowing only lingers it out, but the disease is incurable." A citizen of Auckland said to us, "The necessity for a fresh, additional loan is aggravatingly obvious; but we have no security to offer, for we are nearly beggared." The country may and doubtless will come out of this financial embarrassment all right, for it is rich in animal, vegetable, and mineral products beyond nearly every other country, excepting perhaps the sister colonies of Australia. The exports of 1886 are represented to have exceeded eight million pounds sterling, over one million of which was in gold. The export of meat is annually increasing, and the mutton, from its greater size and fatness, is preferred to that which is produced in Australia. The country is believed to be almost fabulously rich in auriferous deposits, besides which coal of excellent quality is abundant and easily mined; while in the north the kauri-forests yield immense quantities of shipping timber. All that is needed to promote and confirm the prosperity of this naturally favored country is population, — a good class of immigrants to open up the fertile lands, and to produce grain for food and export. But the Labor Unions are jealous of immigration, and strive to prevent it in all possible ways lest it should tend to lower wages. Neither the leaders nor their followers have brains enough to look at the matter in any other light than a thoroughly selfish one. As they outnumber the rest of the community and can therefore outvote them, they are likely for a while to enact laws which will favor their narrow purposes. The principles and system of Democracy were never so challenged before as in this case at Auckland. What is wanted there is one-man power — a despotism, if you will — until affairs can be put into proper course, and people who are too ignorant to know what is best for them are taught a little common-sense. Auckland will be set back ten years at least in the matter of progress by the crisis through which she is now passing. Labor organizations have chosen as usual the very worst time to enforce their arbitrary rule, and must suffer accordingly.

New Zealand as a colony has gone ahead too rapidly, and without counting the cost. It has built railroads too fast; that is, before they are absolutely required, — railroads running straight into the "bush," without any *raison d'être;* and the present reaction is but a natural sequence arising from extravagance. Undoubtedly these "bush" railroads, as they are now called, will help to open up the country through which they run; but even this may be done at too great a cost. Experience has demonstrated the wisdom of a rule the reverse of that which has been adopted here; namely, first to wait for a certain amount of population and business before furnishing the expensive railroad facilities required for their accommodation.

The kauri-tree, though a conifer, — the pine of this country, — is not at all like our North American pine; instead of needles, its foliage consists of leaves of sombre green. The botanists call it *Dammara Australis*. It produces a timber, however, which for some uses is unequalled. It is very slow of growth, is remarkably durable, easily worked, of fine grain, and does not split or warp by atmospheric exposure. We were told that the kauri-tree requires eight hundred years to arrive at maturity. One of the first objects to attract our attention upon landing at Auckland was a number of kauri tree trunks brought to the wharf for shipment. Some of these logs measured seven feet in diameter, and were from eighty to ninety feet in length. To visit the kauri-forests of the Auckland district one takes cars from the city to Helensville, a distance of forty or fifty miles, where the Kaipara River is reached, upon which small steamers ply, taking one directly to the desired spot. Here the busy saw-mills, which are gradually consuming these valuable trees, are so located that vessels of two thousand tons can load at their yards, and with their cargoes pass directly out to sea. It is singular that while this district is the only place in New Zealand where the kauri-trees are found, nearly every other species of tree indigenous to the country is also found here, — among them the rimu, the matai, the white and silver pines, the tooth-leaved beech, and the totara, all in close proximity to the kauri, and together forming a most remarkable conglomeration of species.

It was our good fortune to travel in the kauri-forests with Professor Kirk, Conservator of State Forests, and from him many interesting facts were learned. Here over seven millions of acres are forest-covered. The mills give permanent occupation to five or six thousand men, and the gum-digging carried on close at hand is pursued as a regular occupation by at least two thousand more. The saw-mills, as regards their machinery and capacity, are among the most complete we have ever seen, employing the best modern inventions to facilitate their operations and output, which averages six or seven million feet of dimension-timber annually. There are six of these mills in this immediate locality, each of which has in its own right many thousand acres of land bearing a sufficiency of good timber to supply them for twelve years to come. It is believed that by that time all the kauri-forests of New Zealand will be worked out or exhausted. In anticipation of the failure of this supply for ship's masts and spars, iron is being very generally adopted, and will eventually take the place of wood altogether.

The commercial prosperity of Auckland and its vicinity is largely due to the harvest reaped from these forests. The kauri-tree grows to an average height of a hundred feet, with a diameter of fifteen feet and over. It is a clannish tree, so to speak; when found near to those of other species, it groups itself in clumps apart from them. One often sees, however, large forests where the kauri reigns supreme, quite unmixed with other trees; and beneath the shadow of its limbs there is no undergrowth save the verdant ferns, — Nature's universal carpet for the woodlands here. There are thus created dim perspectives and forest vistas of marvellous beauty.

The kauri gum forms a large figure in the table of exports from Auckland, and the digging and preparation of it for market, as we have shown, gives employment to many persons. The natives have a theory that the gum descends from the trunks of the growing trees, and through the roots becomes deposited in the ground. But this is not reasonable. The gum is a semi-fossilized composition, showing that it has gone through a process which only a long period of time could accomplish. It is usually found at a depth of five or six feet from the surface. It is undoubtedly the fact that the northern part of New Zealand was once covered with immense forests of this gum-producing tree, which have matured and been destroyed by fire and by decay, century after century; and the deposit which is now so marketable is from the dead trees, not the living. Experiments have been tried which prove that the gum exuded by the growing trees has no commercial value. The only evidence to give color to the Maori theory is the fact that the gum is found near the roots of young trees; but it is also found far away from any present kauri growth. It is very similar to amber, for which article it is often sold to unskilled purchasers; but its principal use is in the manufacture of varnish. Amber, it will be remembered, is the product of a now extinct tree of the pine family, whole forests of which are supposed to have been sunken in the Baltic Sea, whence our present supply of the article is mostly derived, and where these forests have been submerged for perhaps twice ten thousand years. The deposits of the kauri gum in the Auckland district seem to be inexhaustible.

On returning to the city we found quite sufficient in and about Auckland to interest and occupy us for a week and more. We made almost daily excursions, sometimes on foot and sometimes on horseback; and when mounted, our day's journey often covered a distance of many miles inland, each time in a new direction.

In our trips afield, after passing through the immediate suburbs of the city, we found outlying cottages where the garden-plats are adorned with English plants in full bloom, succeeded by thrifty farms, well-fenced fields, and highly cultivated meadows. These last were dotted here and there with choice breeds of cattle and picturesque groups of sheep. Some very fine horses were observed in this region; and there are some breeding-farms here solely devoted to the raising of fine animals for the market, — many of which, as the proprietors told us, are sent twelve hundred miles by ship to Sydney, and even still farther, to Melbourne and Adelaide. Notwithstanding this district is the oldest in its settlement by the whites of any in New Zealand, the scenery struck us as being singularly primitive, bold, and beautiful, while the bright, breezy, light, and shadow-casting atmosphere brought out every native grace of form and color. Along the roads one is delighted by the abundance of the marsh-mallow, sweet clover, wild mint, and trefoil, and only sighs for time to gather of them and leisure to enjoy their sweets. Many trees and flowers were noted which were quite new to us, and which the intelligence of our half-breed guide rendered doubly interesting. The natives had distinctive and expressive names for every fowl, tree, and flower before the white man came. There is a lovely little native daisy called tupapa, and a blue lily known by the aborigines as rengarenga; also a green and yellow passion-flower named by the Indians, kowhaia. A glutinous, golden buttercup is known as anata, which is nearly as abundant as its namesake in America. A small white fragrant flower which attracted our attention is called the potolara. All these species are wild. One morning the guide brought us a dew-spangled bunch of them all together, wound about with a delicate sweet-smelling native grass known as karetu, — the *Torresia redolens* of botany.

The immediate neighborhood of Auckland has been almost denuded of the original native trees, and shade is very much needed both for beauty and comfort. Fires and the woodman's axe have swept away the grand old forest and the "bush" which once covered every rod of land in this vicinity. A few English oaks and other imported trees planted by the immigrants are to be seen, besides some California pines, which are universal favorites in this country. At a short distance inland, and especially bordering salt-water inlets, the traveller is surprised and charmed by groups of the pohutukawa, a tree thus named by the Maoris. Like many other blossoming trees of the Southern Pacific, its flowers when gathered have very little individual beauty or attractiveness, its brilliant color-effect being derived from the clusters of bright scarlet stamens, which when seen in mass upon the tree appear strikingly beautiful.

We do not remember to have seen the English lark in any island south of the Equator, but they abound here, and must have been introduced by the early settlers from Great Britain.

Another fact about Auckland struck us as curious. Here we find a rich greensward carpeting hill and dale, field and lawn, which is the growth of imported seed, and which has proved so tenacious as to root out all original and opposing vegetation, and establish itself permanently. Here also may be seen the European thistle, the veritable Scotch article greatly improved by transplanting. The farmers declare that it enriches the ground, — a sentiment which we also heard expressed at Dunedin, — and every one can see for himself that it feeds the bees. New Zealand seems to be adapted for receiving into its bosom the vegetation of any land, and of imparting to it renewed life and added beauty. Its foster-mother capacity has been fully tested, and for years no ship left England for this part of the world without bringing more or less of a contribution in plants and trees to be propagated in the new home of the colonists. The consequence is that we find pines and cypresses, oaks and willows, elms and birches, besides fruit-trees of all sorts grown in Europe, thriving here in abundance, and so thoroughly acclimated as to seem indigenous.

The climate of this region appeared to us very nearly perfect, favoring human life as well as that of the vegetable kingdom. It may be compared as a whole to the climate of the best portions of Europe. It has the soft, genial atmosphere of the south of France and Italy (which is best enjoyed at Nice and Mentone), but none of the chill caused by the piercing mistral of the mountains, nor the scorching blasts of the African and Egyptian siroccos. In seeking to recall a climate which most nearly approaches it, Madeira alone suggests itself. Its range of temperature is more limited than any other place we have visited north or south of the Equator, or in either hemisphere. Summer and winter are here only the dry and the rainy seasons; flowers, vegetables, grapes, in short all plants grow bright and thrifty the whole year round in the open air. Tropical and hardy plants are here equally at home; Scottish firs and Indian palms, oranges, lemons, india-rubber trees, and limes thrive side by side. As we were told in Japan one could do there, so here one can gather a pretty bouquet in the open air any day in the year.

We must not forget to speak of the mineral resources of this Province of Auckland, which were in the early days of its settlement quite unsuspected, but which have turned out to be both extensive and profitable. A gold-bearing range of lofty hills runs northward along the banks of the Thames River, ending on the Coromandel Peninsula. Here several quartz mines are being successfully worked for gold, though the process of disintegration does not seem to be satisfactorily understood. It is well known that not more than half the precious metal which the rock contains is realized by the means now employed for its extraction. In order to obtain the best and latest improvements in machinery designed for this purpose, a representative agent and proprietor of these Thames River mines came to the United States in the same ship with the author, to visit our principal mining centres in the States of Idaho, Colorado, California, and so forth. Coal of excellent quality crops out in various parts of the Province, particularly at the Bay of Islands, and several coal mines are regularly worked. Copper is found here also, and a valuable article of manganese, besides iron, nickel, bismuth, asphaltum, and other minerals. In Poverty Bay petroleum has been discovered in great abundance, and though it is made no special use of at present, it is sure in the near future to be profitably utilized.

The district to which we have just referred as being rich in gold-bearing quartz and other minerals, and which is situated along the banks of the Thames and Waikato rivers, is also productive as a pastoral and agricultural country. A large portion of the land is laid down to grass and other crops, and is well stocked with sheep and cattle. Government has done much to encourage agricultural enterprise among the people of the province, realizing its great importance over all other industries. The remarkable fertility of the soil seconds this purpose, and there are hundreds of square miles of it as level as our Western prairies. We were told of a company called the Waikato Land Association, which was formed not alone for pecuniary profit to its stockholders, but also to advance the pastoral and agricultural interests of the Province. This association owns a hundred thousand acres of rich land which is being drained and brought into the most available condition. We saw the operation going on in the form of extensive and systematic drainage, tree-planting, and other means of improvement upon the company's lands, through the centre of which the railroad runs southward from Auckland.

CHAPTER XVI.

A Journey to the King's Country. — An Experienced "Whip." — Volcanic Hills. — A New Zealand Forest. — A Strangely Afflicted Boy. — Lake Rotorua. — Ohinemutu. — Funeral of a Maori Chief. — Wailing and Weeping. — Moonlight on the Lake. — Wonderland. — Spouting Geysers and Boiling Pools. — Savage Mode of Slaughter. — Maori Houses. — Chivalry and Cannibalism. — Savage and Civilized Life.

HERE in Auckland we were also in the vicinity of the Hot Lake District of North New Zealand, and a week was devoted to a visit to the remarkable points of interest connected therewith. To accomplish this, one goes from the capital of the Province a hundred and thirty miles to Oxford, and thence thirty miles by stage to the native town of Ohinemutu. This route carries the traveller in a southeast course, and leads into the very heart of the North Island, among the Maori tribes. The cars took us over a level country, which however is bounded on either side, five or six miles distant, by lofty serrated hills, presenting a confusion of irregular forms. These hills contain an abundance of mineral wealth in the form of gold, silver, iron, coal, and manganese. Many low-lying marshy fields of native flax were observed, and the Waikato River was three times crossed in its winding course. Large plantations containing several thousand each of young pine-trees of the American species were seen, covering gentle slopes and many broad acres of level land, where Government is endeavoring to establish artificial forests throughout wide reaches of unwooded country. These trees grow more rapidly here than they do even in their native soil. Miles upon miles of this level country were covered only by the low-growing ti-tree and the ever present ferns; the former, being a sort of tall heath, was in some places in bloom, producing an effect as if a light fall of feathery snow had lodged upon the delicate branches. Flocks of sheep and lambs were numerous, but the population was sparse. The whole landscape was lighted up here and there by the bright yellow leaves of the wattle-tree, which contrasted strongly with the black beech, the deep green of the cabbage-palm, and what is called the white-pine, which is totally unlike any pine we ever saw. Several miniature villages were passed through, where a few small European houses clustered in the neighborhood of the railroad depots, consisting of a blacksmith's forge, a grocery-store, a one-story inn, and three or four dwellings. There was plenty of water everywhere. Now it was a small and pretty stream, and again it was a large river's course. At one rural hamlet a rustic water-wheel was revolving, splashing and sparkling in the sunshine with a noisy, gleeful sound, telling how easily and thoroughly these fields might be irrigated. We passed through what is called the Waikato Pastures, a rural district where herds of fine-looking cattle were browsing, and where cheese-making is a flourishing industry. Some coal mines were being worked upon the route, connected by side-tracks with this main branch of the railroad; the coal, it was plain to see, was a good article for domestic use or for manufacturing purposes. Small Maori encampments, composed of a dozen lodges each, were scattered along our way, the lazy, tattooed natives — men and women — lingering about the stations with blackened pipes in their mouths, smoking the rankest sort of tobacco, while they kept up a chattering like Benares monkeys. Why Maori women and savage squaws generally are so fond of wearing men's hats, with a feather stuck into them, we cannot understand; for though serving the purpose of a head-covering, they are far from being ornamental. The awkward Maori men looked doubly outré in their ill-fitting European clothes.

Oxford is the somewhat pretentious name given to the hamlet where the railroad ends, containing five houses, one of which is the Oxford Royal, — a neat but circumscribed inn, affording us a sleeping apartment measuring exactly seven feet wide by nine in length. The stage-drive from here to Ohinemutu — the centre of the geysers, boiling springs, and mud caldrons, and also of the Maori reservation — is by a road a little over thirty miles in length, which we do not hesitate to pronounce to be the hardest to travel that it has yet been our misfortune to encounter. The patient reader will bear witness that we do not often parade the hardships of travel, but it makes our bones ache to recall those seven hours of staging; and yet they were by no means without their compensation. It was the author's good fortune to sit upon the box with an experienced and admirable "whip," — Harry Kerr by name, — who was fully equal to his business. The vehicle was an American stage, the harnesses on the horses were American made, and the stage line was owned by an American, — a resident in New Zealand for many years, during which time he has held a mail contract throughout the country. We travelled lightly, there being no other passenger, and four stout horses forming the motive power; but had not the stage been constructed of the best seasoned material, and put together in the most thorough manner, it would have been left upon the road in fragments before it had completed the trip. The traveller under such circumstances is always more or less dependent upon the intelligence of the driver who takes him through a new country, and we cheerfully acknowledge our indebtedness on this occasion. We can well understand why Harry Kerr is a favorite in the Auckland district.

On leaving Oxford the journey takes one at first through a section of country where the hills were thrown about in the wildest fashion during the ancient volcanic period, causing them to present a grotesqueness of aspect which is quite beyond description. Here the bowels of the earth vomited forth their fiery secretions of molten lava, and as it cooled, it formed itself into countless ridges and hills, no two of which are alike. The road wound over hills, down into gulches, and skirted precipices where to have deviated a few inches only from the proper track would have been instant destruction. As we rose to the summit of some elevation loftier than the rest, the view became expansive. From one of these summits was seen, nearly one hundred miles away on the far horizon, the broad, bold, snow-covered mountain Ruapehu, ten thousand feet high. The last portion of the journey from Oxford to Ohinemutu took us through one of the grandest forests in all New Zealand, extending eighteen or twenty miles without a human habitation or any sign of life, save the flutter of an occasional bird.

In this forest, mingled with tall columnar trees of various species, were seen frequent examples of the fern-tree thirty feet in height and of surpassing beauty, spreading out their plumed summits like an Egyptian palm, while the stem had the graceful inclination of the cocoanut-tree. Well has the fern-tree been called the forest Houri. The picturesque effect of the birches was also remarkable, flanked by the massive outlines and drooping tassels of the rimu, the soft luxuriance of the undergrowth adding charms to the whole. For miles of the way on either side of the road the forest was impenetrable even to the eye save for the shortest distance, presenting a tangled mass of foliage, vines, and branches such as can be matched only by the virgin forests of Brazil or the jungles of India. Ground-ferns were observed in infinite variety, sometimes of a silvery texture, sometimes of orange-yellow, but oftenest of the various shades of green. Here too we made acquaintance with the sweet-scented manūka, the fragrant veronica, and the glossy-leaved karaka, — this last the pride of the Maoris. A dark-colored shrub, with leaves like the orange-tree, their under side being of a quicksilver hue, was pointed out to us by the driver, which though poisonous, as he declared, to horses, sheep, and cattle, is nevertheless eaten by them with avidity whenever they chance to come upon it. Its first effect is to intoxicate them, and it will ultimately prove fatal unless an antidote is given. Many specimens of the lofty rimu-tree were seen, about whose tall white stems a parasitic vine was slowly and treacherously weaving itself, clasping and binding the upright body with such a marvellous power of compression as literally to strangle it, until ultimately the vine becomes a stout tree in place of the original. The most noted and destructive of these vegetable boa-constrictors is the gigantic rope-like rata, whose Gordian knot nothing can untie. The tree once clasped in its toils is fated, yielding up its sap and life without a struggle to cast off its deadly enemy. Many trees were observed whose stems bore branches only far above the surrounding woods, laden with bunches of alien foliage, — parasites like the mistletoe. Indeed, this forest seemed like vegetation running riot; and with its clumps of abnormal foliage, fixed like storks' nests in the tops of the trees, it recalled similar effects seen on the banks of the St. John's River in Florida.

Midway in these almost impenetrable woods, where the soil was literally smothered by vegetation and a wilderness of undergrowth, we came upon a lonely cottage, with a large barn and some outbuildings attached, which had been established by the owner of the stage line; and here our four jaded horses were changed for fresh ones.

At this isolated spot we saw a remarkably handsome boy between six and seven years of age, large and well-formed for one of his years, wearing only a blouse reaching to his knees, — otherwise being entirely without clothing. It was instantly apparent that he was mentally deficient, and his eccentric gambols caused us to make further inquiries. It seems that his mother, an intelligent Englishwoman, four or five months before the boy was born had been so terribly frightened by a furious bull as to throw her into convulsions, from which she was with difficulty restored. The eccentricities of the child began to exhibit themselves as soon as he had reached a twelvemonth, and from that period his actions became more animal than human. He cares only for vegetable food, living mostly on potatoes. The use of the knife and fork he utterly ignores, taking his food from the plate with his mouth, not using his hands. He smells of every new thing or person when first presented to his notice. He will not abide clothing beyond the blouse already spoken of, and when he is restrained in any purpose butts with his forehead like a bull. The boy has never uttered any words distinctly, though he makes half-articulate sounds of assent and negation. Sometimes he walks about with his head extended before him, mooing like a bovine, and on such occasions he takes no notice of any words addressed to him or any attempt to divert him. He is quite mischievous, but not viciously so; it is necessary to keep wire screens over the glass windows, which he would otherwise put his head through when he desired to get into the open air. He was running about the space before the house and roadway when we saw him, and submitted to our kindly caress, even uttering sympathetic sounds in response, while his large black eyes looked into our own with a half-pleading, half-grateful expression. The father told us that the favorite amusement of the boy was tossing small articles high into the air and seeing them fall to the earth. Having this in mind, we commissioned Harry Kerr to purchase a strong ball for the unfortunate child, and to bring it to him on the return trip. The health of the boy has always been perfect, and his strength is equal to that of a youth of twice his age. He has brothers, one older and one younger than himself, both of whom seem to be of even more than ordinary intelligence, and all are over-fond of the unfortunate one.

After leaving the forest and crossing a volcanic mountain, the road winds across the broad reach of table-land which borders Lake Rotorua, whose waters lay shimmering under the warm and brilliant tints of the afternoon sun. We drove for three or four miles along the side of this beautiful and romantic sheet of water, concerning whose one island the Maoris have many curious legends, prominent among which is one nearly identical with that of Leander and the Hellespont, — possibly antedating that classic story, and thus proving that " there is nothing new under the sun." This lake is justly celebrated for its scenic beauty and remarkable surroundings, being about ten miles long by eight or nine in width.

As we approached the quaint little settlement of Ohinemutu, over which floated a heavy sulphurous cloud of steam, a motley cortége was met, consisting of men, women, and children decked in all the gay colors which delight the Maori heart. Their heads were dressed in gorgeous feathers, yellow wattle-blossoms, and other fantastic ornaments, their faces rendered hideous by tattooing. Each of the women had an infant upon her back, held in position by a tawdry shawl arranged in the form of a sack and tied across the breast. These natives called to mind the feather-crowned Crow Indians of the Yellowstone Valley, both races living in a wonderland of geysers, boiling springs, and sulphurous vapor. This display proved to be a funeral procession in honor of a dead chief named Rotohika. Curiosity led us to follow the procession to the grave near at hand, where the ceremony was brief but peculiar. Two of the dead chief's wives knelt by the coarse wooden box which supplied the place of a coffin, and made sacrifice of their long dark locks of hair, cutting them from their heads and placing them in the box containing the body of the deceased. The box was then lowered into the grave, each relative throwing a shovelful of dirt upon it, and others followed, quickly filling up the cavity. The throng then returned to their huts with manifest eagerness, to participate in a grand feast. After the burial is completed the grave is placed under what is termed " tapu," — or in other words the spot is made sacred, to be avoided always; to tread upon it is considered a desecration.

We were told that formerly the burial ceremony of a chief involved the sacrifice of at least one human life. If the tribe had a prisoner of war on hand, his life sufficed. After sprinkling his blood upon the grave, his body was roasted and eaten at the grand feast which followed. The Maori " wakes " his dead after the Irish fashion, the revel lasting as long as the money holds out, and almost any excess is condoned on these occasions, which are characterized by the strangest and most weird dances, the wildest shouts and wailings, the most fantastic distortion of body and limbs that can be conceived of. On the occasion at which we were present the performers, especially the women, seemed to us for the time being to lose their reason, and to become maniacs, exciting one another to a state of frenzy. To listen to the native *tangi*, or wail for the dead, one would think it represented the most natural and heart-broken grief, accompanied as it is by a copious fall of tears; but this is all pretence. It is wonderful how these Maori women can summon such perfect showers of tears at will; we saw them shed Niagaras of brine, which of course deceived no one. It was as purely a mechanical operation as is the work of a hydraulic ram. A wail of grief is started by some one among the mourners, when it is taken up and continued for hours by the others, now one and now another prolonging the note with unabated vigor. Though realizing that this is so largely mere pretence, one cannot listen to the sad note of the *tangi* without a corresponding sense of sorrowful emotion. The present occasion being the decease of a great man among them, drew forth the most exaggerated expressions, and the wailing was at times almost deafening.

The Lake House, presided over by the intelligent and lady-like Mrs. Graham, afforded us every comfort as well as admirable service, hardly to be anticipated in so isolated a spot. The window of our chamber overlooked Lake Rotorua; and as the moon was at its full on that first evening of our arrival, the scene was indescribably lovely. It was an inspiration to stand on the shore of the lake, beholding the heavens above, and their reflected glory in the mirror-like waters below. The wailing, singing, and dancing among the natives had ceased; the performers had rolled themselves in their blankets, and worn out with excess were sleeping; the night and its peace were over all, — and yet it was as light as mid-day. One certainly feels inclined to give New Zealand moonlight precedence over anything of the sort elsewhere. How it silvered the unruffled surface of the lake! So calm, so intense, so dazzlingly brilliant were its shining waters that they seemed to put the stars out of countenance. With a couple of tawny, tattooed natives we took a long, lazy row upon Rotorua at midnight, " the dusky hour friendliest to sleep and silence," permitting the boat at times to float after its own fancy, while we dreamed a dream of peace. So quiet were the scene and the hour that both oarsmen leaned upon the thwarts and slept. It was enchantment verified; one was loath to break the spell by arousing the sleepers and turning shoreward. By and by the silence, only slightly broken by the light dip of the oars, became almost oppressive, and we said, "Give us a song, men! a Maori song;" and those rough, dark-hued rowers broke forth in a low, weird chant as we glided smoothly over the water, seeming to be the only adjunct needed to fill the measure of that midnight hour.

And yet it is difficult to say which was the more inspiring, — the sweet, suggestive hours of the moon's reign, or those of the delicious break of day across the lake, so quickly followed by the sunrise. How responsive were the waiting waters to every fresh hue and color of the returning morn! The moonlight had recalled many thoughts of the past, memories both sad and joyous; while the sunlight was full of hope, promise, and present grandeur. Those of our

A REGION OF WONDERS. 377

readers who have seen at the foot of the Maritime Alps, on the shores of the Mediterranean, the change of night into morning, will most readily understand what the break of day really is over Lake Rotorua.

Once fairly within the area of this south land of varied wonders, the most active volcanic region of the Antipodes, nothing seems too strange to be true; geysers, fumaroles, boiling springs, and dry stones burning hot beneath one's feet, as though the surface of the land covered Nature's chemical laboratory, are all regarded by the visitor as quite the proper thing, — in fact, just what is to be expected. Even the scores of naked Maori bathers, of both sexes, outrage no sense of propriety in this weird atmosphere of Ohinemutu. One seems to be surrounded by a race upon whose semi-civilization the era of clothes has not yet dawned. The Maori inhabitants of Wairoa, the native town which was so recently buried with all its people by a volcanic outburst, had no more reason to anticipate any immediate danger than have these natives on the banks of Lake Rotorua. Indeed, so far as external evidence of subterranean volcanic force is concerned, the inhabitants of Wairoa had not one half the threatening tokens about them that exist here at every turn. Sulphur, alkaline, and iron-impregnated pools of inviting temperature induce one to indulge in frequent baths, and it seems but natural that the natives in their semi-nude condition should pass so much of their time in the water, both sexes mingling in this pleasure as they would do in the ordinary avocations of life. Near to the shore, where the lake is shallow, a boiling spring forces its way to the surface of the surrounding cold water, telling of a submerged fiery caldron underlying the lake at that particular point. It was, however, no more significant than the scores of other steam-holes and spouting geysers which force themselves to the surface all about this sulphurous region. In short, the town of Ohinemutu is built on a thin crust, roofing over, as it were, a vast fiery furnace, whose volcanic eccentricities form the marvel of the locality.

Here then the traveller eats, drinks, and sleeps above a series of suppressed volcanoes. One could not but recall the fate of Lisbon and of half-exhumed Pompeii. Many of these springs and geysers are so hot that a mere touch of the water will blister the human flesh as quickly as contact with red-hot iron. Others are of a temperature suitable for boiling vegetables; and still others by artificial means — that is, the introduction of cool surface-water — are rendered of a temperature suitable for bathing purposes. One must walk cautiously among these boiling mud-pits, open springs, and steam-holes; a misstep might prove instantly fatal. Caldrons lie on either side of the path, within a few inches of where one may be walking all unsuspiciously. A Maori child lately disappeared while playing near some sulphurous jets. A full-grown aboriginal met the same fate not long ago; he had been partaking too freely of intoxicants, and sank into the Stygian darkness without uttering a cry.

One coolly records these facts; but what an awful fate to encounter!

The natural conclusion as to the cause of these remarkable phenomena would seem to be that the waters of the lakes, rivers, and springs descend by various channels to the fiery regions below, and are returned by the force of the steam thus created, bringing up with them the débris which is deposited about the surface. Of the hundreds of these boiling springs only a score or so have been analyzed; no two, however, exhibit the same properties. The various chemical combinations seem to be without limit, and bathing in them is considered to be a specific for some skin-diseases as well as for rheumatic affections. There can be no doubt but that all the virtues possessed by similar springs in Europe or America are equally combined in these of New Zealand, and the list of remarkable cures which they have accomplished is annually increasing.

White faces are here the exception; dusky, bronzed ones, the rule. This is the real home of the natives, and for ages has formed the chief settlement of the Arawa tribe. Nothing could possibly be more grotesque than to see groups of the native women — from the wrinkled old grandams to the girls of a dozen years — bathing at all hours in the warm, steaming pools without any apparent thought of undue exposure. It is their daily, almost hourly resort. As a rule, a blanket forms their only covering; and if they are cold, day or night, they at once resort to the hot springs for warmth. Their chief occupations are literally bathing, and smoking tobacco,— the women using the pipe even more freely than the men. Of regular occupation they have none. A few potatoes are planted and allowed to grow without cultivation, and these with pork form their chief food. Some small lake fish are added to their diet occasionally; but this amounts to very little, as a lake so under volcanic influences, so impregnated by sulphur springs and super-heated waters, as is Rotorua, is not a favorable place for fish breeding.

The revels incident upon a funeral are often kept up for a week or more. To conduct the ceremonies with due éclat for the death of the late chief of whom mention has been made, much extra food was necessary to entertain the visiting representatives of other tribes, men and women, who had come to Ohinemutu. We chanced to witness the preparing of a portion of the feast on the second day after our arrival. A native seized a large pig by the hind leg, in the midst of the animals feeding about among the fern-roots, and pulled him backwards toward the lake. The animal took matters very coolly, much to our surprise, and made no noise about it. Maori and pig thus backed into the water until the man was waist-deep, when he suddenly seized the other hind leg of the animal and threw him upon his back, at the same time putting his foot upon him, thus holding the pig under water for the space of a couple of minutes, until life in the animal became extinct. With the aid of one or two companions, the native then proceeded to chop the pig into small pieces with an axe and a hatchet. A large camp-kettle stood hard by, in which some herbs and a few potatoes with spring water had been placed. Into this kettle the crude, unwashed portions of the carcass were thrust until it was full to its brim, and then a sheet-iron cover was pressed on the top and held down by a couple of large stones. A small fire of chips built upon the hot stones on which the kettle stood in the open air, soon set the pot to boiling, and in half an hour's time the mess was quite sufficiently cooked for Maori taste. It was then devoured eagerly by the hungry mourners who sat round the pot without any attempt at ceremony, and, so far as we could discover, without the use of knives or plates; hands and fingers seemed to be all-sufficient. The natives sometimes partake of bread, when they can get it; but potatoes constitute their chief diet. The little cooking in which they indulge is usually performed by the boiling springs, in which they suspend their potatoes in small wicker nets; and for baking purposes they use the red-hot stones that are to be found in plenty in this vicinity. These broad flat stones are the identical ones on which the natives in the past used to roast their prisoners of war before eating them. It is impossible to bear one's hand on them for an instant; the wonder is that stones subjected to such constant heat do not become calcined and break in pieces.

There are no means for building fires inside the

native cabins, which have little or no furniture; in place of using chairs, the natives squat upon their hams, like nearly all savage races, and most of the Eastern tribes. Their beds are composed of dried fern-leaves, sometimes raised a few inches above the level of the earth floor; but quite as often nothing but the fern-leaves intervene between the body and the ground. The *wharry*, or cabin, is always the same, and contains but one apartment, with a low doorway and an overhanging thatch of dried ti-tree interwoven with long grasses. There is no matting or flooring of any sort upon the ground within the cabin. Ohinemutu is built over a region so heated by internal fires that the earth is dry and warm, — too warm we thought. There is one compensation, however, for the risk of thus building one's home over burning sulphurous regions, — no insects or vermin can exist in these ground-floor huts, which the uncleanly habits of their occupants would otherwise tend to make swarm with such parasites. In these cabins there is sometimes seen a rude attempt at ornamentation in carving, but the images are grotesque, and to us were quite unmeaning, — consisting generally of hideous heads with blood-red lolling tongues and dwarf-shaped bodies. The natives have very little idea of decoration, except tattooing and the wearing of a few personal ornaments.

There is a green stone — nephrite — native to New Zealand, which is prized by the women for personal wear, and which admits of a high degree of polish.

This stone in various shapes is worn as ear-rings, amulets tied about the neck, or made into beads; it is sometimes worn bracelet-fashion about the wrists or ankles. There is another and less common ornament worn by the Maori women; namely, a small pink or white feather thrust through the cartilage of the nose, the ends hanging down on either side, shading the upper lip like a moustache. This recalled the brass and silver rings worn through nose and lips, as seen in South Africa and the Straits Settlements. The young women of the tribes that are brought most in contact with the whites are giving up the tattooing process upon their faces; but those of middle age, or older, are defaced by blue lines about the lower lip and the chin. The pride of the women is to wear a short skirt of some high-colored material, and to wrap themselves in a blanket of the "loudest" pattern, — flaming red or yellow being preferred. The men affect more the dress of Europeans.

The Maoris differ in many essential particulars from most savage races with whom we have chanced to meet. Unlike the American Indian, the Maori is neither treacherous nor deceitful. He does not, like our American savage, foster a spirit of secret revenge, but when his enmity is aroused it is openly displayed and exercised, man-fashion. This has been a tribal trait with the Maoris for centuries. Before declaring war the Maori always gives his enemy fair notice. But for ages he has been accustomed to go to war upon imaginary grievances; or, to put it more clearly, his great object was to make prisoners, and when made, to cook and eat them.

The early Maoris, even so late as sixty years ago, looked upon war — what we should call civil war; that is, fighting one tribe with another — as being the only legitimate object of life. No two tribes, however nearly allied, were proof against an ever present liability to fall out with each other and engage in internecine strife. An authentic anecdote was told to us illustrative of this propensity to fight where no principle whatever was involved. A certain chief of a tribe living near Rotorua received a message from a neighboring chief which he construed into an insult; and he indignantly declared that the sender would not have ventured upon such a message had he not known and counted upon the superiority of the weapons of war which he possessed, which, it seemed, embraced a number of European fire-arms. When this imputation of unfairness and cowardice came to the ears of the first chief, he divided all his weapons into two lots, and sent for his rival to come and choose between them. This done, of course there was no further excuse for not fighting. The tribes fought a long and bloody battle, followed on both sides by a great feasting upon each other's prisoners! Here was united, most indisputably, a spirit of chivalry with that of ferocity. In these days, however, the Maoris have settled down to a life of quiet, and could hardly be more peacefully inclined; they are now as lazy and listless as the Arabs.

It is surprising how well these Maoris got along without civilization. It is fully as surprising to see how they wilt and fade away with it. Whether the white man has been upon the whole of any advantage to them is certainly an open question. They originally possessed a language composed of a copious vocabulary, and also a complete social system that answered their purpose. Their houses, rude as they were, kept out the heat of the summer sun and retained the necessary warmth in winter, — and this in a degree quite superior to European houses. Their food-supply, eked out by cannibalism, was ample though not varied, while their natural condition involved few necessities. Their wars promoted a condition of robustness as well as a spirit of enterprise and activity. But with civilization came rum, tobacco, and laziness. Far be it from us to argue in favor of the savage life above that of the civilized; but to judge these savage races correctly or fairly, we must look at them from their own standpoint, not from ours.

CHAPTER XVII.

The Maori Dog. — A Romantic Island. — Sinking of a Maori Fort. — Volcanic Destruction. — A Country of Boiling Springs. — Idleness. — A Lazy Race of Savages. — Native Religion. — A Fitful Geyser. — Sophia, the Famous Guide. — A Funeral Dance. — The "Haka" Performance. — Maori Improvidence. — Rubbing Noses. — Native Babies. — Church-Going and Card-Playing. — The King's Country. — Eloquent Aborigines. — A Sanitarium. — Sulphur Point. — Future of New Zealand.

THE funeral wailings of the natives during the day were not sufficient to fill the measure of uncanny noise; so at night — those wonderfully bright moonlight nights! — the dogs seemed to feel it incumbent upon them to take up the refrain, and they howled frightfully by the hour together. The Maori dog is quite different from any other specimen of the canine race; he is a mongrel of decidedly conglomerate character, — the most remarkable fact about these creatures being that no two of them are at all alike, or seemingly of the same breed. Why the Maoris keep these dogs we cannot conceive; they certainly have no food to spare for them, and the poor creatures look nearly starved with their thin bodies and protruding ribs. At Ohinemutu every cabin had at least one dog, and frequently three or four of these animals were seen lying before the entrance. They rushed out and barked fiercely at the passing stranger, but there the hostile demonstration ended. Dogs are not more numerous, in proportion to the population, in Cairo or Constantinople, nor more neglected, than here. We suggested to one of the half-castes that it would be possible to utilize these animals for food, but he shook his head knowingly and said, "No, no; him got no meat on him bones." Their pigs run wild, and feed themselves on fern-roots and sweet weeds; but their dogs, not being herbivorous, fare hardly for food.

Unable to sleep on account of these canine disturbers of the night, we rose long before daylight on the third day of our visit to Ohinemutu, and awaking a couple of natives, took a row-boat over to the island of Mokoia, which is situated about four miles from the mainland, toward the centre of Lake Rotorua. This island is itself a sleeping volcano, lying now placidly enough upon the bosom of the waters, but originally thrown up from the bottom of the lake in some past century. Though the natives evidently thought us crazy to abandon a comfortable bed at such an hour, we only gave them the necessary direction and sat down quietly in the stern of the boat. It was just sunrise as a landing was effected on the island, when a sight was enjoyed which had not been anticipated. As the monarch of day showed his face above the volcanic hills, the effect was superb. Mokoia is a well-wooded island, and on the side farthest from Ohinemutu there is some level fertile land occupied by natives; indeed, there is here quite a Maori village.

It was once a favorite missionary station, but as such was long ago abandoned. It is a sort of second edition of the villages lying about the Lake House on the mainland. When the missionaries were here they planted fruit-trees, which are still thriving and annually productive of pears, apples, peaches, and the like. One of the boatmen spoke English after the Maori fashion, and wanted to relate the love-story of the island, the Hinemoa legend; but we knew it already. We did listen, however, to the story of the blood-thirsty chief Hongi, who came hither when Mokoia was the stronghold of a prosperous tribe, and putting them to the sword, killed one half and more in a terrible hand-to-hand fight; after which he and his followers feasted on their bodies for weeks. We got back to the Lake House by mid-day.

The faulty and incomplete traditions of the natives concerning the last eruption previous to that of about a twelvemonth ago which occurred in the Hot Lake District, are entirely unsatisfactory; but the late terrible one which destroyed the beautiful pink and white terraces at Tarawera by one sudden throe of Nature, and by which nearly two thousand square miles of territory were sensibly affected, we know all about. The destructive demonstration lasted only six hours, but during that time the amount of lava, volcanic bombs, stones, and fiery substances thrown out by the burning mountain is beyond calculation. This volcanic outburst seemed to us just what might be expected at Ohinemutu at any moment. What signifies it that matters have remained in their present condition for perhaps a thousand years? The liability to an outburst is none the less on that account. Such is the history of all eruptions: centuries elapse of comparative quiet and seeming immunity from serious danger,— and then comes a great and awful explosion! Confined steam, boiling water, and burning sulphur must somewhere and somehow find vent at the surface. The seething and subdued roaring which never ceases are a constant warning to this effect. And yet here both Europeans and natives live on, and give the possible contingency never a thought.

Within pistol-shot of where these notes were originally made, there was before our eyes a half sunken point jutting out into Lake Rotorua which has "gradually subsided"— ominous words — so that but a small portion remains in view. In former times a *pah*, or fort, stood upon this point, the fate of which is briefly told. One stormy night a hoarse rumbling noise was heard, of more than usual significance, followed by a shrill sound of hissing steam. The trembling earth opened on the border of the lake, and the pah with all its people sank instantly into the raging fires below. No native can be induced to put foot upon what is left of this peninsula at the present day. The place is *tapu*. The visitor explores it alone, while his guide remains at a wholesome distance. Plenty of boiling springs, sulphurous vapor-holes, and seething mud-pools were found distributed over the place where the Maori pah and its people were engulfed.

Although by the late eruption, so far as is known, only one hundred and six persons — natives and Europeans — were destroyed, it included a whole Maori village which was instantly blotted out of existence, as was the pah on the peninsula jutting into the lake. The particulars of the late awful visitation, unequalled in the history of New Zealand, were sad and harrowing to listen to. There were instances where persons, still alive, were dug from the ashes and débris miles away from the crater, after being either buried, or partially so, for one and two days, though none of them survived more than a few hours after exhumation. We were told of an aged Maori whose cabin was miles distant from the burning mountain, who was exhumed after twenty-four hours' burial. He was over one hundred years of age, and survived three days after being recovered.

As to those far-famed and beautiful natural curiosities the Terraces, so completely is the configuration of the country changed for many miles in all directions, that it is quite impossible to discover their former site. An area covering nearly thirty square miles is now but one sad picture of desolation, strewn with ashes and lava, to look upon which was both depressing and awe-inspiring. One bowlder was pointed out to us which must weigh at least a hundred tons, that was thrown a quarter of a mile from the mouth of the crater.

The country over which the boiling springs and geysers occur is about a hundred and twenty miles long by seventeen or twenty wide, their activity varying somewhat at different localities. The fiery region extends beneath the sea after reaching the coast at the Bay of Plenty, being doubtless connected with several remote islands of the Pacific Ocean, — the immediate vicinity of Ohinemutu being apparently the centre of thermal development. It is only necessary in many places to make a hole a few feet deep by thrusting one's walking-stick into the ground, to bring forth a vigorous demonstration of the hissing steam. On first rising from sleep in the morning and looking out upon the remarkable scene, the low-lying dense clouds of vapor all about the hamlet give one the idea that the activity of the underground forces is greater in the night than during the day; but this is probably not the case. Except occasionally, when owing to some great unknown disturbing cause an unusual explosion takes place, the result varies but little at the surface from one year's end to another.

Is idleness infectious? One dallies with time in the midst of these strange phenomena, wandering among the native huts and their lazy, bronzed inhabitants, studying their gypsy life in all its phases. Everything is not quite agreeable, but all is quaint, novel, and interesting. We were shown some of the native carving which was executed a hundred years ago, mostly in the form of war-clubs and idols. There were images representing strange human beings of both sexes; but they were always grotesque, and often disgusting. There was not even an approach to excellence or a spirit of art observable in any of them. A certain consistency is discovered in the manners and customs of this people who live so nearly after the style and laws which governed their ancestors, and which have been carefully preserved for hundreds of years. Superstition is born in a Maori. He is a professed Christian,— that is, in most cases,— and accepts the Bible; but he is apt to give it his own interpretation: yet for that matter how many white religionists there are who do the same! These children of Nature follow their ancestral traditions modified by Christian influences. The original religion of the natives, if we can give it that name, consisted in a dim belief of a future state, quite undefined even in their own minds. It was largely a sort of ancestor worship, according to the missionaries, with a vague idea of some Being higher and better than anything human or finite. The sorcery which was universally practised among them filled up a certain measure of religious conviction and observance; nor is this by any means disused among them to-day. Many of the tribes can read and write, and educational facilities are freely offered to the rising generation by the English Government.

Whakarewarewa — we can write but not pronounce the name — forms another active volcano point, and is situated about four miles from the Lake House. For three days, whenever the eyes wandered in that direction, we had seen the hamlet, which occupies a side-hill, steaming away vigorously, and sometimes got a glimpse of the boiling water spouted high in air. The road thither lies over a perfectly level way in the midst of a plain which was doubtless overflowed by the lake in former times, and which is still so much under water as to be nearly navigable for a small boat. Here we found another tribe of Maoris surrounded by geysers, boiling pits, hot, spluttering, and unwholesome-looking mud-pools, with steam-holes innumerable. What a region of perpetual ferment it is! How busy must be the fiery agencies constantly operating in Nature's subterranean laboratory! Soon after entering the hamlet we passed a clear, blue boiling-pool of great depth, which is improved by the whole community for cooking purposes. In the sides of this out-of-doors stone and earthen cavity indentures had been made, where iron pots and wicker screens could be placed for boiling vegetables and other food.

The action of the largest geyser here was fitful and irregular, subsiding for a few seconds now and then, and again bursting forth with renewed power, throwing a column of boiling water thirty feet into the air with startling effect. We were told that this geyser when in operation often sent up such a column to the height of sixty feet. Much wandering over the earth's surface and knowledge of terrestrial affairs has taught us not to accept unchallenged the statements of even such worthy guides as our veracious Sophia. The fact as confirmed to us by ocular demonstration was quite startling enough, and exaggeration was certainly needless. This erratic geyser emerges from a large opening eight or ten feet in diameter worn through the split rock, and is of unknown depth, — a successful attempt to sound it being impossible, as the spray would envelop the operator and scald him to death.

The water from this geyser overflows a series of bowlders running down into a broad sulphurous basin, in which are many more boiling springs and yawning chasms, with here and there overheated flat stones upon which the natives bake their food. The bowlders and slabs over which the chemicalized waters flow, receive a yellowish deposit of sparkling silica, mixed with crystals of sulphur and gleaming sparks of black manganese, which all together form beautiful colors when the sun's rays break through the clouds of mist and play upon them. We were shown among the rocks a natural stone basin capable of holding thirty or forty gallons of water, into and through which the boiling waters could be conducted at will; and here, according to Sophia, her forefathers used to boil the heads of their prisoners into a palatable soup!

The action of the subterranean forces is more demonstrative here than at Ohinemutu, and the immediate sulphurous effect upon the atmosphere is much more dense. The matter thrown up from the depths consists of crystals of alum, soda, sulphur, arsenic, iron, and other chemicals, which form cones about the several chasms. After passing in and out among these geysers, boiling rivulets, hot springs, and steam clouds, one is glad to reach an elevation where the atmosphere is comparatively clear and pure, and where a long breath may be drawn with a degree of comfort. Standing upon an elevation overlooking the whole strange scene, the air filled with heated spray, steam, and sulphurous gases, forming all together a dense vapor which clouded the sunlight, it was impossible not to recall the picture of Dante's Inferno.

Our cicerone here, as the reader has already been partially informed, was the famous Sophia, a Maori woman who has acted in this capacity for many years, and who, as she herself deposed, was the mother of fifteen children, twelve of whom were still living. Her tattooed face is well wrinkled by the hand of time, though her activity in climbing the different points of interest is marvellous. She speaks English well, is gentle in voice and remarkable for her good manners, taking great care that those whom she conducts through these novel scenes shall see and understand every object of interest. On the green borders of all this volcanic confusion, as we were leaving Whakarewarewa, a fragrant little bouquet of the wild blossoms of the manuka were gathered and offered to us by a Maori girl, who felt so much overpaid by the shilling tendered her in return as to hesitate to receive it.

On returning to Ohinemutu we found extensive preparations going on in the Maori hamlet for a grand dance as a sort of winding-up ceremony to the four days of wailing and feasting over the death of the chief, of whom the reader has already heard. It was curious to see into what a state of excitement the natives could work themselves by means of dance and song. It recalled the infatuation and frenzy of the whirling Dervishes of Cairo. Alcohol could not more thoroughly excite them or stimulate their brains. In these exercises the women far exceeded the men in their extravagance of behavior, — jumping wildly up and down, thrusting out their arms and legs with perfect abandon and apparent unconsciousness, distorting their bodies and features, and twisting themselves generally into most impossible shapes. A dull, monotonous drum-beat was the only musical accompaniment, which was produced from a hollow log, both ends of which were covered with sheep-skin. The perfect concert of action among the dancers was marvellous, the more so because no consecutive purpose could be divined. The most weird and picturesque scene we can recall as witnessed in the Lake District was the performance of one of these dances by moonlight; but it must be acknowledged that the exhibition was more striking than decorous. Belonging to this tribe, and indeed to all that are visited by the whites, there is always a bevy of dancing-girls with a world of passion in their bold, luminous eyes, and a reckless disregard of all delicacy in their behavior, ever ready to perform before strangers for money. Some of these girls have very long, perfectly straight hair and a Jewish cast of features quite in contrast to the typical Maori faces. The indifference of parents to the conduct of their daughters is remarkable even for savages. One great objection to the *haka*, or native dance, is the beer-drinking which invariably accompanies it. The beer is brought from the hotel in an open bucket holding several gallons, and mugs being furnished, the performers partake freely, until by the time the dance draws to a close they are not in a condition to care much for the proprieties.

When one of these Maoris meets another after a long separation, the first thing is the mutual rubbing of noses, after which each of the parties begins to mourn and weep; but when they say good-by at parting, for however long a term, boisterous laughter is indulged in, — for it is a principle with them to speed the parting guest with feast, song, and hilarity. As the dead lies prepared for burial, the nearest relative first, and the closest friend after, rubs noses with the corpse. The natives here are in receipt of a considerable amount of money from the rents of lands, from pensions granted by the Government, and from acting in the capacity of guides, or as boatmen on the lake, and for performing other odd jobs for the whites. But they have no idea of economy or of saving anything for a time of need. The money which they receive goes as fast as it comes into their possession, and mostly for liquor and tobacco. When the money is gone, they will half starve themselves until a fresh supply comes in. After one of their continued wakes, at which food is so recklessly wasted, and all their spare cash expended in drinking and in other excesses, there follows a period of fasting, during which they live upon roots, berries, and stray bits of food picked up here and there. Such is their improvidence, that there are often times when they would absolutely starve were it not for the aid given gratuitously by the whites.

The Maoris at the present time are remarkably peaceable among themselves, — being never known, as we were told by local officials, to quarrel one with another, not even in their cups; for while liquor makes them foolish, it seldom makes them pugnacious. It was noticed that the fathers often carried the infant children on their backs, and in the same style adopted by the mothers. From this and other indications we got the impression that they are very kind to their children. One thing is certainly remarkable: these native babies never cry. We were a full week among them, witnessing their domestic life at nearly all hours, and we never heard the first cry from their lips. The same peculiarity as regards infants was also noticed by the author both in China and Japan.

As has been mentioned already, the funeral of one of their chiefs had drawn numerous representatives from other tribes to Ohinemutu, so that the number of aborigines was largely increased at the hamlet during our stay. The last day of our sojourning here was Sunday, a certain outward respect for which is observed by the natives as well as the few white residents at Ohinemutu. The little rude earthen-floored chapel, where a Roman Catholic priest officiates, was not large enough to accommodate both the resident tribe and their visitors at the same time, so they divided into two parties, — one half attending the services in the chapel, while the other half remained outside squatting upon their hams and playing cards for pennies. This seemed to us to be a little out of keeping with the church-going idea, but the average native is not at all amenable in his feelings to the conventionalities of the whites. Gambling with cards under the shadow of the church presented no anomalous aspect to these waiting worshippers. When the first audience had completed the usual religious exercises, — listening to prayers read in Latin, which of course were "all Greek" to them, — then the card-players changed places with them, and each party did as the other had just done. The afternoon was devoted to foot-ball by the men, and to bathing, gossiping, and smoking tobacco by the women. The food and stimulants had evidently become exhausted, as the visitors prepared to depart to their homes, but they were dismissed as usual with riotous tokens of joy.

The Government now owns a considerable portion of land in the Hot Lake District, which has been purchased at a fair price from the natives. The region called the King's Country contains at least ten thousand square miles, lying within clearly-defined boundaries. Its possession is sacredly secured to the Maoris by treaty with the Home Government of England. The aborigines however would in no contingency permit any encroachment upon their present domain; they would declare open war first, and fight for their rights. It is remembered by the whites that these natives *can* fight when incited to do so by their chiefs, and by a sense of being wronged. This was made clear enough in the early days of the European occupancy, when it cost the English thousands of lives and vast amounts of treasure before peace was finally brought about by the abundant concessions of Sir George Gray, the then Governor. The natives had very rude weapons in those days; now, however, they have fire-arms, and know how to use them. No foreigner can go into the King's Country without a native permit; no white man can travel there without a Maori guide; a murderer or other criminal cannot be pursued thither by a Government officer, except by first obtaining the proper permission. In these reserved lands the Maoris show a bold and warlike front. They enjoy full political rights in the government of the country, and return their own members to the National Assembly from the several districts in their province. The few educated members of the tribe are distinguished for a certain kind of eloquence, and can speak well and forcibly in behalf of the interests of their race. Like our own American Indians, they abound in poetical figures of speech and natural illustrations. Instances were related to us of some of these Maori representatives (generally with more or less European blood in their veins), who had electrified the legislative body to which they belonged, by their eloquent and powerful harangues, and who had more than once carried their purpose to a successful issue, against the manifest popular wish of the Assembly, by their clear force of argument and manly speech.

Government is building a sanitarium at Sulphur Point, as it is called, situated about half a mile from the Lake House. The baths attached to it are supplied with water from springs which are highly charged with chemical matter, each being quite different from the others in its peculiar properties, and supposed to possess special curative powers. There is also here a hospital already in operation under the control of the Government, in which there were a score of patients when we visited it. Several of these were grateful and enthusiastic for the benefit they believed themselves to have experienced by bathing in the ill-smelling waters. Said one to us: "I now leave my crutches under my bed; but when I came here two weeks ago I could not walk across my room without them. Now, however, I walk a mile in the open air, forenoon and afternoon, without any help, and have a grand appetite, with the digestion of an ostrich."

A large town has been arranged for by the authorities in anticipation of the future popularity of these hot springs. Broad, regular, and well-laid out streets have been graded and fenced, having nicely gravelled road-beds, lined with ornamental trees; but there are yet no dwelling-houses here except the very comfortable Hospital structure. There is, however, a grocery store, a Post-Office, and a Town Hall,— these last two being of brick. It seemed to us that the atmosphere of Sulphur Point must always prove an insuperable objection to its being adopted as a permanent home. The constant odor rising from the subterraneous fires not only excites disgust, but is disagreeably suggestive of the nearness to active volcanic agencies. The Lake House is situated upon a gentle elevation, thirty or forty feet higher than the lake, and overlooking the lands all about it; but Sulphur Point is nearly on a level with the water, and is so low that any rise of the lake would inevitably flood it, and it must always be very damp.

Yet invalids have come all the way from the North of Europe to test the advantages of these springs, and, as we were assured by the attendant physician, with almost unvarying success. A railway is constructing from Oxford hither which will connect Ohinemutu with Auckland direct, obviating the necessity for staging, which no invalid should attempt unless the road is in a very different condition from that in which we found it. The railway will doubtless be finished within a twelvemonth.

One must start before sunrise from Ohinemutu in order to reach Auckland on the same day, though the distance is only a hundred and sixty miles, all but thirty of which is by railway. We have shown that the road between the Lake District and Oxford is one requiring time to deal with. When we left the Lake House, the silvery gray of the morning was struggling through the clouds of hot vapor and sulphurous steam which hung over and about the place. The stage lanterns and those in the hands of the attendants cast a weird and fitful glamour all about us. A dog was baying down among the Maori cabins, albeit the hamlet as a whole still slept. The horses brought out from their stable into the crisp morning air were a little restless, and a hostler held the bits of the two leaders. Presently the driver called out, "All right! let them go!" and in a moment more we were rolling smartly away by the borders of Lake Rotorua.

The extended programme was completed, and now our steps would be turned toward distant America.

No intelligent person can be blind to the favorable position of New Zealand or to the promise of its future commercial importance. Situated as it were in the centre of this Austral Ocean, the future highway of the world, it is accessible from all quarters. On the west, not far away, lie the busy harbors of Australia, with which her exchanges of merchandise are constant. Within easy reach of India and China on one side, she has California, Mexico, and South America on the other. To the north lie the hundreds of islands which constitute the groups of Polynesia, notable for their voluptuous climate and primitive fertility. With the opening of the Panama Canal or other available means for crossing the isthmus, New Zealand will lie directly in the highway between Europe and the gold-fields of the great island-continent,—between England and her largest colony. The insular position of the country does not necessarily indicate inaccessibility. The many beautiful islands of the South Sea must sooner or later come under the commercial sway of New Zealand, as they may be explored and civilized. Her admirable harbors, noble estuaries, and navigable rivers are elsewhere unsurpassed. If destined to achieve greatness, these islands, like those of great Britain, will do so through the development and maintenance of maritime power; and with so many advantages as they possess, we predict for them this final accomplishment.

As an attractive country to the explorer and traveller, though so many thousands of miles away from the beaten tracks, New Zealand is rendered accessible by the growing facilities of our times, and certainly combines within itself a grand variety of natural phenomena which nowhere else are so readily reached or more striking to behold. Her soil produces all the vegetation and fruits of the teeming tropics; and yet within a few hours' travel of flower-clad plains, one can ascend mountains as lofty, and behold glaciers as frigid and grand, as in Switzerland or Norway. While perennial verdure characterizes her valleys and plains, her lofty ranges are snow-capped all through the year. In the north she has geysers, boiling springs, heated caldrons, and active craters, as endless in variety as they are countless in number; in the south she has myriads of cool lakes which for beauty of scenery excel the Lake of Geneva, and for depth vie with the famous fjords of Scandinavia,— thus giving us an epitome of the grandest exhibitions of many lands. Her native race is unique, excelling nearly all others in originality, and full of interest to the ethnological student. In the wild Maori country the paths are among a wilderness of boiling waterspouts, and in the open districts of the lower country one is sheltered by fern-trees, tall, graceful, and picturesque. From the crests of burning mountains we may look into regions where sulphurous fires never cease, and by turning the eyes in another direction behold crystal waters tumbling over precipices hundreds of feet in height, to feed the streams which irrigate the fertile plains below.

These marvellous forests, precipitous gorges, lovely rivers, and fruitful valleys have neither legend nor history to lend them fortuitous attractions; but is it not quite as fascinating to tread such unworn lands, to make one's own path in the unbroken forest, and to be brought face to face with Nature in her primal condition? He who has become blasé with travel in Europe, or even in the less worn fields of Asia, may here encounter wonder upon wonder which will be sure to "whet his almost blunted appetite," and to renew in him all the early charms of foreign discovery and travel.

www.ingramcontent.com/pod-product-compliance
Lightning Source LLC
Chambersburg PA
CBHW030558300426
44111CB00009B/1024